The Work of Global Justic

Human rights have been generally understood as juridical products, organizational outcomes or abstract principles that are realized through formal means such as passing laws, creating institutions or formulating ideals. In this book, Fuyuki Kurasawa argues that we must reverse this 'top-down' focus by examining how groups and persons struggling against global injustices construct and enact human rights through five transnational forms of ethico-political practice: bearing witness, forgiveness, foresight, aid and solidarity. From these, he develops a new perspective highlighting the difficult social labour that constitutes the substance of what global justice is and ought to be, thereby reframing the terms of debates about human rights and providing the outlines of a critical cosmopolitanism centred around emancipatory struggles for an alternative globalization.

FUYUKI KURASAWA is Associate Professor of Sociology and Social and Political Thought at York University in Toronto; Faculty Fellow of the Center for Cultural Sociology at Yale University; and Co-President of the International Sociological Association's Research Committee on Sociological Theory. He is the author of *The Ethnological Imagination: A Cross-Cultural Critique of Modernity* (2004).

Cambridge Cultural Social Studies

Series editors
Jeffrey C. Alexander, *Department of Sociology, Yale University*, and Steven Seidman, *Department of Sociology, University of Albany, State University of New York.*

Titles in the series

Tamir Sorek, *Arab Soccer in a Jewish State*

Jeffrey C. Alexander, Bernhard Giesen and Jason L. Mast, *Social Performance*

Arne Johan Vetlesen, *Evil and Human Agency*

Roger Friedland and John Mohr, *Matters of Culture*

Davina Cooper, *Challenging Diversity, Rethinking Equality and the Value of Difference*

Krishan Kumar, *The Making of English National Identity*

Ron Eyerman, *Cultural Trauma*

Stephen M. Engel, *The Unfinished Revolution*

Michèle Lamont and Laurent Thévenot, *Rethinking Comparative Cultural Sociology*

Ron Lembo, *Thinking Through Television*

Ali Mirsepassi, *Intellectual Discourse and the Politics of Modernization*

Ronald N. Jacobs, *Race, Media, and the Crisis of Civil Society*

Robin Wagner-Pacifici, *Theorizing the Standoff*

Kevin McDonald, *Struggles for Subjectivity*

S. N. Eisenstadt, *Fundamentalism, Sectarianism, and Revolution*

Piotr Sztompka, *Trust*

Simon J. Charlesworth, *A Phenomenology of Working-Class Experience*

List continues at end of book

The Work of Global Justice

Human Rights as Practices

Fuyuki Kurasawa

CAMBRIDGE UNIVERSITY PRESS
Cambridge, New York, Melbourne, Madrid, Cape Town, Singapore, São Paulo

Cambridge University Press
The Edinburgh Building, Cambridge CB2 8RU, UK

Published in the United States of America by Cambridge University Press, New York

www.cambridge.org
Information on this title: www.cambridge.org/9780521673914

First published 2007

Printed in the United Kingdom at the University Press, Cambridge

A catalogue record for this book is available from the British Library

ISBN 978-0-521-85724-6 hardback
ISBN 978-0-521-67391-4 paperback

To Toronto and New York City,
urban muses and arenas of a cosmopolitanism
of the everyday

Contents

Figures

Preface

This book, like many others I suppose, was born out of a false start of sorts. A few years ago, wrestling with the legacy of the twentieth century after reading Eric Hobsbawm's *Age of Extremes* and Paul Ricoeur's *La mémoire, l'histoire, l'oubli*, I began researching the aftermath of the atomic bomb blasts in Hiroshima and Nagasaki. While initially interested in what occurred in Japan itself, I rapidly became engrossed in the Faustian tale of some of the US-based physicists who had participated in the Manhattan Project out of which the atomic bomb was invented. Having come to realize the fearsome powers they had unleashed as well as the appropriation of the use of such powers by military and political leaders, brilliant and often mercurial figures such as J. Robert Oppenheimer, Hans Bethe and Leo Szilard felt a sense of responsibility, in differing ways and degrees, for what transpired on those fateful days in August 1945 and for the implications of the existence of atomic weapons for the future of humankind. Remorse was a common reaction, politicization was another – the latter leading to the establishment of what became known as the scientists' movement in the postwar United States and the founding of the *Bulletin of the Atomic Scientists*, among other initiatives. Although the following pages carry few traces of this initial project, I discovered the book's themes through it. In retrospect, what fascinated me was how the scientists' movement grappled with, and eventually developed, a set of public and transnational strategies to respond to the Hiroshima and Nagasaki bombings: bearing witness to the victims' and survivors' suffering, seeking forgiveness, advocating foresight to prevent nuclear warfare, assisting survivors and cultivating a sense of planetary solidarity.

Regardless of how productive a starting-point the scientists' movement may have been, the issues it raised required dramatically recasting the project. Indeed, what came to the fore were questions about the cultivation of a sense of concern for temporally or spatially distant others that, when connected to contemporary struggles for an alternative world order, frame one of the central dynamics of our age: the project of global justice.

However, upon researching this topic, I was struck by the formalist, top-down bias that pervades its scholarly treatment; more often than not, global justice is reduced to a normative endeavour (discovering universal ethical principles), a juridical construct (legally entrenching human rights) or an institutional outcome (designing a new infrastructure of global governance). All of these initiatives are necessary, of course, but their vantage-points from above do not, to my mind, capture the substantive core of what constitutes global justice. For their part, empirical studies of the numerous progressive actors that compose the nascent sphere of global civil society tend to exist in a descriptive register, examining the organizational and strategic dimensions of campaigns and civic associations dedicated to global justice without adequately accounting for the webs of social relations that underlie it.

To address these limitations, I contemplated the idea of conceptualizing global justice as social labour, that is to say, as a reality substantively made up of ethical and political tasks that actors strive to accomplish by confronting difficulties and obstacles. In this manner, the crucial question becomes less the specification of norms, rules and institutional configurations, or the description of progressive forces, than the interpretation of how global justice is enacted – the ways in which groups and persons produce it by engaging in patterns of intersubjective, public and transnational social action that can be transposed across different historical and geographical settings. Hitherto neglected, it is the arduous, contingent and perpetual processes of making and doing of global justice that I want to highlight. Accordingly, the book discusses the work of global justice, and hones in on five modes of human rights practice (bearing witness, forgiveness, foresight, aid and solidarity) in order to grasp how the building of an alternative globalization can proceed. Ultimately, I would argue, we can gain significant insights into struggles to end structural and situational injustices in the world by viewing them as ethico-political practices. Moreover, the critical and substantive approach advanced here supplies widely discussed cosmopolitan ideas with an action-theoretical grounding, one that studies how they are being put into practice from below. The work of global justice, then, represents a manifestation of critical cosmopolitanism.

Despite being wary of self-aggrandizing confessions seeking to generate a facile and clichéd pathos, I must admit that this has not been an easy book to write. The choice of subject ensured that this would be the case, since it required that I devote the last few years to immersing myself in some of the most horrific events and manifestations of structural and situational violence in human history, by whatever means were at my disposal: official reports and first-person accounts, art exhibitions and plays, documentary films and still photographs, among others. That the task has been all-consuming, and at times draining, is clearly insignificant when compared to the experiences of those who perished or survived such circumstances. None the less, the suffering that lies at the heart of this book is haunting in both its intensity and scale. There is little solace, only the appeal to scholars and citizens to relentlessly confront global injustices until they are overcome. What, indeed, could be more pressing for the human sciences today?

The fact that lives could be destroyed with such impunity and that human dignity could be trampled upon so desultorily, not to mention that unjust situations and systemic factors are neither natural nor necessary, is dispiriting and infuriating in equal doses. At the same time, this realization need not, and ought not, result in believing in the metaphysical inevitability of crimes against humanity and instances of structural violence – a view all-too-often shared by stoic fatalists and despondent determinists alike. We need to explain why grave human rights violations continue to occur and reoccur (design, neglect, denial, indifference, etc.), but simultaneously to think about how they could be halted or prevented altogether. Neither great optimism nor pessimism about our current and future state of affairs animates me, although I do want to insistently claim that a just world order exists as a viable project in our age, that is to say, as no more and no less than a historical possibility on the terrain of socio-political struggle.

On another note, while striving to maintain a certain analytical distance from progressive social forces involved in attempting to create an alternative globalization, I must admit being largely sympathetic to the causes they defend and the criticisms they mount about the existing global system. For this, I make no apologies, yet it should not be taken to mean that this book represents a paean to these groups' status as the new emancipatory agents of history, nor even that I am taking at face value their effectiveness or self-understandings as disinterested guardians of human rights; for example, even the most commendable humanitarian non-governmental organizations provide emergency relief to needy populations while keeping one eye on their institutional interests (fundraising, public relations, stature with governments, etc.). To recognize such facts requires a dose of realism, albeit stripped of the *prima-facie* dismissiveness or utter cynicism that passes for critical thinking in some quarters of academia.

I would be remiss if I did not acknowledge the numerous persons who have played a role in the writing of this book. Jeffrey C. Alexander supported the project unstintingly from its inception, with his vast doses of constructive criticism and spirited intellectual engagement. At

Yale University more generally, I have learned much from the community of scholars clustered around the Center for Cultural Sociology; aside from Alexander, thanks are due to Philip Smith and Ron Eyerman, as well as the graduate students there, all of whom have made my stays at the Center stimulating and enjoyable. At New York University and the Social Science Research Council, Craig Calhoun has made his theoretical nous and his vast knowledge of global affairs and the human sciences available to me, while offering encouragement and advice at several stages. I attended Nancy Fraser's graduate course on 'Postnational Democratic Justice' at the New School for Social Research during a crucial period of gestation for the ideas found herein. For their interest in the project and their assistance at various points, I would also like to acknowledge Feyzi Baban, Lucy Baker, Amy Bartholomew, Ulrich Beck, Seyla Benhabib, Bruce Curtis, Peter Dews, Alessandro Ferrara, Roger Friedland, Neil Gross, Sheryl Hamilton, Michael Hardt, Geoffrey Hartman, Morgan Holmes, Axel Honneth, Fuat Keyman, Will Kymlicka, Michèle Lamont, Steven Lukes, Bryan Massam, Abdul Karim Mustapha, Maria Pia Lara, Graça Almeida Rodrigues, Cristina Rojas, Patrick Savidan, Lesley Sparks, Frédéric Vandenberghe, Charles Weiner, Michel Wieviorka and Anthony Woodiwiss. Obviously, none of them can be held responsible for the book's shortcomings. I am grateful to the audiences at lectures and presentations where parts of the argument were first introduced: the American Sociological Association (including its Junior Theorists' Symposium), the Canadian Congress of the Humanities and Social Sciences, Carleton University, the Institute of Philosophy of the Academy of Sciences of the Czech Republic, the International Social Theory Consortium, Koc University, the New University of Lisbon, Wilfrid Laurier University, the World Congress of Sociology and Yale University.

At York University, which remains a rather unique site of interdisciplinarity and theoretically robust critical scholarship, I am grateful to Debi Brock, Gordon Darroch, Lorna Erwin, Ratiba Hadj-Moussa, Gerald Kernerman, Janine Marchessault, Brian Singer, Leah Vosko, Lorna Weir and the outstanding group of graduate students whom I have taught and am supervising. Dean Robert Drummond of the Faculty of Arts provided financial support and research leave. I wrote the bulk of an early version of the manuscript while holding a Fulbright Fellowship at Yale University and New York University in 2003–4, and am grateful to the Canada-US Fulbright Program Foundation and the US Institute of International Education for the opportunity. Through a Standard Research Grant, the Social Sciences and Humanities Research Council of Canada made the entire project possible.

It has been my good fortune to work with superb research assistants, who diligently dug up piles of material and documents – more than I could ever read, yet invariably useful. Many thanks, then, to Albert Banerjee, Sabina Heilman, Patti Phillips, Philip Steiner and Lachlan Story. Additionally, Sabina Heilman formatted the final manuscript and Philip Steiner did the same for the figures. Mervyn Horgan compiled the index, patiently and meticulously. At Cambridge University Press, Sarah Caro, John Haslam, Carrie Cheek and Joanna Breeze have been a wonderful editorial team. The anonymous reviewers for the Press supplied detailed and fruitful comments on the manuscript, which helped me to improve it as well as sharpen its focus. I am grateful to Chris Doubleday for copy-editing the final typescript.

An earlier version of Chapter 3 appeared as 'The Global Culture of Prevention and the Work of Foresight' in *Constellations* 11, 4 (2004), pp. 453–75. Similarly, an earlier version of Chapter 5 was published as 'A Cosmopolitanism from Below: Alternative Globalization and the Creation of a Solidarity Without Bounds' in the *Archives européennes de sociologie* 45, 2 (2004), pp. 233–55. I thank both publishers for permission to reprint portions of these articles.

The book is dedicated to the two cities where I wrote it. There is much talk of cosmopolitanism today, but to witness it being negotiated more mundanely on the streets and in daily life is a source of political hope, and of theoretical humility. As always, I owe my family and friends eternal gratitude for their unflagging support and understanding. And a final dedication goes to Gloria Kim; she knows why.

Introduction: Theorizing the work of global justice

Setting the scene

At the dawn of the twenty-first century, the legacy of the previous one weighs heavily upon us. The 'age of extremes' (Hobsbawm 1994) was marked by great accomplishments, but also by a series of catastrophic developments that in many ways defined our present relationship to it: totalitarianisms of the Left and the Right, war, ecological degradation, genocide, widening North–South disparities, grinding poverty, and so on. The litany is a familiar one, not least because the end of the twentieth century was punctuated by ongoing civil wars, the reproduction of structural inequalities, famines and widespread crimes against humanity in the former Yugoslavia and Rwanda.

Predictably, this predicament has given rise to two sorts of response from progressive quarters. Many are falling prey to a fatalistic *Zeitgeist*, which is itself spawning positions ranging from stoic resignation about the state of the world to a weary and disillusioned cynicism about emancipatory projects, and even a kind of nihilistic despondency. There is indeed little doubt that recent tendencies – the hegemony of neoliberal capitalism, the clash between rival brands of politico-religious fundamentalisms and the assertion of a US-led 'war on terror', or the continuing ravages of the HIV/AIDS pandemic in the global South – only seem to justify the mood of despair. Furthermore, one of the great paradoxes of our epoch originates out of the disjuncture between the multiplication of human rights discourses nationally and globally, on the one hand, and the unrelenting violation of such socio-economic and civil-political rights, on the other – often by the very same actors who drape themselves in humanitarian rhetoric (Chomsky 2003; Teeple 2004).

By contrast, in the wake of the possibilities opened up by the end of the Cold War and the collapse of the bloc-driven logic of bipolar geopolitical confrontation on the world stage, some intellectual circles are championing an unbridled buoyancy. For a brief period in the 1990s, the United Nations Security Council was revived as a relatively effective organ of global governance on account of greater, albeit always tenuous and strategically driven, collaboration between erstwhile rivals. Despite recent setbacks and the vexing lack of enforceability, multilateralism is gaining traction because of a build-up of a vast infrastructure of international agreements (the Kyoto Accord, the International Treaty to Ban Landmines, etc.) and judicial institutions (such as the International Criminal Court and the International Criminal Tribunals for former Yugoslavia and Rwanda). In addition, the formation of a global civil society out of expansive transnational networks of non-governmental organizations (NGOs), social movements and concerned citizens is sustaining a bullish mood among certain progressive thinkers, for whom the civic 'multitude' represents the new agent of history that will radically transform the current world order (Hardt and Negri 2000; 2004).

It would be tempting to follow the lead of pessimists or utopians, yet I want to claim that another path can be trodden – one that, without overstating either scenario, simultaneously recognizes the dire circumstances in which humankind finds itself and the potential for emancipation cultivated by numerous and diverse struggles around the planet aiming to fully and universally realize socio-economic and civil-political rights via an alternative globalization. The project of global justice has come to stand as shorthand for these struggles and their associated discourses, although it should be seen as neither an ill-fated delusion nor a teleological necessity; instead, it represents nothing more, yet nothing less, than a set of emancipatory possibilities rising out of the ashes of the last century. Whether or not these possibilities become actualized depends less on formal normative principles and institutional arrangements than on the work of global justice, that is, how and to what extent civic associations enact the social labour required to counter the sources of structural and situational violence around the planet and to give birth to a different world order. As I will contend throughout this book, the work of global justice is arduous and without guarantees, for it often falls short of protecting the lives of much of the world's population – let alone dramatically improving its material and symbolic standing. Much remains to be accomplished if we are to eradicate crimes against humanity and structural inequalities, while any gains hitherto achieved are merely provisional. For its part, global civil society does not represent a harmonious space where a just world order is bound to flourish, but rather a contested and differentiated site in which actors of opposite political persuasions confront one another; even what might appear as its progressive elements are by no means natural carrier groups of an alternative globalization, since many putatively Left NGOs and social movements are losing their financial and ideological independence *vis-à-vis* governments, international organizations and private corporations, to become fully integrated into an international human rights industry.

If this is the case, then why bother with global justice at all? Two principal reasons come to mind. Normatively, it represents the single most compelling political substantiation of the principle of universal moral equality available today and one of the key 'moral horizons of our time' (Badinter 1998). While it is imperative to recognize that governments and transnational corporations are appropriating humanitarian discourses to advance their own geopolitical or commercial interests, we cannot reduce human rights *per se* to mere instruments of *realpolitik*, Euro-American hegemony or globalized capital. As such, the belief that all human beings are entitled to a full spectrum of socio-economic and civil-political rights, and conversely that abuses of such rights ought not be tolerated because of a territorially unbounded sense of mutuality, is acquiring an enviable ethical weight in many societies. The cosmopolitan stretching of the moral imagination, to the point that distant strangers are treated as concrete and morally equal persons whose rights are being violated or incompletely realized, offers nascent public legitimacy and political traction for the interventions of progressive groups in national and global civil societies. Because of the presence of human rights discourses, these groups can push for greater public debate about the past (how do we remember crimes against humanity, and how do we deal with their contemporary effects?), the present (how should we halt collective suffering in our midst, and how do we achieve a just world order?) and the future (how do we avert eventual humanitarian disasters, and how do we promote the capacities of all?), including challenging systemic sources of inequality and domination.

The second reason that global justice matters is strategic, for if the aforementioned construction of a multilateral human rights edifice on the international stage appears to be a strictly formal development, it does enable progressive forces to use legal means to rein in corporate and state power along democratic and egalitarian lines, or at least to try symbolically to shame institutions violating human rights into respecting their official engagements. Furthermore, radical interventions through the official infrastructure of human rights to contest the hegemony of existing economic and political structures can represent one step toward an alternative globalization, by chipping away at the root causes of humanitarian crises, crimes against humanity and sustained material deprivation. The work of global justice, then, can move beyond what is often the liberal individualist and formalist biases of conventional human rights paradigms, employing existing institutional and legal tools gradually to leverage changes toward a substantial reorganization of economic and political structures and redistribution of material and symbolic resources in line with the cosmopolitan idea of planetary egalitarian reciprocity (Habermas 2003: 369; Woodiwiss 2005: 150n1).

Hence, this book is intended as a contribution to a critical and substantive theory of global justice, one that converts the latter from an ideal steeped in noble sentiments and intentions, or a juridified concept enshrined in multilateral declarations, into an ensemble of emancipatory practices constructed through ethico-political labour. To do so, it examines the social processes and repertoires of collective action that underpin transnational struggles against gross human rights abuses, while also indicating what normative and socio-political steps can be enacted in order to further an alternative globalization. But before turning to these matters more fully, we should consider some of the main paradigms in the vast literature on global justice, which as I shall endeavour to demonstrate in the next section, suffer from either formalism or an absence of theoretical systematicity. Following this discussion is a brief exposition of critical substantivism, the analytical framework that I am proposing to address the flaws of other approaches and to bridge the gap between formalism and empiricism because of its orientation to hermeneutical critique. For its part, prior to supplying a brief overview of each chapter, the final section of this introduction presents critical substantivism's conceptual apparatus: the notions of practice and mode of practice, as well as the action-theoretical model of the work of global justice.

Mapping the intellectual terrain

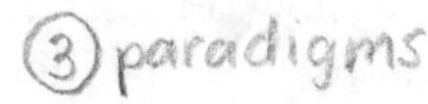

Although a comprehensive review of the multiplicity of writings on global justice is well beyond the scope of this introduction, three key paradigms can be discussed: philosophical normativism, politico-legal institutionalism and global civil society empiricism.[1] What I want to suggest is that, despite vitally contributing to the analysis of global justice, these paradigms have not adequately grasped its substantive dimensions – namely, the fact that it is created out of the labour stemming from modes of ethico-political practice, which provide it with a patterned social thickness, and that it exists as much as an enacted reality than a formal project.

Taking their cue from various sources (ancient Graeco-Roman Stoicism, Enlightenment Kantianism, non-Western humanism, etc.),

[1] More specialized writings on bearing witness, forgiveness, foresight, aid and solidarity are treated in each of the book's five chapters.

philosophical normativists primarily interpret global justice via the prism of the elaboration of a cosmopolitan ethics. This begins from a subject's self-understanding as a citizen of the world and a concerned member of humankind (*'la terre est ma patrie'*), who is conversant with and appreciative of a variety of different socio-cultural settings and their accompanying customs, beliefs, norms and symbolic systems; the prototypical cosmopolitan subject is a well-travelled and open-minded polyglot who regularly negotiates between and crosses cultural boundaries, since nothing human is foreign to her. Of greater direct relevance here is the ethical imperative that follows from this world-dwelling identity, the recognition of universal moral equality. For philosophical normativism, then, human beings are entitled to the realization of the same socio-economic and civil-political rights as well as to enjoy the same freedoms and protections regardless of their specific circumstances or socio-cultural location. Global justice thrives on concern for the well-being of all persons in the world, the faraway stranger no less than the proximate neighbour. More concretely, philosophical normativists specify universal moral principles, such as hospitality and egalitarian reciprocity, that can guide the juridification of international relations for the construction of a peaceful and multilateral world community, and that can legitimate global distributive justice through the reallocation of material resources on a planetary scale.[2]

If they overlap to a degree with the normativist counterparts, politico-legal institutionalists treat global justice as a question of redesigning the world system in accordance with international human rights procedures and cosmopolitan principles. Institutionalism thereby urges the reform or complete overhaul of the existing transnational legal infrastructure and set of multilateral political institutions, in order to increase democratic accountability and socio-economic fairness as well as to tackle problems confronting humankind as a whole (environmental degradation, migration, etc.). Proposals range from a world parliament to multiscaled yet interconnected executive structures with overlapping jurisdictions, and from global citizenship (a status granting socio-economic and civil-political rights and accorded to all human beings) to the enforcement of an international legal regime that would regulate interstate relations and the conduct of powerful transnational private actors (e.g., through taxation of financial transactions or international labour codes). Put succinctly,

[2] For a sample of philosophical normativist writings, see Apel (2000), Appiah (2003; 2006), Beitz (1999), Bohman and Lutz-Bachmann (1997), Dallmayr (2002; 2003), De Greiff and Cronin (2002), Derrida (2001), Habermas (2001 [1998]; 2003), Kant (1991b [1795]), Nussbaum (2002a [1996]), Pogge (1992; 2001a; 2002b) and Singer (2002).

politico-legal institutionalists believe that transforming the official system of planetary governance produces the clearest path to global justice.[3]

Undoubtedly, philosophical normativism and politico-legal institutionalism are vital to elaborate the ethical doctrines, structures and procedural models that undergird an alternative globalization. However, both paradigms suffer from a formalist bias that adopts a view of global justice 'from above', whereby the latter is formulated essentially through prescriptive or legislative means; the protection and attainment of socio-economic and civil-political rights becomes a matter of finding the most compelling universal ethical principles or the best-designed institutional plan. Here, the problem originates from these approaches' social thinness, since they do not supply a sense of how global justice is made from the ground up, that is to say, how socio-political actors situated in dense and meaningful lifeworlds engage in practices to counter structural and situational forms of violence and to advance emancipatory projects. These actors, it should be pointed out, do not necessarily or principally orient themselves toward abstract norms or official institutions and juridified relations, but rather understand what they do as tasks performed in order to face up to severe material deprivations and crimes against humanity, among other perils they encounter experientially. Therefore, formalism skews interpretation away from the social labour and modes of practice that supply the ethical and political soil within which the norms, institutions and procedures of global justice are rooted, but to which the latter is not reducible. Without sufficiently attempting to make sense of these types of social action, neither philosophical normativists nor politico-legal institutionalists can adequately account for what makes up the substance of global justice and for the arduous processes that lead to its constitution in specific moments and places.

Global civil society empiricism represents the third, and rather sprawling, tendency characterizing literature on global justice. Instead of focusing on normative or legal-institutional dimensions *per se*, empirically engaged analysts are drawing a comprehensive portrait of the transnational networks of informal actors (social movements, NGOs and activists) that are driving global justice from below by leading to the formation of a politicized civic realm existing beyond territorial borders. Accordingly, writings in this vein describe in some detail various aspects of global civil society or one of its carrier groups: its composition (the groups that are part of it); its strategic and organizational facets (the

[3] Politico-legal institutionalist writings include Archibugi (2003), Archibugi *et al.* (1998), Beck (2000; 2005), Falk (1995; 2000), Habermas and Derrida (2003), Held (1995; 2004) and Higgott and Ougaard (2002).

strategies, resources and infrastructure that it uses and mobilizes); the political causes and problems it confronts (global warming, war, gender equality, human rights, emergency relief, etc.); as well as its institutional history (defining moments, key figures and gradual build-up of its capacity and linkages). Many studies of global civil society view the latter as the principal agent of an alternative globalization, civic associations generally representing progressive forces that can help counterbalance the role of hegemonic states and transnational corporations in national and world politics.[4] Others, however, are less sanguine, claiming that global civil society is organizationally incoherent on account of the bewildering range of its constituent parts and their lack of coordination or commonality, that it remains an ineffective actor on the planetary stage because of its underinstitutionalization and lack of influence on official decisional bodies, or that it is itself a problematic entity in light of the democratic unaccountability and ideological diversity of its participants (which can include conservative as well as progressive elements), their loss of autonomy in recent years, as well as the scant material and symbolic gains they have produced.[5]

Leaving aside this debate, what is relevant for our purposes is the fact that global civil society empiricism corrects the formalism of other approaches, yet its organizational treatment of civic associations does not supply a sufficiently substantive, action-theoretical perspective on global justice – that is to say, a consideration of the patterns of socio-political and ethical doing and thinking that these civic associations enact. Indeed, these modes of practice establish the social density of global civil society, whereas its political orientation is defined largely by the capacity

[4] See Anheier *et al.* (2001; 2002; 2003; 2004), Clark (2003), Glasius *et al.* (2005), Kaldor (2003), Keane (2003), Keck and Sikkink (1998), Lipschutz (1992), Peterson (1992), Rajagopal (2003), Scholte (2002) and Smith (1998).

[5] The limited impact of global civil society on the world scene is due to a number of exogenous and endogenous factors. Exogenously, civic associations' struggles and campaigns are often neutered by Euro-American states' indifference or hostility because of their narrowly defined conceptions of national interests, by bureaucratic ineptitude or inertia from within the ranks of the United Nations system and by generalized denial or callousness among Western publics (Barnett 2002; Boltanski 1993; Cohen 2001; Farmer 2003; Power 2002a). Endogenously, international NGOs are losing their financial and political independence *vis-à-vis* Western states, domestic governments in the global South, and the United Nations – a process of clientelism that has accelerated because of some organizations' compliance with the US-led 'war on terror' and their calls for a greater number of military interventions for ostensibly humanitarian purposes. In addition, the kind of development aid that NGOs supply can sometimes worsen impoverished populations' already dire circumstances by creating long-term dependence, being diverted to prop up oppressive political regimes, or being utilized by one side in an armed conflict (Baker 2002; de Waal 1997; Ignatieff 2001; Kennedy 2004; Laxer and Halperin 2003; Morris-Suzuki 2000; Rieff 2002; Terry 2002; Weissman 2004).

of transnationally minded NGOs and social movements to engage in emancipatory tasks against dominant forces and obstacles in the current world order. To understand how global justice is made, we need to treat it as more than an amalgamation of progressive networks and actors and turn our attention to the arduous and contingent forms of struggle that compose it. Overall, then, philosophical normativism, politico-legal institutionalism and global civil society empiricism leave what I am calling the work of global justice undertheorized. Let us now turn to critical substantivism, which can address this gap in a variety of ways.

A critical theory of global justice

The substantive perspective on global justice mentioned above can be buttressed by a critical theorization of it, one that aims to negotiate the productive tension between the interpretation of the actual state of human rights struggles today and the evaluation of what these struggles should accomplish and how the existing world order can be organized in an emancipatory fashion; thus, it draws from a tradition of critical hermeneutics that explicitly connects analytical and normative dimensions, as well as interpretive and structural approaches, to examine social phenomena (see Figure 1).[6]

To counter the top-down predilections of formalism that produce an experientially and culturally thin account of socio-political life, the vantage-point proposed here is oriented toward making sense of the realities of participants involved in the social labour of global justice, their intentions, and the meanings they give to this labour. Concretely, this signifies taking seriously the socio-cultural aspects of global justice by beginning theorizing at the phenomenological level of actors' lifeworlds and their intersubjectively produced webs of meaning, in order to supply interpretively thick explanations of what these actors are doing and thinking in situations involving the defence or advance of human rights. In other words, what needs to be understood are the belief-systems that groups and individuals hold and the cultural and socio-political rituals they perform. Indeed, it is only when critical theory aims for hermeneutic

[6] See, *inter alia*, Adorno *et al.* (1976 [1969]), Alexander (2003), Benhabib (1986; 2002), Calhoun (1995), Fraser (1997), Fraser and Honneth (2003), Habermas (1987 [1971]), Honneth (1991 [1985]; 1995 [1992]), Kögler (1996), Rabinow and Sullivan (1987), Ricoeur (1981), Taylor (1985 [1971]) and Walzer (1983). Although it represents a distinctive intellectual constellation, critical hermeneutics regroups thinkers whose work differs in its epistemological emphases. Indeed, some stress the interpretive dimension of the paradigm by primarily aiming to make sense of intersubjectively constituted webs of meaning (e.g., Alexander, Taylor, Ricoeur), while others underscore its orientation to critique of the established social order (Adorno, Habermas, Benhabib, etc.).

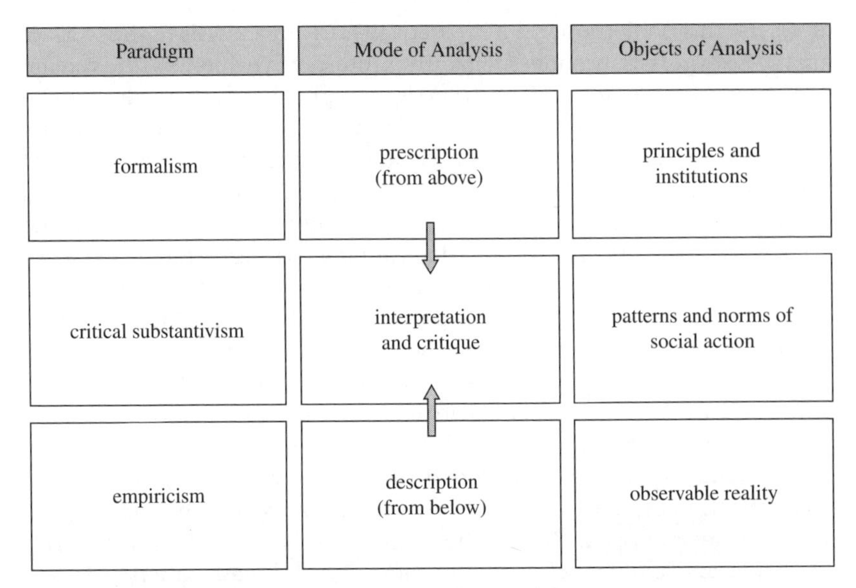

Figure 1. Analytical paradigms of the social.

thickness and empirical engagement that it properly comes to terms with the perils and possibilities related to global justice, and thereby advances normative proposals about an alternative globalization.

Accordingly, each of the chapters in the book draws upon a range of primary and secondary sources to develop its models of the practices of global justice and illustrate how groups and individuals are enacting them. The first chapter, on bearing witness, is framed by writings from Holocaust and Hiroshima atomic bomb survivors, as well as those on the Rwandan genocide and other recent events. The tribulations of post-apartheid South Africa, Chile after the Pinochet regime, Australian treatment of Aboriginal peoples and Jewish–German relations in the aftermath of the Holocaust all supply material for the second chapter, on forgiveness. The study of campaigns to prevent the use of nuclear weapons, environmental degradation and humanitarian crises informs the third chapter, which deals with foresight. Research on the discourses of development and humanitarianism, and especially on the HIV/AIDS pandemic in sub-Saharan Africa, represents the empirical core of the fourth chapter, on the practice of aid. And studies of the various components of the alternative globalization movement help to ground the claims about universal solidarity advanced in the book's final chapter.

However, since other authors have published a plentiful and excellent supply of primary research on, and detailed case studies of, human rights projects, this book proposes a theoretically driven analysis of the work of global justice. If it questions formalism's interpretive thinness, the version of critical theory employed here is no less sceptical of a strictly descriptive empiricism that confines the human sciences to the observation, depiction and explanation of social reality, in a manner supposedly devoid of any normative content (Apel 1984 [1979]; Habermas 1987 [1971]).[7] On the contrary, research is analytically most solid when reflexive about the value commitments that, without determining its interpretation of empirical findings, certainly inform it; in fact, a critical normativity can bolster empirical understanding of socio-political situations or structural forces by helping to identify and assess their emancipatory potentialities and perils. The articulation of analytical rigour and ethico-political commitment is particularly compelling in light of this book's subject-matter, since an exclusively descriptive chronicling of structural injustices and severe human rights violations is of questionable worth if it is not coupled to a reflection on how they can be averted or overcome through various forms of social action. Surely, the ubiquity of famine, chronic poverty, genocide and pandemics, among other kinds of mass suffering in the world, call for normatively and publicly engaged human sciences.

The critical substantivism that I elaborate in this book is organized analytically around a double movement: it begins 'from below' by unpacking and making sense of the social labour of groups and persons implicated in human rights struggles in historically specific socio-cultural contexts, yet proceeds 'upward' to formulate normative reconstructions of what is required ethically and politically of these struggles to advance the work of global justice. Hence, aside from examining the 'actually existing' patterns of socio-political action produced by progressive civil society participants, critical substantivism advocates an extension and intensification of the emancipatory tasks that contribute to an alternative globalization. The latter – which represents a precondition for the universal realization of civil-political and socio-economic rights – is built upon structural transformations of the world order, through the domestic and transnational redistribution of material and symbolic resources, the enshrining of political freedoms and civil rights in vibrant public spaces, and the cultivation of a cosmopolitan sense of concern for the well-being of distant strangers (see the Conclusion for an elaboration). Given how far we find ourselves from such a state of affairs, and the fact that abuses of

[7] This is a common rendition of sociology, championed from within the discipline by those who guard their version of its scientific standing and by those outside of it who classify it as an empirical form of knowledge participating in a broader intellectual division of labour (whereby normativity is the domain of moral philosophers and political theorists).

human rights remain as common as ever and that material conditions are worsening in many parts of the world, I want to interrogate the formalist bias that is pervasive in the human rights industry (namely, international organizations, mainstream NGOs, governments and normativist and institutionalist academic paradigms). But rather than dismiss discourses of human rights *in toto*, we should consider how they can be reconfigured as components of practices assisting emancipatory projects.

The enactment of global justice

To flesh out the action-theoretical component of critical substantivism, I would like to suggest a conceptual framework anchored in the notion of practice, which despite having a lengthy pedigree in the human sciences, often falls in the space between two broad disciplinary traditions: Kantian moral-political philosophy, which views social action as following and derived from normative principles grounded in human reason (e.g., the categorical imperative); and the Durkheimian sociology of morality, which understands social action as an outcome of institutionally prescribed ideals and structurally enforced and sanctioned rules of conduct (e.g., socialization). For our purposes, however, a practice cannot be reduced to adherence to a norm or rule, as cognitivists would have it, nor to the mechanistic execution of a pre-existing structural code (Bourdieu 1977; 1990 [1980]; Taylor 1985 [1971]; 1995). Rather, it represents – and simultaneously produces – a pattern of materially and symbolically oriented social action that agents undertake within organized political, cultural and socio-economic fields, and whose main features are recognizable across several temporal and spatial settings. A practice confronts certain perils (or obstacles) and must therefore enact a certain repertoire of social tasks, the whole forming what I am terming a mode of practice (see Figure 2).[8]

Taking a cue from Bourdieu and Giddens (Bourdieu 1977; 1990 [1980]; Giddens 1984), who seek to avoid the pitfalls of structural determinism and voluntarist subjectivism, the concept of practice is understood here as both structuring and structured. At one level, actors engaging in a mode of practice have the capacity to contribute to the creation, reproduction and transformation of established relations and

[8] The practice-based model advanced here shares some similarities with the paradigm of contentious politics (McAdam *et al.* 2001), notably its comparative and processual analysis of collective political action. However, instead of focusing on strategic action and mechanisms *per se*, critical substantivism put the accent on the arduous, aporetic and normatively oriented labour of enacting ethico-political tasks and confronting perils (via the concepts of mode of practice and of the work of global justice).

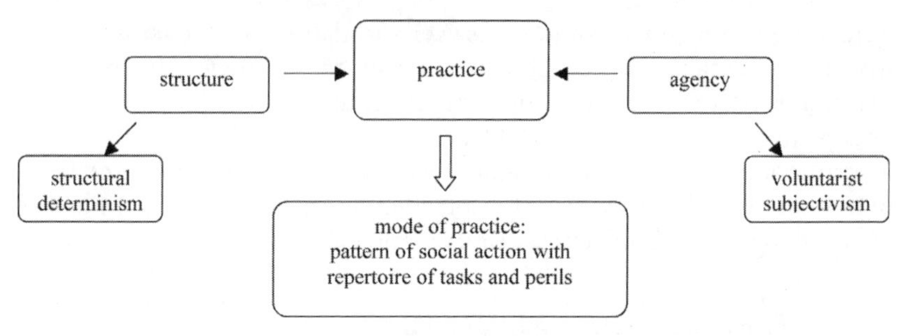

Figure 2. The concepts of practice and mode of practice.

institutional fields of power within which it is located, as well as to the making of new patterns of thought and action that may transcend existing ones. However, a practice is neither a spontaneous act nor the expression of pure free will on the part of agents, who would shape the social world outside of any structural constraints or conditions. Instead, it is located within – and thus structured by – historically transmitted and socially institutionalized forms of thought and action, discourses and relations of power, which have enabling and constraining effects upon a practice's effectiveness and the range of possibilities within which it operates. The extent to which this range of possibilities expands, contracts or remains identical varies in each context within which a mode of practice is performed, according to the terrain of socio-political forces that enframe it and which, in turn, it enframes. Importantly, to acknowledge the productive and creative aspects of a mode of practice is not to treat the latter as an improvisational art that defies taxonomic logic; on the contrary, it is characterized by regularized patterns of thinking and acting that human scientists can identify and interpret.

Intended to signify an ensemble of relations among seemingly disparate elements that forms a whole whose outlines are recognizable across a certain number of geographically and historically distinct circumstances, the term 'pattern' supports a conception of practice that navigates between the aforementioned traps of structuralist and voluntarist accounts of social life. A mode of practice, then, is composed of and framed by patterns of discourses, ethical principles and socio-political rituals. Furthermore, because these patterns can be similar across different settings, modes of practices are characterized by their 'modularity' (Tarrow 2005) – that is to say, the fact that they are transposable across many settings in the world, a specific pattern in one situation being diffused to others. This transferability across contexts is more a matter of creative adaptation of a pattern of social action that originated somewhere else or at another epoch than precise mimesis of it, in response to varying local, national and historical factors. Nevertheless, the enactment of the same mode of practice in different socio-historical environments is defined by a comparable repertoire of ethico-political tasks and perils that agents perform, or to put it succinctly, analogous features among numerous cases. For instance, bearing witness to the Holocaust has served as a template for testimonial responses to the Rwandan genocide; some of the lessons of societal forgiveness in South Africa are being applied in East Timor; the strategies and outlooks of anti-nuclear campaigners have been integrated into foresight about global warming; the campaigns of those living with HIV/AIDS in the global South have inspired Northern activists' demands for a universal right to health; and the worldview of the Brazilian landless peasant movement is one of the backbones of projects of transnational solidarity.[9]

By recognizing that patterns of social action are neither entirely singular (containing a unique combination of elements in each context) nor identical (containing exactly the same combination of elements in all contexts), the idea of modularity or 'transposability' is designed to steer clear of the excesses of nominalism and false universalization; the first would make it impossible to comparatively draw analytical similarities across different manifestations of a mode of practice, whereas the second would generalize a specific configuration of social relations without considering the distinctive features of a given situation. By contrast, the argument about the patterned character of a mode of practice aims for systematicity in its investigation of consistent and regularized configurations of ethico-political relations in several periods and sites, yet is simultaneously adaptable enough to pinpoint significant variations in the locally adapted versions of a mode of practice – which may in turn impact upon the modelling of a mode of practice. In other words, rather than subscribing to analytical notions of complete alterity (nominalist empiricism) or sameness (universalizing structuralism), it is more fruitful to apply principles of similarity and regularity across cases. In the following chapters, then, I examine five modes of practice of global justice: bearing witness (testimonial acts in the face of extreme human rights violations); forgiveness (collective processes by which perpetrators of grave injustices ask to be forgiven and are granted such requests); foresight (farsighted

[9] This is not to claim that the global diffusion of a mode of practice is necessarily unproblematic, as the desire to reproduce a widely publicized and relatively successful response to a global injustice in one setting may be plagued by insufficient consideration of local, national and historical particularities in another setting (e.g., the imposition of South Africa's post-apartheid efforts at reconciliation in societies where impunity for crimes against humanity is rampant).

forms of prevention of, or protection against, atrocities and disasters); aid (assisting persons living through humanitarian crises); and solidarity (the creation of a sense of global responsibility and a planetary consciousness). Each of these five modes of practice of global justice is composed of a finite repertoire of material and symbolic perils and corresponding tasks, which are present in many apparently disparate sets of circumstances across the world.

Bringing to light the repertoires of tasks and perils that constitute the modes of practice of global justice is meant to underscore the *work* of global justice, that is to say, the fact that the latter should be conceived of less as an abstract norm or institutional outcome than a multidimensional, socially and historically constructed project produced by various forms of social action and ethico-political labour.[10] Thus, I want to build upon an emerging sociological and action-theoretical approach to cosmopolitanism and human rights (Beck 2005; 2006; Calhoun 2002; Gilroy 2005; Woodiwiss 2005) in order to argue that the crucial question not only concerns how global justice is legislated from above through normative ideals or procedural-cum-organizational arrangements, but also how its imperfect manifestations function in concrete socio-cultural settings; what matters, then, are the ways that progressive civil society participants attempt to put global justice into practice by confronting difficulties and obstacles that characterize the labour of bearing witness, forgiveness, foresight, aid and solidarity. It is in the performance of tasks and the confrontation of perils defining these modes of practice that the socio-political and ethical thickness of global justice lies, and ultimately, the prospects of an alternative globalization. Likewise, this framework supports a substantive conception of human rights, whereby the latter function as more than ontological attributes which we enjoy as members of humankind or entitlements that are legislated on our behalf by states or international organizations; they are, just as significantly, capacities that groups and persons produce, activate and must exercise by pursuing ethico-political labour.

Focusing on the work of global justice therefore serves as a corrective to formalism, for it directs analysis toward how agents located in socio-political and normative fields put into practice emancipatory projects at various scales (whether framed through or outside of human rights

[10] The action-theoretical notion of the work of global justice draws from a variety of sources: Arendt's treatment of the faculties of thinking, willing and judging (Arendt 1978; 1992); Ricoeur's analysis of the work of memory, which is itself inspired by Freud's discussion of the work of mourning (Ricoeur 2000); Balibar's suggestive idea of 'worksites of democracy' (Balibar 2004 [2001]: 156–7, 172–3); and Boltanski's examination of love and justice as social competencies (Boltanski 1990).

discourses). At the same time, *contra* descriptive empiricism, this same focus can help sustain a critical substantivism that grounds global justice in the already existing patterns of discourses, rituals and belief-systems of progressive national and transnational civic associations, while simultaneously informing a reconstruction of the normative horizons that are necessary and possible for the five modes of practice to advance the vision of an alternative globalization.

Integral to the work of global justice is the fact that struggle represents the core of its enactment – and this, using two meanings of the term. In the first instance, relations of power structure the fields of action within which modes of practice operate, as actors strive to obtain and retain material and symbolic resources and to exercise strategies through which to advance their interests and have their worldviews recognized by governments, international organizations and ordinary citizens. Far from being inherently progressive spaces, national and global civil societies are contested arenas; they certainly contain an impressive range of feminist, humanitarian and social justice movements, but also terrorist and religious fundamentalist organizations among its less savoury elements. Thus, what results from the work of global justice is largely determined by socio-political struggle between such forces.

The second sense in which struggle captures the functioning of the work of global justice concerns the latter's Sisyphean character, namely, the fact that it essentially consists of perpetually difficult, even flawed and aporetic, labour. Indeed, as I understand them, modes of practice of global justice cannot permanently or completely overcome the socio-political and normative perils that constitute them (as enumerated in Figure 3), but must instead constantly and contingently begin to confront them anew by attempting to enact a variety of tasks; no moment of transcendence, finality or perfection awaits those who perform these tasks, which aim as much to curb or avert grievous human rights abuses as to create a more just world order. In this respect, what we need to recognize is that such labour fails to assist human beings at least as frequently as it succeeds in doing so, and that its effectiveness has been hitherto rather modest when we consider the state of the world today. Over the last decade, despite certain promising institutional developments in the field of human rights and the increasing prevalence of human rights discourses in public spheres, severe global injustices regularly occur. Consequently, the recurrence of both structural and situational forms of violence continues to subject populations in the global South to material and symbolic deprivations, including extreme poverty, famine, crimes against humanity, and epidemics, on an all too frequent basis. None the less, acknowledging difficulty and contingency does not

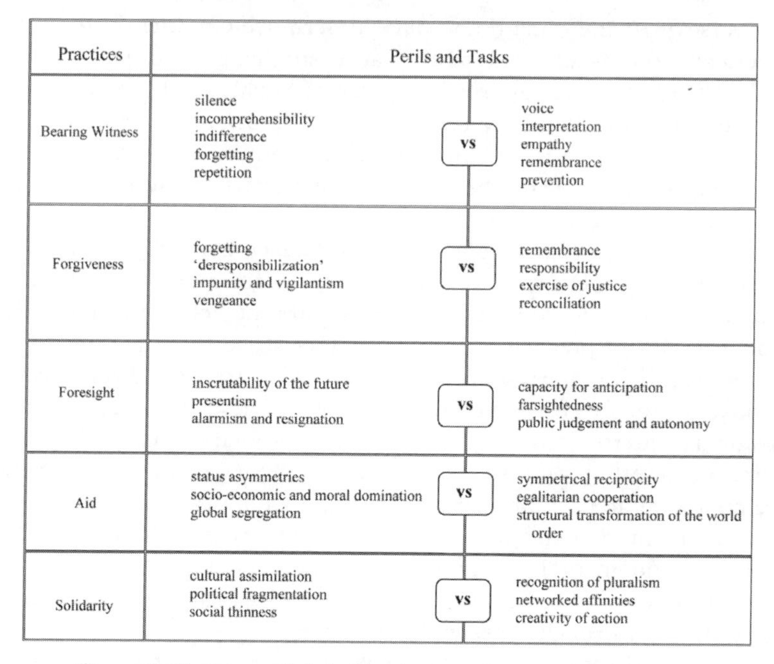

Practices	Perils and Tasks		
Bearing Witness	silence incomprehensibility indifference forgetting repetition	vs	voice interpretation empathy remembrance prevention
Forgiveness	forgetting 'deresponsibilization' impunity and vigilantism vengeance	vs	remembrance responsibility exercise of justice reconciliation
Foresight	inscrutability of the future presentism alarmism and resignation	vs	capacity for anticipation farsightedness public judgement and autonomy
Aid	status asymmetries socio-economic and moral domination global segregation	vs	symmetrical reciprocity egalitarian cooperation structural transformation of the world order
Solidarity	cultural assimilation political fragmentation social thinness	vs	recognition of pluralism networked affinities creativity of action

Figure 3. Practices of global justice.

imply that the work of global justice is thereby futile or that we must resign ourselves to the status quo. On the contrary, these realities bolster a critical substantivism that views bearing witness, forgiveness, foresight, aid and solidarity as imperfect and enduring types of social action – rather than abstract ideals toward which we can strive – performed with resilience on messy terrain, in the face of dangers that incessantly threaten to engulf them.

A constellation of practices

As suggested in the previous section, we can begin to make sense of the bewildering diversity of human rights struggles and projects for an alternative globalization by regrouping them into five modes of practice, the tasks of which, when enacted, constitute the work of global justice (see Figure 4).

Without making a claim to comprehensive coverage of the field of global justice, the model proposed here has the merit of incorporating five patterns of socio-political and normative action that are particularly

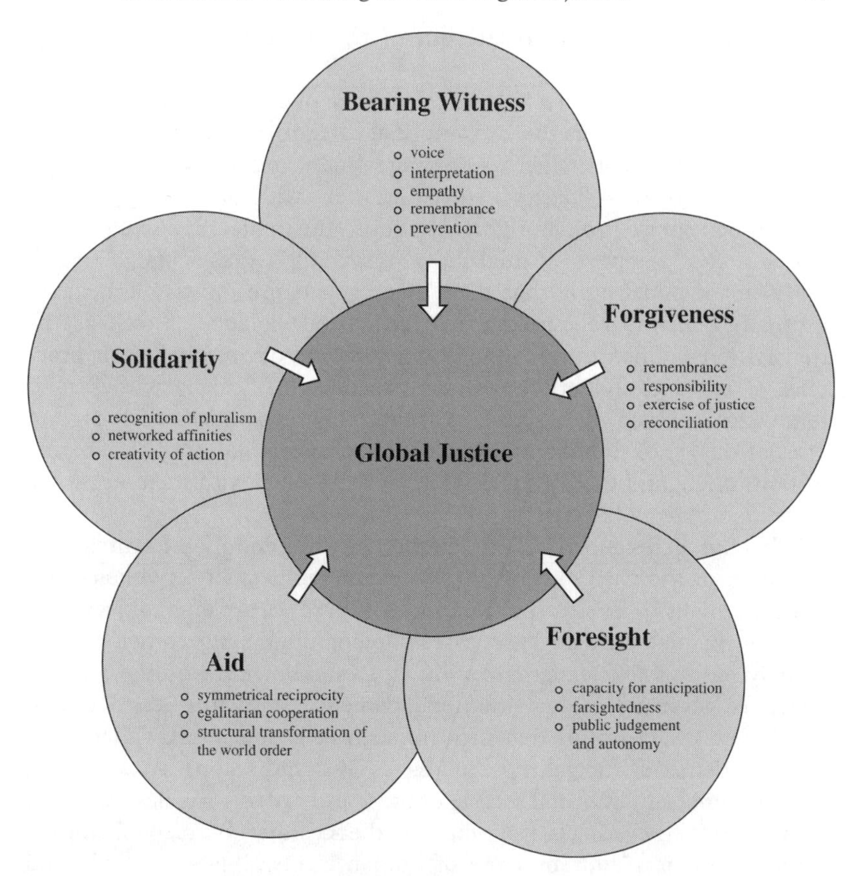

Figure 4. The work of global justice.

salient in many societies and for which actors mobilize noticeably intense social labour; more and more progressive forces are organizing their struggles in the form of testimonial gestures, forgiving, preventing harm, lending assistance and developing a planetary consciousness. In a similar vein, the schema covers a large swath of the progressive civic associations and institutions that participate in the enactment of global justice: these include eyewitnesses, diasporic ethno-cultural communities and media outlets (for bearing witness); survivor groups, truth commissions and transitional justice NGOs (for forgiveness); environmental movements and humanitarian NGOs (for foresight); public health and emergency relief organizations (for aid); and multiple players in the alternative globalization movement (for solidarity). What emerges, then, is a picture of the ways that these agents and structures are gradually constructing global civil society out of transposable configurations of thought and action.

The constellation of five modes of practice of global justice renders in action-theoretical terms the conventional categories of civil-political and socio-economic rights: whereas bearing witness and forgiveness concern the former, aid and solidarity involve the latter – with foresight applying to both dimensions of human rights. However, the model that I am proposing adopts a 'perspectival dualism' (Fraser 1997; Fraser and Honneth 2003) in demonstrating that these two aspects are indivisible because mutually constitutive; resistance to structural violence as well as the transnational redistribution of material and symbolic resources, via practices of aid and solidarity, sustains processes of bearing witness and forgiveness, which themselves facilitate the recognition of past and present-day mass human rights violations that is required if assisting distant others and cultivating a sense of reciprocity with them are to be possible on the global stage.

What binds this constellation together are three common features of all instances of the work of global justice: intersubjectivity, publicity and transnationalism. Firstly, the five modes of practice are intersubjective in that they involve dialogical processes of recognition between two parties, namely, groups that experience, anticipate and/or inform others about instances of structural or situational violence (eyewitnesses, activists, media, etc.) and groups that pick up such calls and convert them into political demands (social movements, NGOs and so on). Accordingly, within formal and informal sectors of the world order, struggles for global justice strive to construct politicized audiences that, by recognizing the claims of victims and survivors of human rights abuses, are able and willing to take steps to stop or avert such abuses. Secondly, the work of global justice draws upon civic associations' capacity to invent and sustain public spaces at the local, national and transnational levels, which are designed to foster wide-ranging democratic participation and citizens' involvement in processes of debate and deliberation about human rights and an alternative globalization. I am using an expansive definition of these worksites of global justice, in order to include public arenas as varied as art exhibits and international tribunals, in addition to protest marches and media outlets transmitting accounts of given humanitarian crises. Such spaces are simultaneously enabling of modes of practice and produced by them, for civil society actors' initiatives publicize global injustices and try to impact public opinion about them. Thirdly, due to the efforts of these same civil society actors, the work of global justice is being transnationalized to the extent that public and political awareness of cases of situational and structural violence is crossing borders in significant ways. Of course, the local and national aspects of modes of practice of global justice remain just as meaningful as ever, but the transnational dimension is superimposing itself atop them and thereby adding another layer of socio-political struggle and normative claims. In fact, activists may sometimes bypass their 'home' nation-state when unfavourable or hostile circumstances result in the domestic non-recognition or misrecognition of their claims (e.g., because of governmental denial or public indifference). In such instances, civic associations can 'scale up' by appealing for transnational support and drawing upon legal and institutional avenues, whether in the form of advocacy networks, multilateral treaties, intergovernmental organizations, international courts or other states – in turn putting 'rebound' pressure on recalcitrant domestic governments.[11]

The design of the schema illustrated in Figure 4 facilitates a sequential and cumulative order of exposition of its components, in order to demonstrate how each form of ethico-political labour flows out of, and overlaps with, its predecessor. For its part, the substantive core of global justice, the repertoire of tasks and perils of which the five modes of practice are composed (see Figure 3), supplies the organization of the book's chapters. Indeed, I begin by discussing bearing witness, which is foundational for the other practices; without public acknowledgement of atrocities and structural injustices in the past and the present, achieved through testimonies, the prospects of forgiving and being granted forgiveness, of exercising foresight, of offering aid and of developing a sense of solidarity without bounds are circumscribed. But bearing witness is significant for its own reasons, given how prevalent testimonial acts have become as means to respond to crimes against humanity since the latter half of the twentieth century. Using the theoretical framework formulated here, Chapter 1 considers five difficulties and matching endeavours that underpin testimonial labour. The first of these is the possibility of silence regarding gross human rights abuses, which eyewitnesses can oppose by communicating their experiences to attuned audiences. Yet because of their character as limit-experiences, such abuses can become seemingly incomprehensible – thus the importance of trying to make sense of them dialogically to bridge any representational and experiential gaps that may exist between eyewitnesses and audiences. While necessary, this sort of cognitive understanding cannot address commonplace indifference toward the suffering of distant strangers, which is why testimonial labour aims to cultivate public empathy and concern for the victims of structural

[11] Keck and Sikkink (1998: 12–13) identify this phenomenon as a 'boomerang pattern' of activism.

and situational violence. Aside from these risks, collective forgetting of catastrophes remains a looming problem against which civil society groups oppose rituals of mnemonic institutionalization and routinization, whereas they can guard against the danger of public complacency by pushing for the prevention of future atrocities.

The book's second chapter examines the practice of forgiveness, which has also become a focal point of the work of global justice in recent years; this is particularly so in transitional and post-transitional societies, where truth commissions are blossoming. Contrary to the widespread belief in forgiveness's intimate links to societal amnesia, the labour of forgiveness supports witnessing's emphasis on collective remembrance via historical investigation and mnemonic reconstruction of past injustices. Once a reasonably complete historical record is produced, actors are in a position to take responsibility (in the case of former perpetrators and supporters of massive human rights violations who acknowledge wrongdoing) or apportion it (in the case of democratically representative institutions in post-transitional situations). Opposing 'deresponsibilizing' tendencies such as unrepentance (the refusal to accept responsibility) and collective guilt (the assigning of equal responsibility to all citizens), forgiveneness can be based on a framework that distinguishes between criminal, moral and political layers of responsibility, and on a consequentialist ethic. Nevertheless, the prospect of impunity for perpetrators and the resulting danger of vigilantism require that those engaging in the practice of forgiveness adopt a model combining retributive and restorative aspects of justice, including the redress of structural relations of domination between former perpetrators and victims. Moreover, civil society participants can hold the temptation to seek revenge against those who inflicted mass suffering at bay by working toward peaceful co-existence or even reconciliation, albeit always under the aegis of the rendering of justice.

If witnessing and forgiveness are both geared toward past human rights abuses, a prospective form of social action is also coming to the fore in world affairs; its practitioners, who are inspired by a kind of dystopian imaginary defining the current epoch, strive to anticipate and prevent future instances of structural and situational violence. This mode of practice of global justice, which I have termed foresight, is the subject of the third chapter. To oppose a sort of radical indeterminacy asserting that the future is utterly inscrutable, certain progressive NGOs active in global civil society are developing a capacity for the early detection of, and warning about, potential humanitarian crises. Despite the possibility for anticipation, actors engaging in the labour of foresight often encounter a presentist bias in Euro-American societies, expressions of shortsightedness or simple callousness about the future. In response, civic associations are trying to cultivate a public ethos of intergenerational responsibility, which draws upon citizens' moral and cognitive skills in pushing for a farsighted version of cosmopolitanism. At the same time, since state and civil society groups can manipulate farsightedness to convert it into alarmist fearmongering or make it degenerate into resignation, progressive forces must try to anchor it to norms of precaution and justice that feed public debate about the eventual shape of a different world order.

But what happens when foresight fails, when populations face grave crises threatening their very survival (famines, epidemics, etc.)? At that point, as Chapter 4 contends, the practice of aid, of humanitarian assistance to distant strangers placed in situations of extreme vulnerability and mass suffering, becomes crucial. What is notable, however, are the recent transformations in the framing of aid, whose legitimacy rests less on troubling notions of charity or failed policies of 'Third World development' than on the concretization of global socio-economic justice. Having said that, the creation and accentuation of status asymmetries between donors and recipients of aid represent ever-present dangers due to gaps in expert knowledges and socio-economic resources, which specific elements of global civil society groups are striving to contest by pursuing participatory assistance projects in the global South (guided by the principle of symmetrical reciprocity). And because aid has served as a tool of Western socio-economic domination and moral regulation of regions and populations, forms of assistance participating in the work of global justice must attempt to foster egalitarian modes of North–South cooperation, based on local decision-making and democratic empowerment of marginalized groups. Furthermore, to counteract neoliberalism's accentuation of transnational processes of spatial and socio-economic segregation, progressive global civil society participants are viewing aid as a part of broader struggles to structurally transform the current world order in the direction of an alternative globalization.

The book's fifth and final chapter covers the practice of solidarity, which in many ways represents both the starting-point and culmination of the work of global justice, given the significance to emancipatory visions of a cosmopolitan sense of concern for all human beings and belief in a shared fate. Yet fostering solidarity without bounds is a precarious endeavour, not least because many thinkers believe it to be a by-product of a social homogeneity that transcends difference in the name of cultural assimilation. By contrast, certain actors in the alternative globalization movement are advocating the recognition of planetary cultural heterogeneity as a means to forge solidaristic ties, while simultaneously demonstrating that the embrace of pluralism need not produce a debilitating fracturing of political projects; the labour of transnational solidarity is currently adopting features of a dense web or network of intersecting affinities and shared interests among progressive sectors of global civil society, without constantly resorting to calls for greater sameness among participants. Whilst this may well be the case, many advocates of a pluralist cosmopolitanism maintain a rather thin and formalist version of solidarity that is premised upon a minimalist global consensus on normative or procedural grounds. To my mind, this is to overlook how and to what extent social action can generate ties between persons and groups via processes of public deliberation, participation in political struggles and initiatives, as well as aesthetic appreciation. This sort of solidaristic labour can sustain a thicker and more experientially meaningful version of cosmopolitanism – a cosmopolitanism from below.

In light of this overview of the different chapters, it should be clear that the following pages' sequential treatment of the five modes of practice is a heuristic device rather than a suggestion about their discrete or self-contained status. In fact, they are characterized by a considerable degree of overlap and interdependence, to the point of being mutually constitutive; engagement in one mode of practice is facilitated a great deal by the performance of the labour that defines the others and, conversely, the inability or unwillingness to enact one of them renders its counterparts more difficult to enact while weakening the prospects of an alternative world order. Taken together, then, bearing witness, forgiveness, foresight, aid and solidarity form a distinctive constellation of normatively and socio-politically emancipatory actions, which take part in the arduous, contingent and perpetual undertaking that is the work of global justice.

1 A message in a bottle: on bearing witness

> The paradox here is that if the only one bearing witness to the human is the one whose humanity has been wholly destroyed, this means that the identity between human and inhuman is never perfect and that it is not truly possible to destroy the human, that something always *remains*. *The witness is that remnant.*
>
> (Agamben 1999: 34)[1]

Introduction

Our examination of the practices that constitute global justice begins with bearing witness, for testimonial acts undergird and create the ethical and socio-political conditions under which the other modes of practice considered in this book can exist. Indeed, without the labour of groups and persons struggling to give voice and respond to mass abuses of both civil-political and socio-economic rights, the pursuit of global justice would rapidly grind to a halt. As we shall see in the chapters to follow, bearing witness to past, present and future structural injustices and atrocities is necessary for forgiveness to be envisaged, for farsighted warnings about potential catastrophes to be heeded, for aid to those in need to be forthcoming and for solidarity with distant others to be built.

Aside from grounding other modes of practice, bearing witness merits attention in its own right. Its prevalence and impact today can hardly be ignored, for we inhabit what commentators have variously described as 'the era of the witness' (Wieviorka 1998) and 'the age of testimony' (Felman and Laub 1992: 206). The history of the last century is replete with testimonial litanies of human suffering: from colonialism and slavery to the Holocaust and the Gulags, from the Armenian to the Cambodian genocides, from the Chinese Cultural Revolution to South African apartheid, from Hiroshima to South American dictatorships. And the recent past hardly offers any respite: Ethiopia, Tiananmen Square, the former Yugoslavia, Rwanda, East Timor, Chechnya, Iraq, Darfur – all events

[1] Italics in the original.

whose perception has vitally been shaped by eyewitnesses.[2] What becomes clear, then, is that beyond an 'archive fever' (Derrida 1996), the world is consumed by a more generalized witnessing fever whereby public spaces have been transformed into veritable machines for the production of testimonial narratives and evidence (of a visual, oral or textual variety). Nowhere is this more so than in the budding realm of global civil society, which has been both deluged by such claims and itself partially created by them.

Consequently, witnessing fever has taken hold in a variety of fields of intellectual endeavour. It is a key preoccupation in what could be termed the realist arts – that is to say, those explicitly concerned with factual depictions of reality (documentary film-making, journalism, autobiographical writing, etc.).[3] Moreover, the theme of bearing witness has sprung forth as a key source of inspiration for creators in the fictionalizing arts, which attempt either to transfigure reality or break with it (e.g., literature, theatre, cinema, painting).[4] Within academic circles, an already imposing body of work on the topics of collective memory and testimony has appeared over the past two or so decades.[5]

Despite this cacophony of voices and abundance of material, bearing witness has hitherto not been conceptualized as a form of social action and thought performed in response to human rights abuses and composed of similar ethical and socio-political patterns across different historical and cultural settings. Hence, we need to theorize the social labour that composes testimonial acts and their reception by audiences; in particular,

[2] Obviously, this is not to suggest a facile moral equivalence between these different events.

[3] For instance, one could think of the tradition of war photography stretching from Robert Capa to James Nachtwey, John Hersey's *Hiroshima* (1985 [1946]), the writings of Primo Levi (1988; 1996), or yet again Alain Resnais's *Night and Fog* (1955). *The Last Just Man* (dir. Steven Silver, Canada, 2001), *Shake Hands with the Devil* (dir. Peter Raymont, Canada, 2004), *War Photographer* (dir. Christian Frei, Switzerland, 2001), and *What Remains of Us* (dir. F. Prévost and H. Latullipe, Canada, 2004) are four recent and outstanding documentaries on the subject of bearing witness to catastrophe today. On the importance of documentary cinema as a form of memorialization, see Rabinowitz (1993).

[4] In the field of cinema alone, three exceptional works can be mentioned: Alain Resnais and Marguerite Duras's *Hiroshima mon amour* (1959), Jean-Luc Godard's *Eloge de l'amour* (2001) and Atom Egoyan's *Ararat* (2002). Of course, as these films imply and find troubling, the line between the realist and fictionalizing arts is sometimes blurred (Kurasawa 2004a).

[5] See Agamben (1999), Coq and Bacot (1999), Felman and Laub (1992), Friese (2000), Hatley (2000), Hartman (1996), Huyssen (2000), LaCapra (1994), Le Goff (1992), Levi (1988), Levy and Sznaider (2002), Maclear (1999), Oliver (2001), Rabinowitz (1993), Ricoeur (2000), Sturken (2002), Yoneyama (1999) and Young (1993), as well as the journal *History and Memory*. Maurice Halbwachs is the author of two pioneering studies in the field of collective memory (Halbwachs, 1994 [1925]; 1997 [1950]) upon which much current-day work is based. Pierre Nora's (1984–92) multivolume *Les Lieux de mémoire* project is a landmark in the historiography of memory in modern France.

I argue that bearing witness consists of five interrelated tasks that confront corresponding perils: voice against silence, interpretation against incomprehension, empathy against indifference, remembrance against forgetting and prevention against repetition. This action-theoretical framework enables us to comprehend how actors situated in specific contexts construct and struggle for human rights, as well as to pinpoint the seemingly paradoxical character of the endeavour. On the one hand, what must be acknowledged from the outset is that eyewitness accounts about severe human rights violations have more often than not fallen on deaf ears, whether those of the Western public, states or international organizations. As a number of important studies demonstrate, denial, bystander apathy, *realpolitik* calculus, lack of political will, bureaucratic 'deresponsibilization', and even 'compassion fatigue' are the common reactions to testimonial pleas regarding mass suffering (Barnett 2002; Cohen 2001; Moeller 1999; Power 2002a). On the other hand, such testimonies continue to multiply and to gain visibility around the world as bearing witness becomes one of the primary mechanisms through which persons and groups are combating global injustices in both the civil-political and socio-economic realms. To capture these two dimensions fully, it is useful to view bearing witness as a Sisyphean process that is intrinsically fragile and fraught with difficulties, perpetually encountering and attempting to work through the perils mentioned above without necessarily overcoming them permanently. Accordingly, the capacity to act as an eyewitness to disaster and to elicit effective responses from others only exists as a possibility on the fraught terrain of global justice. Yet the very existence of this possibility warrants attention, and should be better understood.

As such, after briefly considering the pivotal role of bearing witness today, this chapter outlines the theoretical apparatus to analyse it as a mode of practice of global justice. This is followed by a discussion of the first task of testimonial acts, eyewitnesses struggling against silence by speaking out about and communicating their experiences to audiences that are both able and willing to listen to them. In the fourth part of this chapter, I discuss the interpretive labour through which the two parties involved in the practice attempt to bridge the representational and experiential gaps separating them in order to achieve some measure of common understanding, thereby challenging the incomprehensibility of catastrophes. The next task, that of cultivating empathy among testimonial audiences in order to overcome indifference to distant suffering, is then pondered. The chapter's last two sections consider the remaining components of testimonial practice: collective remembrance via mnemonic institutionalization and routinization aimed at undermining the tendency toward forgetting; and to warn against complacency as well as engage audiences in preventing the advent of future global injustices. Thus, I am positing that a consideration of the five tasks that constitute the work of bearing witness – namely, voice, interpretation, empathy, remembrance and prevention – enable a systematic envisioning of what this mode of practice has accomplished and what remains to be done if it is to contribute to the realization of global justice.

The significance of bearing witness

There is no question that bearing witness occupies a privileged and foundational place among practices of global justice. Indeed, it is striking to note the extent to which some of the towering moral figures of the past century correspond to its great eyewitnesses: Primo Levi, Rigoberta Menchú, Aleksandr Solzhenitsyn and Nelson Mandela, among others – names that evoke resistance to the loss of human dignity intrinsic in atrocities and structural injustices and, conversely, cultivation of the universality of socio-economic and civil-political rights.[6] The sheer determination of eyewitnesses to survive in order to inform others about extreme abuses of these rights seems like a rare attribute, but the abundance of testimonial expressions from all parts of the globe makes clear that it consistently manifests itself among ordinary persons. Why, then, has it become so meaningful in our age?

The answer is to be found in the conjunction of a number of developments in the realm of global justice. In the first place, since the adoption of the Universal Declaration of Human Rights by the United Nations' General Assembly in 1948, the discourse of human rights is now ubiquitous in many national and transnational settings, generating socio-political spaces hospitable to the production, circulation and reception of testimonies about global injustices. Despite being seriously deficient with regards to socio-economic rights, the domain of international law devoted to identifying and prosecuting crimes against populations on a mass scale has blossomed in the aftermath of the Second World War – as has the corresponding judicial capacity to incorporate eyewitness accounts into investigations and trials against perpetrators of such crimes.[7] To wit, the pivotal role of testimonies in the various national truth and reconciliation commissions inspired by the pioneering South

[6] Todorov (2000) discusses several remarkable persons who, when confronted with systemic evil in the twentieth century, opted for 'the temptation of the good'.

[7] The concept of 'crimes against humanity' was introduced between the two world wars and first extensively used during the Nuremberg and Tokyo tribunals. For its part, the term 'genocide' entered our lexicon in the second half of the twentieth century, being officially consecrated with the adoption of the United Nations' Convention on the Prevention and

African experiment, in the International Criminal Tribunal for the former Yugoslavia (ICTY) established in 1993 and that for Rwanda (ICTR) founded a year later (both under the auspices of the United Nations), in the newly formed International Criminal Court in The Hague, and last but not least, in attempts at extra-territorial prosecution of persons accused of committing crimes against humanity.[8] Western states and international organizations have undoubtedly promoted witnessing fever, positioning testimonies as the very core of a strategy whereby societies and their populations can embark upon a collective process of acknowledgement of and reckoning with dark moments of their histories. Accordingly, international criminal tribunals and truth and reconciliation commissions sanction the institutionalization of bearing witness as a way of moving forward after mass trauma (as will be discussed in Chapter 2).

In addition, several human rights and humanitarian NGOs (e.g., Amnesty International, Human Rights Watch, Oxfam) are implementing awareness and fundraising campaigns in which eyewitness accounts of atrocities, famines and extreme poverty feature prominently, thus dramatically raising the visibility of testimonies in civil society and governmental sectors.[9] The explosion of mass communication flows linking different regions of the globe represents another important factor, since the transnational reach and coverage of media outlets, coupled to the instantaneity of their reporting and in spite of their high levels of corporate concentration, potentially swells the number of public stages for various forms of testimony (the ubiquity of 24-hour television news channels being the most obvious indication of this trend). For its part, the spread of visual recording technologies – chiefly those of the

Punishment of the Crime of Genocide in 1948. On Raphael Lemkin's fifteen-year campaign to have this neologism recognized by the international community, see Power (2002a: 17–60). Nevertheless, Ignatieff (1998: 90–2) argues that the zenith of liberal internationalism was the brief post-Cold War period of the early 1990s – which faded with the failed or belated interventions in the former Yugoslavia and Rwanda.

[8] In addition to the South African Truth and Reconciliation Commission, which held proceedings between 1995 and 2002 (www.doj.gov.za/trc), other similar commissions have been created in, *inter alia*, East Timor, Peru, Chile, Ghana and Sierra Leone. For the ongoing former Yugoslavian and Rwandan tribunals, see, respectively, www.un.org/icty and www.ictr.org. For the International Criminal Court, see www.icc.int. On extra-territorial prosecution, see Silber (2003). The most famous case of this occurred in 1998, when the British government arrested and detained former Chilean dictator Augusto Pinochet in London in response to an arrest warrant issued by Spanish judge Baltasar Garzón. After a series of complex deliberations and rulings, Pinochet was eventually released and allowed to return to Chile in 2000 because deemed medically unfit to stand trial in Spain.

[9] On the role of formal institutions, agreements, social movements and non-governmental organizations in global politics, see Alexander (2002: 49–51), Dunne and Wheeler (1999), Falk (2000) and Keane (2003).

photographic and video camera – is popularizing the documenting of human rights violations, which becomes accessible not only to victims themselves, but to freelance reporters, NGO workers and even ordinary citizens.

Finally, it should be mentioned that the coming into being of the age of witnessing is a response not only to the multiplication of mass human rights abuses, but also to growing recognition of them and the intensification of the modern anxiety toward social forgetting – the prospect of an impoverishment or erasure of collective memory that has inspired Euro-American thinkers and artists throughout the twentieth century.[10] The advent of mass media valuing distraction, the 'live' and the immediate over historical and mnemonic depth sustains the intense temporal self-referentiality of our times, resulting in a presentism where very little exists outside of the horizons of a perpetual now (something tackled more fully in Chapter 3). Further, the gradual passing away of eyewitnesses who directly experienced some of the atrocities of the past century only heightens the already disquieting realization that catastrophic events can never be perfectly restituted in the present. For many, the dying of the light of the last survivor able to claim 'I was there' means that we are already 'in search of the lost century', as Jean-Luc Godard puts it in echoing the title of Proust's masterpiece.[11] Bearing witness, then, has been enlisted in the war against societal amnesia and a faulty or opportunistically selective remembrance of the past.

Theorizing the work of bearing witness

Having briefly reviewed the socio-historical context within which the era of testimony has arisen, I would now like to propose a theoretical conceptualization of the practice of bearing witness. If formally shaped by juridico-normative principles and institutional frameworks, its substantive dimensions are supplied through patterns of social thought and action; in other words, it is in the labour of bearing witness, rather than in testimonies' procedural or organizational features, that lies the greatest concentration of ethical and socio-political density. Accordingly, in order to frame the following discussion, we can summon a celebrated prose passage from the Jewish Eastern European poet Paul Celan:

[10] See Huyssen (2000) and Ricoeur (2000) on the contemporary culture of memory and the converse fear of forgetting. For instance, the three films already mentioned (by Resnais and Duras, Godard and Egoyan) place the problem of societal and individual forgetting at their core.

[11] *De l'origine du 21e siècle* (dir. Jean-Luc Godard, France, 2000).

> A poem, as a manifestation of language and thus essentially dialogue, can be a message in a bottle, sent out in the – not always greatly hopeful – belief that somewhere and sometime it could wash up on land, on heartland perhaps. Poems in this sense too are underway: they are making toward something. Toward what? Toward something standing open, occupiable, perhaps toward an addressable Thou, toward an addressable reality. (Celan 2001: 396)

Using Celan's allegory of the poem as a message in a bottle, we can ponder how bearing witness embodies the three features of all practices of global justice: intersubjectivity, publicity and transnationalism.

Firstly, witnessing is an intrinsically dialogical process of recognition involving both eyewitnesses and their audiences, the two parties engaging in the labour of address and response through which they constitute each other's roles.[12] It is initiated by eyewitnesses, who take on the representational task of attempting to restitute and transmit their firsthand experiences of the then and there of human rights abuses in order to resist the dangers of silence, incomprehension, indifference, forgetting and return; they write messages, place them in bottles and send them out to sea. However, *contra* monological or individualizing explanations that view testimony as the outcome of personal conscience or of a solitary, heroic stand, what should be stressed is the intersubjective character of the practice of bearing witness. Integral to the testimonial performance is an appeal to an audience that must in turn respond to it, for both the roles of addressee and addressed are constructed through mutual recognition. Those having lived through a particular situation or event only become eyewitnesses to it if and when institutional sanctioning or popular acknowledgement of their status occurs; the bottle must reach land, and others must both read and understand the message it contains. At the same time, a moral asymmetry exists at the heart of the process, the normative and political responsibility embedded in the practice of bearing witness lying with audience members. For the mode of practice to be effective in advancing or protecting human rights, a group of actors must heed testimonial calls to reflection and action by responding to eyewitnesses' appeals. These actors pick up the bottles washed up on land, decipher the enclosed messages, ponder them and intervene accordingly with the aim of alerting the world, making sense of what has taken place, cultivating empathy, remembering and preventing the reoccurrence of

[12] On the paradigm of recognition, see Honneth (1995) and Taylor *et al.* (1994). Though not directly employed here, the Habermasian concept of discourse ethics has sustained the most theoretically and normatively sophisticated analysis of the dialogical character of social life; see, among others, Benhabib (1992) and Habermas (1990). To this extent, my argument runs counter to Oliver's (2001) claim that the witnessing is 'beyond recognition'.

the immediate or structural circumstances that are at the root of suffering.[13]

This chapter also underscores the vitally public character of the practice of bearing witness. Rather than approaching it through a psychologizing, individualizing or therapeutic lens (as a means to deal with trauma, for instance),[14] we can insist upon the essential dimension of publicity that defines testimonial labour – a collective process occurring in and through public spaces (Arendt 1998; Habermas 1989a; 1996: 329–87).[15] The dialogical cycle of address and answer between eyewitnesses and their audiences, as well as the establishment of relations of recognition between the two parties, are publicly oriented affairs that citizens and states undertake in a multiplicity of sites and through diverse means of communication (ranging from museums and courts to books, photography, films and television, electronic and print media).

What has not always hitherto been recognized in the literature on bearing witness is its transnational orientation, which increasingly involves and draws upon institutional and social relations that exist beyond the territorial borders where human rights abuses or struggles are taking place. While they are grounded in local and national settings – and thus take on particular meanings – testimonial appeals are also increasingly being addressed to a global imagined community composed of diasporic cultural groups, states, NGOs, social movements, multilateral organizations, media outlets and concerned citizens in the four corners of the earth. In turn, these actors frequently play determining roles in acknowledging and publicizing atrocities, as well as initiating judicial procedures on behalf of victims and survivors. First visible in the globalization of Holocaust remembrance (Huyssen 2000; Levy and

[13] Levi makes this duty of response explicit, as well as the moral asymmetry embedded therein, in a poem reformulating the Shemá (the prayer that is central to Judaism) (Geras 1998: 15–17): 'You who live safe/ In your warm houses,/ You who find, returning in the evening,/ Hot food and friendly faces:/ Consider if this is a man/ Who works in the mud/ Who does not know peace/ Who fights for a scrap of bread/ Who dies because of a yes or a no./ Consider if this is a woman,/ Without hair and without name/ With no more strength to remember,/ Her eyes empty and her womb cold/ Like a frog in winter./ Meditate that this came about./ I commend these words to you./ Carve them in your hearts/ At home, in the street,/ Going to bed, rising;/ Repeat them to your children,/ Or may your house fall apart,/ May illness impede you,/ May your children turn their faces from you.' (Levi 1996 [1958]: 11) A different translation of this poem is provided in Levi (1995). Deuteronomy contains the original lines of the Shemá.

[14] See, *inter alia*, Perlesz (1999).

[15] For our purposes, the differences between their understandings of the public domain – namely Arendt's emphasis upon agonistic pluralism, which vividly contrasts to Habermas's more overarching and consensual vision of publicity – can be bracketed. Also, see Boltanski's (1993) strongly public conception of the voicing of distant suffering and responses to it.

Sznaider 2002), this transnational phenomenon comes strongly into play today when national governments or populations are either unable or unwilling to take responsibility for the performance of mass crimes and the prosecution of their perpetrators (e.g., in Chile, Argentina, Peru, Cambodia, Rwanda, Chechnya, the former Yugoslavia). In such cases, outside actors can pressure, assist or even intervene in domestic or international settings to try to ensure that the plight of eyewitnesses is not ignored; in fact, awareness of testimonials in global civil society is becoming a precondition for the realization of a similar process at the level of the nation-state. Put differently, the principle of transnational publicity nurtures and sustains the work of bearing witness, which is greatly enhanced by the existence of global public spaces responsive to distant suffering and itself expands the number and kinds of such spaces.[16]

The practice of bearing witness and its three dimensions (dialogism, publicity and transnationalism) are defined by asymmetries of power within national and global arenas, which enframe the socio-political production and reception of testimonial acts. If, ideally, all demonstrably truthful accounts of severe human rights violations should compel audiences to engage in the work of bearing witness, the reality is that global civil society responses to appeals are inconsistent and selective. Some messages in bottles are read and prompt strong constructive responses, while many others are ignored or generate little more than generalized indifference: which experiences of injustice are widely known, and which ones are ignored?; which forms of evidence about, narrative versions of, and claims of, injustice are accepted, and which are rejected?; what kind of interventionist, retributive, commemorative or compensatory action is taken during or in the aftermath of horrific events or structural problems?; and more broadly, who decides such matters and in whose interests, and what effects do such decisions have?

Referring to universal ethical norms and rules of accuracy only provides limited answers to such queries. Instead, we should put into play a notion of socio-political struggle between groups and persons bearing witness, for hierarchies along lines of gender, race and ethnicity, class, nationality and religion noticeably impact upon testimonial practice. Eyewitnesses and the communities to which they belong can exercise power to varying extents and mobilize vastly differing levels of material and symbolic

[16] About the emergence of a global civil society and a transnational ethics tied to the protection of human rights and humanitarian responses to distant suffering, see, *inter alia*, Boltanski (1993), Cohen (2001: 222–77), Dunne and Wheeler (1999), Falk (2000), Habermas (2001), Held (1995), Ignatieff (1998; 2001), Keane (2003), Levy and Sznaider (2002) and Singer (2002).

resources in order to gain and retain access to, support from, and influence over, 'external' actors (such as the media, states, NGOs and international organizations). This delimits the testimonial strategies employed to transmit messages to national and global audiences, as well as the retributive and restitutive demands presented to such audiences – strategies and demands that depend upon uneven capacities to meet and comply with procedural requirements and expectations (the pursuit of prosecution and compensation through appropriate channels, the satisfaction of evidentiary rules in judicial systems, etc.).[17] Relations of power are also closely implicated in determining a particular group's success or failure in institutionalizing mnemonic sites and rituals of commemoration, as well as in eliciting broad public awareness of and participation in the latter; one can think, for instance, of the limited impact of most indigenous groups that have been bearing witness to genocidal and discriminatory policies in the Americas and Oceania. In addition, the relative weakness or strength of audiences shapes the scale and type of popular and official reaction to testimonials, since addressees actively participate in the socio-political construction of human rights abuses through a number of means: expansion of established public spaces to accommodate testimony or creation of new ones for this purpose (e.g., the International Criminal Court, the 2005 Live 8 concerts and the Internet); publicizing certain violations to the international community or neglecting them; narrative structuring through approval or denial of specific interpretations of events; assistance in the collection, validation and presentation of evidence; building support or opposition from other groups and institutions; and deciding what appropriate responses, if any, should be pursued.[18] Endorsement or collaboration by powerful actors on the national and international stages can make the work of bearing

[17] A major flaw with formal legalism of this kind is that its demands cannot be met by many subordinate social groups that have been legitimate victims of mass injustices. Forensic, documentary and eyewitness evidence may have disappeared, been destroyed by perpetrators, or deemed invalid or unreliable by the judicial system – or it may be impossible to collect precisely because of such groups' lack of material and symbolic resources. In these instances, witnessing appeals may be deemed to fall below the minimal threshold for official recognition to be possible.

[18] It is relatively unproblematic for states to recognize particular atrocities or structural injustices if they are not directly implicated in perpetrating them, or if granting such recognition does not indirectly threaten their geopolitical and socio-economic interests. Along the same lines, populations are quite willing to do the same if their involvement or complicity is not in question. The converse case, whether for governments or civil societies, is exceptional – something that is additionally complicated by the fact that public arenas may contain widely differing, even seemingly incommensurable, testimonial claims about particular events (as in the case of the Armenian genocide or the Israeli–Palestinian conflict).

witness possible, whereas their hostility, obstruction or indifference – or, yet again, the aid of exclusively weak players – can render it virtually futile. Put simply, global asymmetries of power have a determining impact upon whether a given message in a bottle is read or cast off, acted upon or ignored.[19]

Thus, as previously mentioned, the labour of bearing witness is composed of continuous and arduous confrontations with a set of perils: silence (what if the message in a bottle is never sent or does not reach land?); incomprehension (what if it is written in a language that is undecipherable?); indifference (what if, after being read, it is discarded?); forgetting (what if it is distorted or erased over time?); and repetition (what if it does not help to avert other forms of suffering?). These foundational aporias of testimonial practice cannot be permanently overcome, yet actors can work through them in particular settings by engaging in a corresponding series of ethical and socio-political tasks: giving voice to human rights violations, interpreting them, developing empathy with eyewitnesses, remembering abuses and preventing their return. Let us see how each of these processes participates in constructing the project of global justice.

Speaking out: confronting the abyss of silence

The initial and most elementary aspect of the labour of bearing witness consists of defying the silence and denial that frequently accompany massive human rights abuses, whether these be perpetrated through systemic injustices or atrocities. Since the second half of the twentieth century, tactics of destruction of the possibility of testimony have flourished, including, at their most ruthless, the organized slaughter of eyewitnesses (for which the infamous phrase 'ethnic cleansing' has come to stand) or yet again, their mass imprisonment, suppression and censuring. Those responsible for such crimes treat forensic and documentary evidence in a similar manner, at the same time as they pursue policies of annihilation of the geographical spaces associated with targeted populations (neighbourhoods, communal sites or entire cities and regions) or their reappropriation through renaming, reuse or rebuilding. In addition to erasing the traces of a people's existence and severing their ties to

[19] See Power (2002a) on the potential influence of the United States in preventing or stopping genocide, which contrasts with its actual role as a bystander state. Obviously, none of these considerations immunizes bearing witness from manipulation or distortion through false testimonies, something that states and groups can invent or support to advance their interests.

certain territorial entities, atrocities can thereby be hidden from the outside world by reshaping the theatres in which they are committed. Not to be overlooked is the obliteration of the lifeworlds of victim groups, from the splintering of intimate bonds between families and communities to the banning or replacing of socio-cultural beliefs and practices (e.g., language, religion). Always mindful of a potential audience, those seeking to silence eyewitnesses often turn to outright deception or misinformation by casting doubt over the veracity and reliability of the latter's accounts and of any potentially damning piece of evidence.

Faced with this void, the two parties bearing witness struggle to name and publicize catastrophic events and situations, to bring knowledge of what happened to the world at large. Consequently, speaking out strives to publicly establish and record basic facts about the existence of human rights abuses, or correct established narratives about them (via truth commissions and trials, for instance) (Cohen 2001: 227–8). What drives many eyewitnesses to confront instances of structural and situational violence is the prospect of communicating testimonials of their plights through visual or written means, in order to inform and warn others. Aside from having firsthand experience of such injustices, victims and survivors who bear witness accept the burden of representation thereby entailed – sometimes at the cost of considerable physical danger or emotional and mental anguish. Audiences composed of political leaders and civil society actors have responded in a multiplicity of ways: denouncing what has occurred or is occurring, intervening to put an end to suffering, assisting eyewitnesses to be set free or escape to locations where testimony is possible, smuggling out evidence of mass crimes from places where they were perpetrated and even amassing and ensuring the archival preservation of this kind of evidence.

Despite their importance, fact-finding and record-setting activities are but the point of departure for national and global audiences, who can grant or deny recognition to testimonials. In fact, states, multilateral organizations, NGOs and social movements create or enlarge public spaces for bearing witness according to their material and symbolic power and those of the groups being victimized, as well as enabling or obstructing access to such public arenas by assessing the 'value' and gravity of human rights violations and selecting which ones are 'worthy' of outside support. For witnessing to be effective, then, certain addressees must assume the task of listening to testimony and broadcasting it to the general population or decision-makers, of reading the message in a bottle and being radically open to heed its call. Over the last few decades, the development of global civil society and its national counterparts means a growing possibility that eyewitness accounts will be noticed by carrier groups – if not necessarily acted upon either by ordinary citizens or political figures. But genuinely to hear a message of this sort demands that civil society actors be willing to learn from it, that they pay careful attention to the forms of representation of catastrophic experiences and explanations of structural violence. In other words, audience members can strive to decentre their own worldviews, suspend their preconceptions and enlarge their horizons in order to be in a position to receive eyewitnesses' narratives, which may well lie beyond what the former knew or imagined (Young 1997). Accordingly, those bearing witness refuse to concede to ignorance and take refuge in the falsely comforting belief that 'we did not and could not know'. By assuming a testimonial duty of speaking out on behalf of victims and survivors who may not be able to do so themselves, or by denouncing human rights abuses wherever they occur, nationally and globally based civic associations produce a potentially knowledgeable, or at least minimally aware, world community. Civic networks transmit messages in bottles, continuously narrowing the circles of those who can legitimately or plausibly claim to be in the dark about global injustices.

The threat of incomprehension and the labour of interpretation

If the task of giving voice and listening to testimonies of severe human rights abuses is what puts the work of bearing witness into motion, making sense of the experiences of those subjected to such abuses is equally laborious. Indeed, although an eyewitness's message may have been written and sent, it is not inherently decipherable by others. Lurking in the shadows is the prospect of incomprehension or misunderstanding, for testimony is routinely confronted to the communicative limits of words and images in the face of extreme suffering and socio-economic want. Among other factors, this is what fuels the much discussed crisis of representation in the humanities and social sciences, which Adorno's (1981: 34) famous dictum about the barbarism of writing poetry after Auschwitz anticipated.[20] What sorts of oral, visual or textual devices can adequately and justly render the intensity and scale of global injustices? And how can Western audiences, made up of ordinary citizens and

[20] Adorno elaborated upon this declaration elsewhere (1982 [1962]: 312–13), while subsequently qualifying it in *Negative Dialectics* (1973 [1966]: 362–3). To my mind, it is not intended as a prohibition of representation of the Holocaust, but a warning against its aestheticization (and that of horror more generally).

political leaders, come to comprehend events and situations far removed from their everyday lives?[21]

Groups and persons bearing witness in global and national civil societies routinely encounter two sorts of interpretive gaps. The first is experiential, since the extreme character of global injustices frequently exceeds the bounds of the familiar and ordinary frames of reference that most potential or real audience members use to function (Felman and Laub 1992: 84–5; Ricoeur 2000: 207, 222–4, 475). In such instances, communication between testimonial parties cannot automatically draw or fall back upon a shared lifeworld, the pregiven or typical repertoire of background symbols, meanings, beliefs and assumptions that Husserl (1970: 145) termed the 'natural attitude' and through which understanding is generated. Additionally, the restitutive and reproductive inadequacies of any and all technologies of representation (e.g., visual artefacts, oral testimony, textual documentation) become glaring when dealing with mass suffering – something that more simplistic theories of representational realism gloss over, asserting instead the fullness of meaning carried by these technologies or their unproblematic correspondence to what actually took place.

The second interpretive gap is historical and cultural, applying specifically to the distance between the then and there (of particular situations where human rights have been or are being violated) and the here and now (of later generations or distant persons bearing witness). Historical estrangement is always a factor with which audiences living in the aftermath of mass suffering in a particular society must contend, yet the transnationalization of testimonial practices accentuates the possibility of geographical and socio-cultural misunderstanding and undecipherability. For populations living in eras or places seemingly far removed from those where a particular global injustice occurred, the latter's meaning in the eyes of those directly affected by it is never easily captured or transmitted; over time and across space, such meaning for a given society or community can be elusive, as can a grasp of the extent and intensity of suffering in the then and there. The evocative and reconstructive powers of representational mechanisms employed by testimonial actors in global and national civil societies may fade, to the point of threatening the interpretive bond that the labour of bearing witness attempts to construct. To wit, the fact that the impact of the words 'Auschwitz',

[21] On the representational aporias of extremity, see, among others, Agamben (1999), Felman and Laub (1992), Friedlander (1992), Friese (2000), Hartman (1996), LaCapra (1994), Langer (1991), Levi (1988; 1996), Lyotard (1988), Maclear (1999) and Oliver (2001).

'Hiroshima', 'Kigali' and 'Srebrenica' varies in different epochs and societies.[22]

The two gaps mentioned here nurture an additional interpretive peril of the work of bearing witness, namely, the Western news media's tendency to oversimplify a given global injustice in order to gain an audience and keep its attention. Since Euro-American readers and viewers may not easily comprehend sudden acts of mass violence or systemic problems in remote places, media coverage often veers toward the packaging of formulaic or sensationalist narratives and images that leave little room for the experiences of eyewitnesses and the circumstances surrounding their ordeals to be represented in all their complexity (Moeller 1999). Such coverage may even become an obstacle to proper understanding of human rights violations, which can be obscured by reports that fall back upon clichés and derogatory stereotypes about non-Western peoples and societies.

None the less, I want to contend that acknowledging the difficulties of wrestling with incomprehension does not imply slipping into a form of cynicism or despair regarding the unrepresentable – and thus supposedly unintelligible – nature of global injustices. On the contrary, the work of bearing witness consists precisely in pursuing the sort of interpretive labour that strives to represent and make sense of these injustices, which exist at the thresholds and in the recesses of language, speech, writing and image. The struggle to portray and grasp extreme suffering marks testimonial practices' ethico-political stakes, for as Friese (2000: 174) puts it: '[w]hat happened cannot be represented and has

[22] Witnessing's two interpretive gaps are lyrically rendered in Marguerite Duras's screenplay for Alain Resnais's film, *Hiroshima mon amour*. The opening dialogue of a story about an affair between two nameless characters (He, a Japanese architect, and She, a French actress) set in the shadows of the atomic bomb dropped on Hiroshima, goes thus: 'He: You have seen *nothing* in Hiroshima. Nothing./ She: I have seen *everything*. Everything.' (Duras 1960: 22) With its categorical play of affirmation and denial between the two protagonists (and his rebuttals of her claims to completely understand Hiroshima), this exchange serves to caution us against believing in the necessary adequacy of representational techniques. Accordingly, Duras and Resnais suggest that extreme suffering cannot be readily restaged for or understood by others; even firsthand experience of the explosion in Hiroshima does not enable testimonial actors to express and convey the full horror of the event, which remains in excess of representation. In her preface to the screenplay, Duras (1960: 10) makes this point herself: 'Impossible to speak about Hiroshima. The only thing that can be done is to speak about the impossibility of speaking about Hiroshima. Knowledge of Hiroshima being posited *a priori* as an exemplary illusion of the mind [*esprit*].' Moreover, the socio-cultural differences between the two characters underscore the complexities of bearing witness, notably the idea that audiences can put themselves in the place of eyewitnesses in a straightforward manner. For a more detailed (and deconstructive) interpretation of *Hiroshima mon amour* in relation to similar issues, see Maclear (1999: 141–57).

nevertheless to be addressed/written-towards and be made present'.[23] Hence, bearing witness should be conceived as a dialogical process according to which eyewitnesses and their audiences jointly create modes and public spaces of 'in-betweenness' where they meet in their efforts to comprehend atrocities and structural violence, if only partially and temporarily. For testimonials to fulfil their normative and socio-political potential, the communicative exchange between the two parties should encapsulate the sheer otherness of a gross human rights abuse in a way that does not trivialize or domesticate its extremism. Conversely, this radical alterity and the aforementioned interpretive gaps cannot become unbridgeable chasms, which would effectively segregate the event or system in the realm of the inhuman and the incomprehensible – thereby shielding it from critical public scrutiny in national and global civil societies (Alexander 2002; Felman and Laub 1992: 232). Stated differently, a global injustice is neither fully captured by, nor does it utterly escape from, testimonial interpretation; it exists somewhere between these two poles, where groups active in national and global civil societies can work toward its representation and understanding.

How, then, does the interpretive portion of the practice of bearing witness to global injustices generally unfold? Eyewitnesses and their audiences engage in an exercise that simultaneously evokes the differences and similarities between them. On the one hand, testimonies endeavour to get across the exorbitant singularity and acuteness of such injustices, their complete rupture from the everyday lives of most citizens in the Western world. They are also wary of 'banalizing' human abuses by unproblematically translating them into established worldviews and frameworks of understanding of daily life, advocating instead a transformation of our perceptions of these to incorporate extremity. Descriptions and images of mass suffering are juxtaposed to the taken-for-granted meeting of basic socio-economic and civil-political rights in Euro-American societies. The message in a bottle's rendition of political and structural violence thus puts participants in global civil society and the general public face-to-face with severe human rights violations

[23] See also Adorno (1982 [1962]: 312) and Agamben (1999: 32), who writes: 'But why unsayable? Why confer on extermination the prestige of the mystical?' Celan's (2001) poetry derives much of its appeal from taking up this struggle to represent the unrepresentable and working through it. He did so by remoulding language, extracting new meanings out of existing words, as well as inventing startling allegories and symbols that fragmentarily allude to the Holocaust's actual horror. Another instance of linguistic invention in the face of extremity is the Japanese word *hibakusha*, literally 'explosion-affected persons', which was adopted after the Hiroshima and Nagasaki atomic explosions to refer to several categories of persons affected by them (Lifton 1991: 6–7).

(starvation, genocide, etc.), which erode the dignity of victims to the point of utterly dehumanizing them; Levi's (1996 [1958]) qualified and doubt-ridden formulation, 'if this is a man', speaks to just this point.[24]

On the other hand, interpretive labour aims to construct bonds of similarity between the two parties bearing witness across experiential, historical and socio-cultural divides. While eschewing the dilution or trivialization of global injustices for the sake of making them readily understandable, eyewitnesses must nevertheless try to make their experiences intelligible to others. For transnational publics and future generations, testimonies can reconstruct the political, economic, cultural and social circumstances that nurtured human rights violations, offer thick descriptions of what life is or was like, or yet again offer glimpses into the lifeworld of those who are or were directly affected. It can even, to assist in understanding, draw upon parallels with better-known, more locally familiar or more recent events (for instance, the Holocaust serving as a template to sound the alarm about late twentieth century and early twenty-first century genocides). Generally speaking, to be successfully publicized and to garner responses from political leaders and lay audiences, then, firsthand accounts of a particular injustice must describe the socio-historical specificity of its causes and consequences, while at the same time gesturing to its universal significance and impact.

Ordinary citizens as well as actors in national and global civil societies share the burden of interpretation, participating in the public, transnational labour that attempts to bridge the two previously mentioned gaps to create spaces of 'in-betweenness'. Encountering testimonies about mass human rights abuses in all their otherness, audiences displace or suspend their own understandings of the ordinary and the normal. To decipher the message in a bottle, they listen to its content, study it and learn more about the context within which it was written.[25] Accordingly, they can develop representational and sense-making initiatives as well as support the establishment of devices and institutional resources assisting testimonial reconstruction, such as inventing or expanding procedures and organizations capable of explaining, preserving and broadcasting oral and visual records to the world at large.

None of this implies a perfect reversibility of positions, whereby audiences would believe that they are easily and completely able to place

[24] See Agamben's (1999: 58–60) similar reflection on this passage. For doubts about the 'humanness' of victims of Hiroshima along the same lines, see Hersey (1985: 60–1).

[25] The importance of a specific testimonial message and the ways to characterize it are themselves dialogically constructed, since those bearing witness must re-establish and reassert them for each generation and in various socio-cultural settings.

themselves in the shoes of victims and survivors of human rights abuses. Still, the latter groups should not be portrayed as embodiments of pure otherness alienated from humankind because of the acute suffering and cruelty to which they have been subjected; they remain men and women, simultaneously like and unlike those to whom they appeal (Agamben 1999; Todorov 1996: 277; Yavenditti 1974: 37). Even in transnational situations, witnessing allows ordinary citizens to develop their imaginative and reflective capacities to come closer to and gain a better understanding of extremity than could otherwise be possible. This, in turn, can result in a broadening of horizons that dwells in and confronts the reality of global injustices; as Levi's (1996 [1958]: 11) exhortation to reflection demands of us, '[m]editate that this came about./ I commend these words to you.'[26]

Indifference and the cultivation of empathy

One of the most daunting challenges for the practice of bearing witness is the persistence of collective indifference to global injustices, Western political leaders' and ordinary citizens' inability or unwillingness to acknowledge and respond to testimonial appeals by distant strangers. Complicating matters is the selectivity (and thus inconsistency) of such outpourings of concern, which answer some pleas in remote locations while ignoring many more. As Cohen (2001) has explained, cognitive denial of human rights abuses (that is to say, the failure or refusal to acknowledge their factual existence) is but the simplest manifestation of a multifaceted problem, which includes both emotional and implicatory counterparts (respectively, not feeling concern or care about others' suffering, and ignoring the moral and political implications of acknowledging such suffering). While a comprehensive analysis of the absence or blocking of transnational empathy would take us beyond the scope of this chapter, a few relevant considerations should be mentioned.

At the most general level, the modern age is characterized by the invention or acceleration of numerous mechanisms of psychological, emotional and social distancing that immunize or shield most persons from the suffering of others – even when the latter are geographically proximate, let alone when they live across the world.[27] Accordingly, to the

[26] Another translation of this passage (Levi: 1995) reads: '[c]onsider that this has been'. To this extent, both characters in *Hiroshima mon amour* are mistaken; She has seen neither nothing nor everything, but *something* – something that, through the interaction between them as the story unfolds, becomes a form of testimony.

[27] See Arendt (1994), Bauman (1989; 1995), Cohen (2001), Scarry (1985) and Tester (1997).

differentiation of social spheres, socio-cultural fragmentation and increased spatial scale of everyday interactions can be added the expansion of certain extreme forms of moral individualism (e.g., utilitarian or neoliberal discourses about the maximization of self-interest), according to which a subject is solely responsible for his or her own well-being. Conversely, the widespread application of purposive-instrumental rationality in modern social life has led to its formalizing depersonalization, to the point that perpetrators of and bystanders to global injustices can transfer responsibility for their actions and decisions onto socio-political institutions (notably the bureaucratic obligation to follow established orders, procedures and regulations); the conclusions drawn in Arendt's famed study of the Eichmann trial are no less revealing today, as Barnett's (2002) examination of the organizational sources of inaction within the United Nations during the 1994 Rwandan genocide unequivocally demonstrates.

Modern nationalism may well have aimed to foster a sense of 'imagined community' (Anderson 1991) in order to counter the alienating effects of excessive individualism on the one hand and the depersonalization of social relations on the other, but its assertion of solidarity with one's fellow citizens within territorially circumscribed societies is based on a claim of sameness ('I care about them because they are like me') that proves to be an obstacle to empathy toward those perceived as different because living outside the bounds of the nation-state. Moral distancing is also facilitated by the casual ethnocentrism and racism of vast swaths of the Euro-American population, which rarely concern themselves with human rights abuses in Africa, Asia and South America; minor incidents in the North Atlantic region (a grisly murder, the death or trial of a celebrity, etc.) are granted extensive media coverage and regularly elicit outpourings of public grief, while the unfolding of tragedies of massive proportion in the Southern Hemisphere (e.g., famine, genocide, civil war) barely merit an afterthought.[28]

For their part, Western governments and international organizations routinely show evidence of institutional indifference by putting their own geopolitical and socio-economic interests ahead of the need to address global injustices. This failure of political will represents a clear case of organizational denial, for political leaders and diplomats take refuge behind claims of a lack of adequate knowledge ('we did not know what was happening') or an obligation to respect proper institutional channels

[28] Ignatieff (1998: 32–3) mentions 'the newsroom rule of thumb that one British, American, or European life is worth – in news value – a hundred Asian or African lives'. See also Cohen (2001: 169–77).

and protocol ('we had to follow the rules') in order to justify their disinclination to devote adequate resources and time (such as the sending of military personnel or negotiators, or the reform of the global financial and trading system) to deal with the underlying sources of human rights abuses (Cohen 2001: 161–3; Power 2002a).

Despite various predictions about the benevolent effects of planetary communication flows on rapprochement between the world's peoples, indifference remains a feature of the global village in the epoch of transnational media. In fact, it may well be that the proliferation of testimonial practices carried by such media produces 'compassion fatigue' (Moeller 1999) among Western readers and viewers, who are bombarded with narratives and scenes of suffering from the four corners of the globe on a regular basis. Oversaturation and overexposure can transform even the most concerned of citizens into morally and emotionally blasé or numbed spectators, who develop a disturbing tolerance to the daily regime of atrocities and structural violence served up in morning newspapers and on evening newscasts. The routinization of representations of extreme suffering means that their threshold of toleration climbs ever higher, whereas a sense of helplessness in the face of seemingly inevitable or intractable global injustices ('they will always occur' or 'the issues are too complicated') makes the general public turn away from testimonial pleas.[29]

Although collective indifference to distant suffering remains a formidable force in the world today because of the persistence of numerous forms of denial, transnational bonds of empathy with and responsibility toward groups and persons outside of conventionally defined moral communities (local, national, gender, class, ethnic, religious, etc.) are being forged. Certain diasporic ethno-cultural networks, NGOs and transnational social movements have been able to bring attention to severe human rights abuses and cultivate a sense of concern for the well-being of faraway persons within large sectors of global civil society. To gain a hearing from Western citizens and their governments, however, these actors must generally possess high levels of symbolic and material resources, or at least employ eyewitnesses and representatives living in societies where they have entry-points into international media outlets, public discussion and socio-political institutions. Testimonial practices can help to 'bring a tragedy home' and 'put a human face' on global injustices, even to the point of shifting public opinion – albeit rarely to an extent that would compel Euro-American governments and international organizations to act promptly and substantially to stop or prevent such

[29] See Cohen (2001), Geras (1998), Hartman (1996: 99–101), Ignatieff (1998: 29–30) and Tester (1997).

injustices. Here, the belated yet eventually sustained responses to the 1984 Ethiopian famine and ethnic cleansing in the former Yugoslavia (Ignatieff 1998: 10, 21–2) contrast favourably to East Timorese, Tibetan, Rwandan and Chechnyan pleas, which have fallen on deaf ears for the most part.

Hence, first-person accounts of human rights abuses have a greater probability of fostering national and transnational empathy when inserted into parallel institutional mechanisms, notably those within public sites of commemoration of past injustices (e.g., museums) as well as politico-legal performances addressing crimes against humanity (official apologies to victims, trials, truth and reconciliation commissions, etc.). In addition to describing and encouraging civil society discussion about the experiences of victims and survivors, sites and performances of this kind enact and publicize human rights discourses and norms of responsibility toward distant others; the principle of universal equality may thereby be evoked if and when states and international organizations recognize past wrongdoings toward given populations and groups while taking restitutive measures in response.

Testimonial masterworks that are successful in eliciting vast empathetic responses – such as Lanzmann's *Shoah* (1985), Levi's writings (1988; 1996), Hersey's *Hiroshima* (1985)[30] and Menchú's (1984) autobiography – invoke the audience's sense that the occurrence of a particular global injustice is intolerable because it shatters collective responsibility for the well-being of our fellow human beings. They are written, filmed, edited and assembled in ways that involve viewers and readers in the unfolding dramas they recount, in addition to shaking these groups' bystander roles in the face of mass suffering. At the same time, in organizational terms, these works' production of popular empathy depends upon their gaining approval from opinion-makers (reviewers, prominent intellectual and political figures, etc.) and being distributed through media channels reaching broad sections of the general public.[31]

The labour of bearing witness functions by fostering the moral imagination of different audiences, and simultaneously constructing the latter via 'symbolic extension' and partial 'psychological identification' with the

[30] *Hiroshima* is a journalistic account of the lives of six survivors of the atomic bomb dropped on the city, told from their own perspectives. Originally published in a 1946 issue of the *New Yorker*, and reissued in book form that same year, it received widespread public attention in the postwar United States. On this phenomenal success, see Boyer (1985: 204) and Yavenditti (1974: 31–2).

[31] A famous case in point is the editing of Anne Frank's diary by her father, Otto Frank (to make it more palatable to a general audience), as well as its conversion into a Broadway play and Hollywood film. See Alexander (2002: 35) and Frank (1996).

plight of eyewitnesses (Alexander 2002). The creation of transnational empathy requires the cultivation of both emotional and formally rational capacities among publics; this is something that testimonial actors in global civil society understand well, given their simultaneous appeals to the hearts and the minds of others. Accordingly, we can draw upon expressivist and rationalist traditions of thought, which although frequently viewed as incommensurable, are in fact both essential to explain the sources of a nascent cosmopolitan moral imagination.[32]

From an expressivist vantage-point, human nature – and more specifically, engrained moral sentiments triggered by the self's conscience and inner voice – is the most reliable source of empathy toward distant strangers.[33] We care about others and feel compassion toward them because we are able to recognize our common capacity to experience suffering, and because we possess, in Rousseau's (1973 [1755]: 73) words, 'an innate repugnance at seeing a fellow-creature suffer'. If we should be wary of sentimentalizing claims to compassion, testimonial accounts of various sorts (eyewitness narratives and memoirs, journalistic pieces, documentary films, etc.) are especially well suited to the task of awakening human concern in relation to global injustices, for they represent phenomenologically rich descriptions, exposing readers and viewers to others' plight (Alexander 2002: 34–7; Rorty 1989: 94). By reconstructing the socio-historical setting of a given situation of injustice and the lifeworld of affected persons and groups, the most effective instances of bearing witness aim to draw audiences in, to dwell provisionally in the emotional, mental, physical and spiritual universes of survivors and victims. For

[32] The expressivist designation is borrowed from Taylor (1989: 368–90), who also provides an account of how Shaftersbury and Hutcheson initiated an inward turn that located humankind's moral sources in our innate sentiments (Taylor 1989: 248–65). Expressivism and rationalism both launched Western modernity's anthropocentric displacement of the foundations of human empathy away from the divine. By contrast, in a theocentric perspective, our sense of concern for our fellow human beings stems from a recognition that we are all creatures of God.

[33] Expressivism stretches from Hume (1969 [1739–40]), Adam Smith (2002 [1759]) and Rousseau (1973 [1755]) during the Enlightenment to Boltanski (1993), Bauman (1993; 1995) and Rorty (1989; 1998a) more recently. See Arendt's (1963: 70–89) discussion of the importance of pity (as a sentiment) and compassion (as a passion) toward the poor for the French Revolutionaries. She argues that the flip side of pity is solidarity, for it is a principle guided by reason – something that is akin to her Kantian idea of 'enlarged mentality' discussed below. Rorty's position is problematic in two ways: firstly, it overstates the role of the emotions in achieving solidarity (and therefore excludes the rationalist route explained below); secondly, the evocation of an emotional response includes, in his words, 'the manipulation of sentiments' (Rorty 1998a: 176) without reference to overseeing criteria of normative judgement – therefore not ruling out dubious or illegitimate kinds of sentimentalism and demagogy. I would like to thank Amy Bartholomew and Maria Pia Lara for drawing my attention to these points.

instance, in the aforementioned works of Lanzmann, Levi, Hersey and Menchú, what comes across to audiences is less the structural dimensions and full scope of the situations they describe than the subjective experiences of being present in the then and there – the sights, sounds, smells, tastes, emotions and thoughts that accompany horror and systemic violence, the daily struggles to survive, resist, help others and make sense of extremity.

It thereby becomes possible for viewers and readers to connect to the vulnerability and pain of their fellow human beings, who beyond their historical and socio-cultural specificities, remain persons of flesh and blood, of heart and soul, of despair and hope – human, all-too-human. This is the normatively thorny message that Levi's poem carries: if we recognize the outlines of a man (or indeed, a woman) in his account of the lives of Holocaust victims and survivors of Auschwitz, then we are morally bound to respond to it. Otherwise, our capacity to feel compassion for others has been lost, and with it, our very humanity.[34] I would hasten to add that this partial identification with another's plight need not result in a misleading belief in moral and social symmetry between the two parties, according to which their roles can be perfectly reversed ('I feel your pain because I can place myself in your shoes').[35]

Though compelling at one level, expressivism tends to underplay the role of public dialogue and reflection in the formation of transnational empathy. Thus the fruitful corrective that rationalism provides, which – whether in the guise of the notion of enlarged mentality (Kant), of fusion of horizons (Gadamer) or of discourse-ethical reciprocity (Habermas)[36] – locates the development of the moral imagination in the capacity and willingness to listen to others, to attempt to put ourselves in their place, to consider their positions and even to bridge the socio-cultural and

[34] James Nachtwey, one of the world's pre-eminent war photographers, encapsulates this argument at a different level:

> [E]veryone cannot be there, and that is why photographers go there – to show them, to reach out and grab them and make them stop what they are doing and pay attention to what is going on – to create pictures powerful enough to overcome the diluting effects of the mass media and shake people out of their indifference – to protest and by the strength of that protest to make others protest. (Nachtwey 1985)

[35] In the dialogue of *Hiroshima mon amour*, one finds a warning against this sense of effortless emotional identification with the experiences of victims and survivors of atrocities:

> She: I have always cried over Hiroshima's fate. Always.
> He: No. Over *what* would you have cried? (Duras 1960: 26; italics in original)

[36] Rationalist contributions to theories of empathy include Arendt (1968; 1992), Benhabib (1992), Gadamer (1960), Habermas (1990; 1996), Kant (2000 [1790]) and Rawls (1971), despite the significant differences among them.

normative distance between addressers and addressees. While this model must be tempered by a recognition that this bridging is always partial because locations in a national or global social field are never perfectly reversible (Young 1997),[37] the bounds of moral communities can be extended beyond local and national borders via the reflexive labour consisting of the attempt to be open to, engage with and grasp the very different plights of remote strangers.

Rationalism allows us to explain the creation of transnational empathy for the victims of global injustices by referring to the intersubjective process whereby audiences engage with and interpret eyewitnesses' appeals, thereby making it possible for the former to recognize the validity or legitimacy of testimonies by referring to universal human rights norms (or at least basic standards of human dignity). Levi's (1996: 11) previously cited invocation ('[m]editate that this came about./ I commend these words to you.') points in this direction, piercing the veil of indifference by requesting that his readers reflect and carefully consider the experience reconstructed for them. Indeed, the expansion of political leaders' or ordinary citizens' ethical horizons can result from their awareness that the events or systems that eyewitnesses describe violate such existing norms and standards, which must themselves occasionally be revisited to incorporate unprecedented kinds of mass suffering. Additionally, transnational socio-political institutions, laws, treaties, and declarations can serve as the formal grounds for empathetic responses to atrocities and unjust circumstances in remote parts of the world.[38] Because it articulates a notion of the equal worth of all persons, the discourse of universal human rights put forward by the United Nations, NGOs and social movements since the middle of the last century aims to promote a sense of concern and responsibility for the well-being of persons and groups around the planet. Granted, this ideal has been instrumentalized for other purposes or ignored by the very institutions producing it. Further, it is far from being realized since the term

[37] Both Arendt (1968: 220–4; 1992: 70–7) and Benhabib (1992) emphasize the possibility of reversibility of perspectives between parties. However, if pushed too far, this insight can overlook asymmetries of power by presuming that anyone is able to directly imagine and put themselves in everyone else's shoes – a belief that is especially problematic in the case of global injustices, which are produced by structural forms of violence reproducing relations of domination between parties.

[38] This is not to say that we should solely rely on institutionally created normative guidelines, to the extent that society is turned into what Bauman (1989: 175) terms a 'factory of morality'. If they can help to broaden the moral imagination, socio-political institutions can conversely narrow it down by blunting sentiments and legitimizing prejudices that reinforce social distancing. Neither one of these facets is intrinsic to institutions, whose orientation and effects are subject to socio-political struggles.

'humankind' remains a stubbornly abstract signifier (especially when contrasted to the more readily coalescing appeals to community, ethnicity, nation and religion that circulate around the world). None the less, egalitarian universalism has made some headway; the entrenchment of the categories of 'crimes against humanity' and 'genocide' in international law and the wide adoption of the Millennium Development Goals by governments, for instance, have made it easier for global civil society actors to condemn injustices and appeal to the public to respond to them.

Forgetting and the duty of memory

We should now examine how the practice of bearing witness attempts to foster modes of collective remembrance that counteract the effects of mnemonic erosion in the face of global injustices. Indeed, in addition to their giving voice, creating understanding and cultivating empathy, testimonial acts are vitally directed toward confronting the perpetual danger of institutional and public forgetting of instances when the human rights of certain groups were severely violated. Most pernicious is deliberate historical distortion, either through the physical destruction of a group's sites of memory or the textual rewriting of the past.[39] The latter is performed by 'assassins of memory' (Vidal-Naquet 1992) who aim to deny, manipulate and falsify history for their own politico-ideological motives. These pathological kinds of historical revisionism – of which Holocaust denial is the most common – are particularly troubling in that they aim to undermine the very fabric of bearing witness. Aside from 'reinterpreting' certain events and settings by intentionally misreading or blatantly fabricating facts to support their case, mnemonic denial seeks to discredit both eyewitnesses and actual evidence of mass human rights abuses. When it is not outrightly refuting the occurrence of such abuses, revisionism of this sort minimizes their scale and impact in order to exonerate those responsible and 'justify it away' by providing fictitious or deceptive reconstructions of the socio-political context within which they took place.[40]

A seemingly more benign, albeit in some instances no less questionable, type of collective amnesia originates from a state or part of a population wanting to 'leave the past behind and move on', to start afresh and embrace a new dawn in the twilight of mass suffering. Though

[39] Touching upon the first instance, Ignatieff (1998: 177) writes: 'Who, after all, is left to remind the winners that someone else once owned these houses, worshipped here, buried their dead in this group? Ethnic cleansing eradicates the accusing truth of the past.'

[40] For a detailed analysis of different types of collective denial, see Cohen (2001: 132–9).

understandable in light of the fact that revisiting global injustices can be a source of acrimony and conflict between groups within scarred societies, the will to forget more often than not represents a refusal to acknowledge human rights abuses and the roles of perpetrators and bystanders – as we will see in Chapter 2. At a different level, the aforementioned and unintended fading of the past due to the passage of time, and the consequent widening of the temporal and experiential gaps between the here and now and what preceded it faraway, can undermine societal remembrance. Worse still is the generalized sense of complacency that greets mnemonic impoverishment, the self-referential presentism of an outlook that only concerns itself with the here and now.

Regardless of whether it is purposeful or inadvertent, collective forgetting produces long-term consequences that are similar to those of silencing. Neglect of the material and ideational sources of remembrance can result in widespread ignorance of a global injustice for generations living in its aftermath. At various intervals following massive human rights abuses, sites of collective memory (cities, neighbourhoods, buildings, museums) can be razed, built over, reappropriated, ignored or left to decay until they become unrecognizable. The same can be done to archives documenting limit-experiences, which can be destroyed, hidden or allowed to collect dust without being consulted. Commemorative cultural beliefs and practices (including entire languages or specific words) can be prohibited, lost or abandoned, making the entrenchment of collective memory and its intergenerational transmission difficult, if not entirely impossible (Wieviorka 1998: 17–79).

Lest we forget global injustices, then, the 'work of memory' (Ricoeur 2000) represents an integral part of the practice of bearing witness. Aside from seeking to establish and shore up remembrance of past human rights abuses, testimonial acts aim to honour victims and survivors of such abuses.[41] For groups and persons in national and global civil societies, the task consists of acquiring what Duras (1960) lyrically termed 'an unconsolable memory', that is to say, a memory that refuses to capitulate to the tides of time wearing away at it by perpetually engaging in the process of commemoration. Since collective memory is a dynamic and shifting socio-political construct that eyewitnesses and audiences

[41] A passage from Sankichi Toge's (1990: 307) 'Poems of the Atomic Bomb' captures this dimension of remembrance: 'The stillness that reigned over the city of 300,000:/ who can forget it?/ In that hush/ the white eyes of dead women and children/ sent us/ a soul-rending appeal:/ who can forget it?' At the same time, Levi (1988: 83–4) contends that the survivors of an atrocity ('the saved') struggle to speak incompletely on behalf of those who perished ('the drowned'), who are its only genuine witnesses. On this seeming paradox, see also Agamben (1999).

produce dialogically, actors must permanently recreate it for each generation and in different cultural settings.[42] Additionally, the work of memory increasingly stretches across territorial borders, for several diasporic communities and transnational social movements enact rituals commemorating human rights violations in locations that are remote from where they originally occurred; in fact, this deterritorialization and restaging may be necessary in order to counter state- or civil society-sanctioned strategies of forgetting implemented at the sites where such violations were committed.

Therefore, the mnemonic component of testimonial labour is structured by symbolic and material struggles on national and global stages, in order to determine who and what is institutionally remembered (and, conversely, forgotten). To guard against historical revisionism, the practice of remembrance of global injustices takes place through the textual or audio-visual recording of eyewitness accounts,[43] the safeguarding of physical and documentary evidence (in archives, court documents, museums, etc.) and the regular reaffirmation of the validity of sources of information. Over time, especially after the firsthand protagonists have passed away, those bearing witness can continue to search for and collect new evidence while reacquainting later generations with the historical record as means to resist the desire to discard the past. Testimonial acts can defy the customary sense of historical estrangement by creating public sites of memory, and by supporting the reproduction of sociocultural means of recording and communication of past events and situations (via oral narratives, literature, visual arts, music and languages, among others).

Essential to all this is the ritualization of commemoration, the establishment and regular performance of public ceremonies of collective remembrance such as memorial days or events, school-organized visits to sites of memory and the broadcasting and circulation of testimonies

[42] Habermas (1989b: 233) has put it thus:

> First, there is the obligation incumbent upon us in Germany – even if no one else were to feel it any longer – to keep alive, without distortion and not only in an intellectual form, the memory of the sufferings of those who were murdered by German hands. It is especially these dead who have a claim to the weak anamnestic power of a solidarity that later generations can continue to practice only in the medium of a remembrance that is repeatedly renewed, often desperate, and continually on one's mind.

[43] An outstanding example is Yale University's Fortunoff Video Archive for Holocaust Testimonies, which was established in 1981 and now includes more than 4,200 interviews. See Hartman (1996: 133–50), Langer (1991), Wieviorka (1998: 140–50) and the archive's website: www.library.yale.edu/testimonies. Of a different order and scale is Steven Spielberg's Survivors of the Shoah Visual History Foundation, founded in 1994 and currently holding more than 50,000 recorded testimonies. See www.vhf.org.

within public spaces.[44] Rituals of this kind may begin from below within particular communities or social movements, yet they must often be sanctioned by governments, international organizations or mainstream civil society coalitions to gain more widespread popular appeal and participation. Public commemorative performances challenge temporal and spatial distancing from past situations of mass suffering by restaging traces of them for present-day audiences and helping the latter make sense of their root causes and consequences.[45] The plunging back into history fosters a mnemonic sensibility at the heart of bearing witness, resulting not in a single, unified and comprehensive commemorative whole, but a patchwork of overlapping, contested and competing collective memories of injustices.

Never again: parrying the return of evil

Bearing witness to global injustices culminates in struggles to avert the repetition of situations of mass suffering for those living in other times and places, a possibility that arises when warnings about the future in a testimonial message in a bottle are not heeded. Thus, to the perils of ignorance, incomprehension, indifference and forgetting should be added that of political and public complacency or well-wishing naïveté, whereby some believe that violations of socio-economic and civil-political rights are bound to become increasingly rare in our 'civilized' and prosperous age: the persons responsible for crimes against humanity in the past have been punished, the structural causes that led to certain events were unique (a version of historical nominalism) and humankind has learnt from its mistakes. However comforting such Pavlovian fables may be, they do not stand up to historical scrutiny.[46]

[44] A well-known instance of ritualization is the two-decade-long silent vigil and walk by the Mothers of the Plaza de Mayo in Buenos Aires, which is directed toward public acknowledgement and remembrance of the thousands of Argentinian 'disappeared persons'.

[45] On the socio-political and aesthetic issues surrounding the memorialization of Hiroshima, see Hogan (1996), Lifton and Mitchell (1995), Maclear (1999) and Yoneyama (1999); for the Holocaust, see Alexander (2002: 52–5), Habermas (1989b), Hartman (1996), Langer (1991), Vidal-Naquet (1992) and Young (1993); for 11 September, see Sturken (2002). As the latter points out, the widely acclaimed 'Portraits of Grief' series that appeared in the *New York Times* as obituary tributes to the World Trade Center victims, as well as the home-made posters of the missing plastered around New York City, were two public manifestations combining mourning and remembrance.

[46] On the international community's failure to prevent and put a stop to the 1994 Rwandan genocide, see Alfredo Jaar's (1998) remarkable artistic project and Power (2002a: 329–89). On the possibility of the reoccurrence of genocide more generally, see Levi's (1988: 86–7, 199) rather pessimistic reflections.

This is why the testimonial labour that civil society actors generate is directed toward puncturing or disrupting self-delusions about the impossibility of human rights abuses occurring here and now, as well as interpellating the general public to guard against the reoccurrence of such abuses. Accordingly, 'never again' is an expression of the will aimed less at what was than what is and what could be. The three dimensions of temporality are inextricably intertwined here, for only by bearing witness to the past can groups in global and national civil societies understand the significance of global justice in the present and aim to realize it in the future. We remember those who suffered and died in order to be vigilant in the name of others who live in our midst and will come in our wake. 'It happened, therefore it can happen again: this is the core of what we have to say.' (Levi 1988: 199) Of course, the task of prevention of future global injustices can only be contemplated if and when the other components of the work of testimony are accomplished, that is, when the message in a bottle is sent and read, when it is interpreted and understood, when it creates empathy and when it inscribes instances of suffering into the collective memory of societies.

As will be argued in greater detail in the subsequent two chapters, it is in its orientation to the present and future that bearing witness lays the groundwork for other practices of global justice. Persons and groups who survived instances of human rights abuses often testify in order to demand the juridical, institutional and existential conditions producing global injustices be altered. The accumulated impact of eyewitness accounts and public responses can create concerted pressure to prosecute persons responsible for atrocities – prosecutions that may no longer be territorially circumscribed. Punishment consequently neutralizes the capacity of particular figures to inflict further harm (e.g., through imprisonment, bans on running for public office), but it may also operate as a deterrent against others contemplating crimes against humanity by demonstrating that impunity is not always already guaranteed. Moreover, criminal trials or investigative commissions incorporating testimonies are noteworthy as rituals of collective condemnation of atrocities that simultaneously publicize as well as reaffirm a national or international community's adherence to established humanitarian principles, and may result in the invention of novel normative-cum-legal frameworks designed to avert the recurrence of atrocities.[47]

Actors bearing witness to human rights abuses direct their appeals institutionally, that is, toward structural transformation of the socio-political

[47] For instance, see Arendt (1994) and Wieviorka (1998: 81–3, 95–8) on the pedagogical functions of the Eichmann trial.

and economic systems that contribute to these abuses. They struggle to dismantle the entire 'machinery of evil', the coercive instruments (the military, police, etc.), ideological environment (media, formal education and other assorted socializing bodies) and social policies ('free market shock treatment', debt repayment schemes, and so on) that are at the root of global injustices of which they were the victims. While this process of systematic rooting out and change can only be completed by states or international organizations, it is often thrust forward by civil society actors; one can think, *inter alia*, of the peace movement in relation to Hiroshima and the Cold War, the Chilean diaspora with respect to Pinochet's bloody dictatorship or social justice organizations demonstrating the effects of structural adjustment programmes on ordinary people in sub-Saharan Africa. In addition, testimonial practices can serve as a catalyst to the development of entirely new official arrangements and formal treaties intended to challenge the structural causes of mass suffering in the future, such as the International Criminal Court and the Millennium Development Goals. Likewise, national truth and reconciliation commissions – in which bearing witness plays a key function – are designed to preclude the repetition of the past by shedding light on it, inviting collective gestures of catharsis to deal with societal trauma within publicly sanctioned spaces (admission of guilt and remorse on the part of perpetrators, descriptions of victims' suffering, healing between groups, etc.), as well as assisting states and international organizations to formulate the foundations of societal reconstruction.

The third, and perhaps the most elusive, preventive task to which persons bearing witness appeal consists of demands for widespread civic engagement to avert future global injustices, a sensibility that can be cultivated via the labour of listening, interpretation, developing empathy and remembering past human rights abuses. Testimonies often express the hope that cognitive and moral progress can be achieved, that human beings can learn from history by reflecting upon and realizing the tragic costs of denial, complacency, indifference and forgetting.[48] Correspondingly, civic associations frequently employ eyewitness accounts to awaken the conscience of ordinary citizens and political leaders, thereby searching to

[48] Nachtwey (1985) puts it thus:

> It has occurred to me that if everyone could be there just once to see for themselves what white phosphorous does to the face of a child or what unspeakable pain is caused by the impact of a single bullet or how a jagged piece of shrapnel can rip someone's leg off – if everyone could be there to see for themselves the fear and the grief, just one time, then they would understand that nothing is worth letting things get to the point where that happens to even one person, let alone thousands.

trigger the inner voice that prompts us to act in order to avoid becoming mere bystanders to severe abuses of socio-economic and civil-political rights.[49] Conversely, as the practice of bearing witness indicates, failure to speak out and intervene makes us 'metaphysically guilty' (Jaspers 1947). To concern ourselves with preventing harm being done to distant others is not merely a juridical or institutional project, then, but an existential possibility that may help blunt the judgement of future generations.

Conclusion

Bearing witness is one of the defining practices of the work of global justice in our age, for multiple actors are engaging in testimonial labour in response to violations of their civil-political and socio-economic rights in different parts of the world. Sustaining this era of witnessing has been a gradual institutional build-up and set of socio-political struggles in numerous arenas, through certain states' adoption of collective testimonial mechanisms (such as truth and reconciliation commissions), the development of transnational juridical frameworks (international law and tribunals dealing with genocide, crimes against humanity and war crimes, and the International Criminal Court), as well as the involvement of a host of groups located within global civil society (diasporic networks, non-governmental organizations and social movements). As a mode of normatively and politically directed social action, bearing witness is constituted through its confrontations with a host of perils constantly threatening to submerge it: silence, incomprehension, indifference, forgetting and repetition. By way of a publicly framed dialogical process that often crosses socio-cultural and territorial borders, the two parties engaged in testimonial labour are enacting a pattern of social action composed of the tasks of speaking out and listening, representing and interpreting, creating empathy, remembering and preventing. Witnessing cannot and should not be looked upon to rectify the injustices of the past, nor even as a cast-iron 'method' for avoiding future ones, yet it points toward the possibility of resisting them in various ways.

[49] On how Amnesty International integrates these existential appeals in its human rights campaigns, see Cohen (2001: 196–221) and Geras (1998: 19–23). Pastor Niemöller's (1995) famous words hauntingly express the existential and ethical costs of ignoring the call of conscience: 'First they came for the Jews/ and I did not speak out/ because I was not a Jew./ Then they came for the Communists and I did not speak out/ because I was not a Communist./ Then they came for the trade unionists/ and I did not speak out/ because I was not a trade unionist./ Then they came for me/ and there was no one left/ to speak out for me.'

The making of a case for the importance of bearing witness should not be mistaken for a minimization of the tremendous challenges that it continues to face in many societies today, where atrocities and structural injustices are still occurring with distressing frequency despite their coming to light via testimonial means. Numerous victims' voices are being silenced or ignored, indicating that relations of power in national and global civil societies seriously impact upon the selectivity and inconsistencies of the circulation and reception of testimonies. To speak of the unspeakable and represent the unrepresentable remains as daunting as ever for eyewitnesses, and so too does the task of making sense of experiences that, in the scale and intensity of the suffering they reveal, lie well beyond many human beings' ordinary cognitive capacities. Compassion fatigue via media oversaturation and generalized indifference to the plight of distant strangers persists, for even the advent of a discourse of cosmopolitanism and of an increasingly active global civil society has yet to cement a widespread sense of concern for and responsibility toward the vulnerable – wherever they may live. Albeit tempered by diverse initiatives fostering a 'politics of just memory' (Ricoeur 2000: 1), attempts to rewrite history and the will to forget lurk everywhere. And the horrors of the past did not prevent crimes against humanity or situations of material deprivation from taking place in the last few years, putting in doubt the 'enforceability' of the laudable declaration of 'never again'. Most damaging of all remains the fact that testimonial practices regularly fail to overcome implicatory denial, since in a majority of instances, citizens, states and international organizations refuse to take action when they become aware of human rights abuses.

Nevertheless, I want to insist that we should not conflate this facing up to what may well be inescapable aporias of bearing witness with a sense of futility about the latter. More than ever before, an array of actors are finding that testimonial strategies offer them fruitful avenues to confront these perils and thereby create ethico-political responses to global injustices. As messages in bottles multiply and spread across the face of the earth, some segments of the world's population are answering back by taking on the tasks of listening and reading, deciphering and reflecting, empathizing with eyewitnesses, remembering their suffering and averting further harm. Current testimonial labour strives to broaden the participation of citizens across territorial borders by establishing public spaces where eyewitnesses' accounts can be widely broadcast and audiences can more easily recognize them. Hence, global civil society represents a key arena where human rights abuses are being denounced, where warnings about them are transmitted and where mobilization against them is taking place. What remains to be accomplished, then, is an effective politics of witnessing, whereby testimonial actors are able to awaken Euro-American public opinion and thereby leverage recognition of global injustices to bring pressure to bear on domestic and international institutions. In the pall of Auschwitz, Adorno (1982 [1962]: 312) declared that '[t]he abundance of real suffering tolerates no forgetting'. And, I would add, as long as human beings are subjected to unjust and life-threatening conditions, no end or limit to the work of bearing witness.

2 The healing of wounds: on forgiveness

Thus forgiveness is as strong as cruelty; but it is not stronger than the latter. (Jankélévitch 1998 [1967]: 1149)

Introduction

To write about forgiveness in an age of injustice and vengeance is far from obvious. The mirroring rhetoric emanating from global terrorism and the 'war on terror' would seem to indicate that the 'settling of scores' with those designated as enemies is an overwhelming force of political discourse and action today. According to many political leaders and their followers, to forgive is at best a sign of weakness equivalent to capitulation to or appeasement of foes, and at worse is tantamount to aiding and abetting the latter. At this historical juncture, then, it is all too easy or convenient to disregard the possibility that forgiveness represents a mode of practice of global justice that can assist actors to work through some of the most egregious manifestations of mass human rights violations in recent memory.

Indeed, over the last decade or so, states and international organizations have increasingly fostered the institutionalization of official mechanisms of forgiveness in societies emerging from situations of structural violence and pervasive abuses of civil-political rights. With widely varying degrees of success, forgiveness has been pursued in post-totalitarian and post-authoritarian settings (in the former Soviet Union and Central Europe, or much of Central and South America), after the collapse of comprehensive systems of socio-cultural domination and segregation (e.g., South Africa under apartheid, Australia's treatment of indigenous peoples), in the aftermath of conflicts marked by the commission of mass atrocities (Sierra Leone, East Timor, etc.) or connected to governmental apologies and reparations for acts of violence committed on foreign territories (such as Chinese and South Korean requests in relation to Japanese state crimes during the 1930s and 1940s).[1] Despite certain promising developments, however, we need to be cautious when assessing officially prescribed instances of forgiveness, which always risk being instrumentalized or appropriated for other political purposes and thereby represent expedient yet flawed 'quick fixes' decoupled from the work of global justice.

Just as interesting, I would argue, is how forgiveness is taking shape from below to become a vital component of the 'advocacy revolution' (Ignatieff 2001) in the domain of human rights, as social movements, non-governmental organizations[2] and ordinary citizens active in national and global civil societies are pressing their home governments and overseas ones to move in this direction.[3] Even demands for public apology in the case of longstanding grievances and hitherto unaddressed injustices – whereby civic associations insist that states recognize their wrongdoings and compensate victims or their descendants symbolically and materially – are becoming caught up in the vortex of forgiveness, whether in the case of the colonization of the global South, the genocide of indigenous peoples of the Americas and Oceania, slavery, the mistreatment of sections of a domestic population (removal of Aboriginal children from their families in Australia and Canada, or internment of so-called 'enemy

[1] As is well known, the Japanese government has only partially acknowledged and apologized for the conduct of its military personnel and political leaders over this period of time, during which massacres, acts of torture, forced labour, 'medical experiments', systematic rape and terror campaigns against civilian populations in parts of Asia (the most notorious incident being known as the 'Rape of Nanking'), as well as the sexual enslavement of Asian women (so-called 'comfort women') in Japan itself, occurred. Japan's stance has considerably hampered the normalization of its diplomatic and cultural relations with its neighbours, whose leaders and citizens are still debating whether they can fully forgive under such circumstances. For documents relating to this, see Brooks (1999: 87–151).

[2] Among the most prominent NGOs involved in processes of forgiveness are the New York-based International Center for Transitional Justice, www.ictj.org (accessed 15 April 2004) and the South African-based Institute for Justice and Reconciliation, www.ijr.org.za/trans.html (accessed 15 April 2004).

[3] For example, one can cite the popular groundswell of protest greeting the Australian state's continued refusal to apologize for the systematic and forced familial removal and state detention of Aboriginal children (a group referred to as the 'stolen generations'), a policy that lasted from at least 1910 to 1970. The public outcry must be understood in the context of the publication, in 1997, of *Bringing Them Home*, a widely discussed report by a commission of inquiry into this practice. See National Inquiry Into the Separation of Aboriginal and Torres Strait Islander Children from Their Families (1997), available at www.austlii.edu.au/au/special/rsjproject/rsjlibrary/hreoc/stolen (accessed 21 March 2004). The government's decision has sidetracked the project of reconciliation between Aboriginals and non-Aboriginals in Australia. To keep the project of reconciliation alive, civil society groups have organized a national 'Sorry Day' held yearly on 26 May – the anniversary of the report's release – when marches take place across the country to demand that the government reverse its stance. In the United States, the issue of reparations for the enslavement of the ancestors of present-day African Americans continues to be a source of debate and controversy (Allen 1998; Brooks 1999: 309–90; McGary 2003).

aliens' in North America during the Second World War) or war crimes committed against civilians (Japanese atrocities in Asia, French ones in Algeria, American ones in Vietnam and Cambodia, etc.) (Lefranc 2002). The net outcome of these struggles is to multiply institutionalized 'worksites of forgiveness' where state and civil society initiatives converge, most noticeably via the numerous truth commissions in transitional settings, and to advance forgiveness as a viable option under certain circumstances.[4]

To forgive and be forgiven, then, stands as one of the five defining socio-political dynamics of the work of global justice, without which the construction of an alternative globalization would be seriously jeopardized. Its significance is all the more striking given the particularities of mass atrocities and systemic injustices, for which restitutive measures are inadequate and retaliatory ones are inappropriate; full 'compensation' to victims and their relatives is illusive, whereas the primaeval law of punitive equivalency ('an eye for an eye') directly produces vicious circles of vengeance and human slaughter.

And yet, because they employ either juridico-political or theologico-philosophical perspectives, most paradigms of analysis interpret forgiveness as a legal outcome or moral principle while failing adequately to consider the socio-political and normative labour that underpins it. By contrast, I am claiming in this chapter that we should think of the work of forgiveness in order to conceptualize how it can contribute to global justice, which also enables us to avert two common pitfalls of existing arguments on the topic. Firstly, instead of being imposed or sweepingly and instantly mandated from above (by states or international organizations), forgiveness can be seen to represent a laborious social practice from below through which actors in national and global civil societies attempt to confront serious difficulties constantly threatening its political viability and ethical soundness. If, returning to this chapter's epigraph, we cannot take for granted that forgiveness is stronger than cruelty, then we need to study how it can be constructed in all its fragility and complexity – including recognition of the fact that it is not inherently desirable, and may in fact perpetuate injustices when dispensing with specific normative conditions to be discussed

[4] The phrase 'worksites of forgiveness' is partially derived from Balibar's (2004) notion of 'worksites of democracy', which places a greater emphasis on political practice as opposed to ideals *per se*. Hayner (2001) analyses no less than twenty-one national truth commissions, with several others having been created or under consideration since the book's publication. On the South African Truth and Reconciliation Commission, see, *inter alia*, Boraine *et al.* (1997), Krog (1998), Rotberg and Thompson (2000), Tutu (1999) and Villa-Vicencio and Verwoerd (2000).

below.[5] Secondly, rather than placing the burden of forgiveness on the party against whom wrong has been committed, forgiveness is best viewed as collective labour that aims to convert an original situation of moral asymmetry (stemming from the fact that those seeking forgiveness have severely violated the human rights of others who can grant it) into one of socio-political symmetry, in which both parties can meet as relative equals.

Therefore, the following pages are organized into five sections, the first of which elaborates on the idea of the work of forgiveness as a dialogical, public and transnational practice of global justice. In the remainder of the chapter, I turn to a consideration of the four perils and corresponding tasks that are constitutive of the practice of forgiveness. As such, the second section problematizes the commonplace assumption that forgiving requires forgetting, the deliberate or passive inducement of societal amnesia in order to lay grievances about the past to rest. On the contrary, I make a case for forgiveness through collective remembrance, the reckoning with past injustices by way of their reconstruction and reinterpretation; only when a society has produced a reasonably comprehensive and just account of its history through the participation of perpetrators, bystanders and beneficiaries in public truth-telling exercises can it contemplate forgiveness. The third section of the chapter considers the task of the practice of forgiveness that follows after the filling out of the historical picture, namely, the apportioning and assuming of responsibility for human rights abuses. Civic associations concerned with global justice frequently encounter two dubious and polarized alternatives at this stage, either unrepentance (the refusal of wrongdoers to acknowledge responsibility and apologize for what they did) or collective guilt (all citizens are equally guilty of committing atrocities or supporting systemic

[5] Lest the argument presented here be misunderstood, I should specify that it is only meant to apply in situations where massive human rights violations have ended or been mostly overcome and a transition to democratic rule has been initiated. As such, I am not making a case for the inherent and universal merits of forgiveness, which is both ethically inappropriate and politically debilitating under circumstances whereby authoritarianism, armed conflict and/or systematic and officially sanctioned social injustices continue unabated. We should keep in mind that the idea of forgiving can be and has been abused or manipulated, even becoming an instrument of subjection to authoritarian rule and quashing of opposition to such rule. Forced apologies were a common feature of purges and show trials under Stalinism in the Soviet Union and during the Cultural Revolution in China, with staged events where dissidents were coerced to confess their supposed crimes and errors, and thus beg forgiveness from the people for 'anti-revolutionary' activities. Furthermore, as will be discussed subsequently, forgiveness is more usefully understood as an ethico-political practice requiring certain socio-historical conditions: the reconstruction of the past, the acknowledgement of responsibility, the achievement of justice and the move toward reconciliation.

injustices). To escape from this false dilemma, I propose a three-pronged model of criminal, moral and political responsibility that is matched to the roles of perpetrators, bystanders and beneficiaries, respectively. Moreover, as groups and individuals are discovering, an apology or demand to be forgiven should be evaluated less on the basis of wrongdoers' apparent motives (an intentionalist judgement) than on the effects of gestures of repentance upon these wrongdoers' readiness to accept responsibility and make amends for their actions (a consequentialist judgement).

In the fourth section of the chapter, I consider the possibility that perpetrators of human rights violations may remain unrepentant and refuse to apologize. In response, many civic associations have demanded that the exercise of justice take place through domestic and international institutions. What I suggest to avert the corresponding dangers of impunity and vigilantism – that is to say, of unconditional amnesty and blanket immunity from prosecution for humanitarian crimes, on the one hand, and of citizens taking the law into their own hands to extract punishment, on the other – is a dual framework advocating retributive justice for those who are criminally responsible and restorative justice for those who are morally and politically responsible for wrongdoing. In addition to insisting on holding individuals publicly accountable, this approach tackles past structural injustices by advocating symbolic and material redress to victims and survivors of such injustices.

Finally, the fifth section deals with how parties living in the wake of global injustices run the risk of being engulfed by revenge, and how practices of reconciliation can stem this dynamic if they are preceded by performance of the other tasks of the work of bearing witness (historical reconstruction, acknowledgement and attribution of responsibility and the rendering of justice). Furthermore, far from consisting of the restoration of a mythical original state of harmonious unity between citizens, reconciliation can be viewed as a process of socio-political constitution through which civil society actors attempt to create a just social order. In order to preserve the pluralist character of transitional societies and resist calls for unanimity and uniformity, we should differentiate between two equally valid versions of reconciliation: a negative and thin one marked by former enemies agreeing to refrain from violence, and thus peacefully yet minimally co-existing with one another; and an affirmative and thick version whereby parties collaboratively participate in establishing a new moral and socio-political order, one that reintegrates all citizens as civic and political equals and is designed to dismantle socio-economic structures that have contributed to the marginalization of formerly victimized or subordinate groups.

But before examining in detail each of the four reciprocal ethico-political tasks described above that can convert moral asymmetry into socio-political symmetry, I want to begin by establishing the distinctiveness of an action-theoretical notion of a mode of forgiveness contributing to the work of global justice.

Forgiveness as an ideal and a practice

Despite the prominence of discourses of forgiveness in contemporary domestic and world affairs, the formalistic character of the two principal paradigms of interpretation of it – which I shall term the juridico-political and theologico-philosophical models[6] – leads them to perceive forgiveness more as an ideal than a mode of practice, thereby neglecting how it is constituted by patterns of social action grounded in the labour of groups and individuals in global and national civil societies responding to human rights violations.

The juridico-political model, which informs the functioning of modern legal systems dealing with human rights abuses, is built around a strict calculus of equivalent and individualized exchange. From a retributive angle, forgiveness is premised upon the meting out of punishment to perpetrators of criminal acts in a manner that is precisely calibrated in its proportionality to these acts. For instance, both courts and the general population in the West commonly speak and think in terms of forgiving someone if and when the debt he or she owes to society is paid back – a debt that is measured according to the gravity of the crime, generally converted into the length of the period of incarceration. Even in its restorative dimension, the juridico-political model is imbued with a logic of individualized exchange, since forgiveness requires a former perpetrator to carry out measures that restore what a criminal act threatened or violated, or the legal specification of the exact condition under which release from a social debt can be officially granted (in the case of an amnesty for politically motivated violence or war crimes, for example).

At least three flaws animate this juridico-political conception. First and foremost, it does not convincingly account for what is the crux of forgiveness for mass injustices: a moral asymmetry that cannot be made to fit easily, and may even violate, norms of equivalence and proportionality. Regardless of whether it is framed in the language of retribution or restoration, the debt paid by those responsible for systematic human

6 This is not to say that the two models are completely separate from one another. In particular, theologico-philosophical discussions of forgiveness have begun to influence its juridico-political understanding.

rights violations intrinsically falls short of the calculative norm of full compensation for what is owed; even the sentencing to death of a perpetrator often pales in comparison to the scale and intensity of suffering he or she inflicted on others (Digeser 2001). Furthermore, legalism awkwardly captures the normative and socio-political processes that underpin the practice of forgiveness and may eventually result in a symmetrical relationship between the forgiving and the forgiven party.

Secondly, the juridico-political model's individualizing thrust (i.e., its focus on criminal responsibility) is designed to assess a specific person's suitability to be forgiven, in accordance with the gravity of the crime, the expression of remorse and the severity of the compensatory measures. It is therefore much less well suited to coming to terms with structural factors, the socio-cultural and political forces that produce mass injustices and consequently with considerations of collective acknowledgement and responsibility for such injustices.

Relatedly, the third problem with the juridico-political model stems from its formalism, according to which it envisages forgiveness as a top-down outcome of state sovereignty, something that a government and its leaders, or the legal system, can grant or deny citizens. As a result, what is missing is an appreciation of the labour of forgiveness from below, whereby actors in national and global civil societies put forward demands to apologize and forgive that eventually trickle upward to states and international organizations, which may only act as facilitators or mediators of popularly initiated gestures. Conversely, *pace* legalism, the socio-cultural fabric of forgiveness cannot simply be woven by official decrees from above, for its viability is determined by how it is perceived by ordinary citizens and various civic institutions. To be effective, rituals and discourses of forgiveness must be the subjects of wide-ranging public debate, deliberation and acceptance (through the media, social movements, etc.).

Largely in reaction to the calculative and legalistic biases of the juridico-political paradigm, a theologico-philosophical model of forgiveness has underscored the latter's aporetic and utopian character (Derrida 2000; Jankélévitch 1998 [1967]). According to this line of thinking, the paradoxical impossibility and purity of forgiving another for the unforgivable is what supplies the act with an ethical valence that enables it to confront radical evil. To forgive, then, is to unconditionally and unilaterally bestow a gift onto another, in a disinterested fashion with a discrete normative validity; it must be performed for its own sake, and valuable in and of itself. Similarly, the theologico-philosophical framework represents forgiveness as an infinite gesture, one without qualification, completely and absolutely releasing the doer from whatever deed he or she has committed in the past. In fact, any expectation of reciprocity or return on the part of the forgiving party, or yet again any attempt to place conditions upon or limit the reach of this gift, corrupts and poisons its essence. From the same vantage-point, forgiveness is a sudden, dramatic and unpredictable occurrence carrying little warning or build-up, as it wipes the moral slate clean in one fell swoop to utterly alter the relationship between forgiving and forgiven parties.[7]

While theologico-philosophical arguments are useful in insisting on the 'hyperbolic' nature of forgiveness (Lefranc 2002: 145), they suffer from a social reductionism that abstracts the practice from its cultural and political moorings, and thus, from the labour that is constitutive of it. Consequently, these kinds of arguments tend to conceive of forgiveness as a monological enterprise undertaken by the forgiving party, who bestows his or her gift upon the forgiven without any intersubjective engagement between them. Likewise, the ethical burden of forgiveness falls squarely upon the shoulders of this same forgiving party, who must demonstrate a self-abnegating righteousness toward former wrongdoers, independently of what they may believe or how they may act (e.g., whether they acknowledge responsibility). Because of its socially reductionist stance, the theologico-philosophical model veers toward a voluntarism that understands forgiveness as a free gesture of will, where a subject has the ability to make a *tabula rasa* of the past by substantially and permanently transforming existing socio-political relations in a particular setting. Forgiving, therefore, represents an absolutist principle, to be completely and freely granted or else to perish because of its soiled normative purity.

Having discussed the limitations of the two main theoretical approaches to forgiveness, we can now consider how it can be more fruitfully interpreted as a social practice constructed through ethico-political labour from actors in national and global civil societies. Thus, the notion of the work of forgiveness extends Wiesenthal's oft-cited formulation of forgiveness as an 'act of volition' (Wiesenthal 1976: 99) by stressing the fact that historical

[7] It should be noted that the theologico-philosophical outlook on forgiveness occasionally adopts a more nuanced – and somewhat ambiguous – position. For instance, one of the key advocates of this perspective during the twentieth century, Vladimir Jankélévitch, left a central tension unresolved in his own writings on the subject. His major work on forgiveness (Jankélévitch 1998 [1967]) makes a strong case for an ideal-typical conception of the latter as unconditional and infinite, whereas the last chapter of that same book and his shorter, polemical essays (Jankélévitch 1986) written in reaction to the invisibility of the Holocaust in postwar France, advocate a much more circumscribed notion of forgiveness. According to the latter, certain acts of radical evil are unforgivable, or, at the very least, forgiving them is conditional upon perpetrators' repentance and their demands for forgiveness to victims and survivors.

wounds will not heal themselves, but may be healed if groups and individuals accomplish a series of normative and socio-political tasks. In other words, what matters is less the formulation of an abstract principle of forgiveness or the realization of a perfect outcome than the performance of forms of social action. Like the other practices of global justice, those of forgiveness taking place in different settings around the world are bound together by three common traits: dialogism, publicity and transnationalism.

The labour of forgiveness for human rights abuses is intersubjective in that it involves mutual recognition of the ethical merit of the claims of each concerned party, the forgiving (victims and survivors of these abuses) and the potentially forgiven (perpetrators and beneficiaries). Forgiveness functions to the extent that social actors directly involved in the process address, listen and respond to others' experiences and demands, and through mechanisms of collective deliberation and argumentation, can recognize the validity of their respective roles. Conversely, if and when a party refuses to ask for or grant forgiveness – and thus to recognize appropriately and sufficiently the other party – then the practice fails or remains in suspense.

Secondly, the various aspects of forgiveness in its collective manifestations unfold in public spaces. Civil society actors struggle to initiate practices of forgiveness by publicly advancing claims for official apologies and compensatory measures in response to systematic social injustices and violations of human rights; in fact, debates and discussions about the legitimacy and representation of such claims (do they have any merit, and should they be recognized?; who is identified as a victim and a perpetrator, and who is authorized to apologize or forgive?) have become vital forces in the public life of many societies. In order to acquire sufficient symbolic and moral weight, a particular demand to forgive or the granting of forgiveness must include the participation of a critical mass of ordinary citizens through various civic institutions prior to being sanctioned by states or international organizations. And not to be overlooked is the fact that the long-term impact of practices of forgiveness, their capacity to prevent the return of massive human rights abuses (and perhaps even to lead to lasting reconciliation between parties), is largely determined by the extent to which post-transitional societies can cultivate a range of democratically and social justice-oriented civic associations, public fora and independent media outlets.[8]

[8] See, for instance, the 1991 Report of the Chilean National Commission for Truth and Reconciliation, which made recommendations to this effect. The report is available at www.nd.edu/~ndlibs/eresources/etexts/truth (accessed 14 March 2004). See also Hayner

The third common feature of practices of forgiveness is their growing transnationalization. Although predominantly occurring and involving players within specific nation-states, forgiveness is also becoming less territorially bounded. Heads of state and religious leaders, ranging from former US President Clinton and Britain's Queen Elizabeth II to the Pope, have selectively apologized or asked to be forgiven for past injustices committed against the peoples of various countries (Gibney and Roxstrom 2001). The victims and survivors of humanitarian wrongdoing, or their descendants and supporters drawn from global civil society, are often spread across the world in the shape of diasporas and advocacy networks that articulate grievances sustaining a politics of forgiveness in domestic settings; the roles of Chilean communities overseas in relation to Pinochet (Burbach 2003), international media and human rights groups with regard to the crimes of particular regimes in Africa, Asia and South America (Bass 2000: 33; Crocker 2000: 109–18; Hayner 2001: 200–3), or less benignly, the mounting tension between Jewish and Arab communities in Europe and North America over the Israeli–Palestinian conflict, are all examples of this tendency. Civil society actors have closely scrutinized and demanded public accountability from governments, monitoring the progress of criminal prosecutions and institutional reforms designed to address past injustices, as well as standing on guard against the return of abuses. Certainly, some of the pivotal discursive and institutional resources upon which these players draw are of a transnational character, ranging from statutes of humanitarian law and norms of human dignity to international expertise and financial assistance (for national truth and reconciliation commissions) and experiments in extra-territorial prosecution. Audiences for nationally based processes of forgiveness are also being transnationalized, whether as external monitors in transitional situations (the United Nations or regional multilateral organizations, human rights groups, journalists, etc.) or as interested parties hoping to transfer the lessons of a particular experience to their own countries. Indeed, certain pioneering efforts, such as the South African Truth and Reconciliation Commission, are serving as templates for similar experiments in other contexts (East Timor, Sierra Leone, etc.).

Highlighting the dialogical, public and transnational characteristics of forgiveness helps us to focus on how it represents a mode of social practice of global justice. Simultaneously, I would argue, we can overcome the

(2001: 324). Gibney and Roxstrom (2001: 927) rightly criticize the inadequate publicity for President Clinton's 1999 quasi-apology to Guatemala for the US government's involvement in the country's civil war – an apology that did not attempt seriously to involve the citizens of either Guatemala or the United States itself, and thus received little domestic attention.

abstraction of both the juridico-political and theologico-philosophical models by identifying the dynamics of normative and socio-political reciprocity that exist at the heart of just kinds of labour of forgiveness. This labour begins with collective acknowledgement of the morally asymmetrical quality of the relationship between the two parties, since those requesting to be forgiven are criminally, ethically and politically responsible for inflicting suffering on those who can forgive them as well as for benefiting socio-economically and culturally from such suffering and subordination; succinctly put, perpetrators and beneficiaries of human rights abuses are morally indebted to victims and survivors. None the less, the practice of forgiveness also functions because formerly victimized groups and official institutions accept the adoption of a logic of non-equivalence that refrains from pursuing a response that would be proportional to the violence of the original act.

However, by viewing forgiveness as a practice, I want to demonstrate that the burden of working toward it does not lie with these formerly victimized groups, who are under no obligation to forgive and cannot be legislated to do so from above. On the contrary, it is those seeking to be forgiven who bear most of the burden by attempting to convert previous hierarchies into structural conditions of socio-political and cultural equality in post-transitional settings; they cannot, *a priori*, expect forgiveness as a gift or demand it as a right (Minow 1998: 17). Instead, they perform a number of ethico-political tasks (i.e., reconstituting the past, acknowledging responsibility, making amends and participating in reconciliation) that prepare the ground for the possibility of reciprocation on the part of injured parties, who may respond in kind by accepting participation in the labour of forgiveness. Without such work by former perpetrators and beneficiaries, the gift proffered to them would go to waste. Moreover, by asking for forgiveness in and through the enactment of these tasks, groups that formerly perpetrated or benefited from grave injustices contribute to a symbolic levelling of the social field. No longer above the law, they – like all other citizens – subject their actions to collective judgement, public deliberation being the mechanism through which the symbolic value of their appeals to be forgiven will be assessed. Hence, if they inadequately perform these same tasks, their requests for forgiveness may well be unsuccessful in swaying public opinion or, more crucially, may be declined by survivors of their crimes (Ricoeur 2000: 626).[9]

[9] The absence of reciprocity and continuing moral asymmetry between parties explain Jankélévitch's famous exclamation of outrage toward the Nazis: 'Forgiveness! But did they ever ask us for forgiveness?' (Jankélévitch 1986: 50).

Since the situations we are considering here are underpinned by socio-political struggles aiming to convert morally asymmetrical situations into socially symmetrical ones, we need to speak of a politics of forgiveness. Various groups mobilize symbolic and material resources in national and global civil societies in order to create political circumstances favourable to the recognition of processes of apology and forgiveness. Such struggles may occur prior to a political transition (and indeed may contribute to such a transition via the overturning of an authoritarian regime or the end of a civil war, for instance), or in already-established democratic settings where civic associations voice their demands for apology and seek to gain domestic and transnational support for formal recognition of these demands. But to refer to a politics of forgiveness should not be conflated with cynically reducing the latter to an exercise of power, a mechanism of domination and legitimation of an unjust social order that would coercively extract pardon from victimized groups or manipulate them into forgiving to ensure the impunity of those responsible. To reiterate what I contended above, the practice of forgiveness is enframed by the requirements of global justice; it is enacted through ethico-political labour that strives toward social symmetry and the consequent realization of human rights for all. As we will see below, then, a substantive process of forgiveness is inseparable from struggles to eliminate structural injustices and foster a radically democratic social order.

To understand better how the practice of forgiveness informs the work of global justice, this chapter presents it as consisting of a series of four interrelated socio-political and normative tasks that confront matching perils: the reconstruction of the past against collective forgetting; the acknowledgement of responsibility against denial of it; the rendering of justice against impunity and vigilantism; and the possibility of reconciliation against vengeance. With some variations due to differing circumstances, groups and individuals in many societies enact these four identifiable patterns of social action, which are transferred from one worksite of forgiveness to another. Because these patterns undergird the labour of forgiveness in our age, each should be examined in turn.

Reconstructing the past and the temptations of amnesia

In the aftermath of severe human rights abuses, the initial peril that the practice of forgiveness encounters is encapsulated in the popular saying 'forgive and forget', which binds the two forms of action together so that forgiveness is believed to be best served through the deliberate and active pursuit of collective amnesia. As certain political leaders and civil society members in transitional situations have asserted, to forgive implies letting bygones be bygones, consciously turning the page on the past in order to escape from its clutches. What, some ask, is the point of dredging up a painful history that, in any case, cannot be reversed? Yet these arguments all too easily slip into the sorts of strategies of historical silencing and forgetting discussed in Chapter 1: explicit denial and distortion of certain events and policies, and liquidation of evidence to that effect; state censorship and interdictions on speaking publicly about the past, ostensibly because it represents a source of national disunity and conflict; and implicit socio-cultural taboos against bringing up acts of violence and injustice, with the violation of these taboos being perceived by many citizens as 'muckraking' that destabilizes their everyday lifeworlds and is likely needlessly to shame or embarrass particular individuals by 'singling them out'. What these varied rationales share is the idea that the rupture with a corrupt moral and social system requires the erasure of, or drawing of a curtain over, the past; the baby of history is thereby thrown out with the bathwater of the old order and the human rights violations committed under it. Furthermore, as many analysts and victims have contended, the conscious and officially sanctioned undermining of collective memory is a form of symbolic violence and social injustice that reasserts the moral and political dominance of erstwhile perpetrators and beneficiaries, whose versions of history prevail over those of their victims in post-transitional settings (Améry 1995). Likewise, it establishes dubious precedents according to which those responsible for atrocities can commit them with impunity and supporters of systemic injustices can retain their ill-gotten socio-economic, political and cultural gains without fear of penalty or accountability (Crocker 2000: 133).

The problems of linking forgiving and forgetting become visible through another maxim, 'time heals all wounds', which appears in some discourses that support a vision of forgiveness as a passive act of historical omission producing societal amnesia. Actors in transitional societies only need to let the irreversible march of time erode collective memory and widen the gulf between past events and present circumstances. However, what these discourses fail to appreciate is that although chronological distance may tame the experiential and emotional vividness of mass suffering (and the accompanying intensity of first-order emotions of anger, revenge and hurt), it does not in any way diminish or undo the injustice of the act or system that created such suffering or absolve those who perpetrated and benefited from it (Améry 1995; Jankélévitch 1998 [1967]; Murphy and Hampton 1988: 23). If they follow this line of thought, civil society groups may consequently be lulled into the falsely comforting conviction that they can let the passage of time perform the labour of forgiveness on their behalf, effectively undercutting the possibility of ethical and socio-political transformation. Similarly, the preference for historical drift leaves the past unaddressed; it thereby takes on the status of a ticking time bomb, temporarily buried but liable to explode at any moment when actors stumble upon it or decide to utilize it for nefarious purposes. To be sure, it is just such an escape from the task of addressing repressed or neglected historical grievances that has lent fuel to several recent ethnic and religious conflicts, by allowing groups bent on 'settling scores' in the name of ancestral humiliations to revive and manipulate such grievances (Bhargava 2000: 53–4).

Some advocates of forgiving through forgetting favour what amounts to interpretive amnesia. A society can acknowledge and remember the raw facts about injustices in its past, but ought to obscure or downplay explanations of why they occurred. More often than not, the results are a sanitized and palatable rendition of history, made into a senseless or questionable narrative that can neither be properly understood nor strongly condemned. This occurs by stripping events of their socio-political context and cultivating ambiguity about their underlying causes in order to avoid 'blaming' specific persons and institutions (so that the leaders of the Chilean dictatorship can conveniently exempt themselves from prosecution for its iron-fisted rule, for instance), or worse still, by an *ex post facto* reframing and rewriting of history that, under the guise of promoting societal harmony, ends up supporting a revisionist justification of past wrongdoings (so that the Pinochet regime becomes the embodiment of a heroic stand against socialism, or South African apartheid is transformed into a project of 'racial' co-existence whose good intentions went awry).

It seems clear, then, societal amnesia and the neglect of the past endanger the possibility of forgiveness. On the contrary, as many victimized groups have demanded, forgiving begins with the work of memory, the plunging back and reckoning with history in order to reconstitute its fragments and properly confront the proverbial skeletons in a nation's or group's closet. Only after truth-telling and commemorative acts and institutions enable a transitional society to produce better and fuller accounts of its past can parties be in a position to ask for or grant forgiveness, with the objective of creating a different present and future (Abel 1991: 226; Shriver 1995: 7). Yet historical reconstruction requires institutional capacity-building in such settings, where a public sphere with effective concepts of truth and transparency was often the first casualty of a state regime or perpetrator group. Democratic institutionalization draws on both domestic and transnational resources, whether to fund fact-finding endeavours, to provide expertise and structural support or to repair damaged capabilities and create new ones.[10] In fact, as the examples of truth commissions in South America and Africa indicate, investigating and reconstituting the past are processes that lay the foundations for the existence of functioning public spheres in transitional societies, by virtue of supporting civic participation and democratic debate through formal institutions (commissions and tribunals) and their informal counterparts (public fora, social movements and the media). Most basically, these organizations enable citizens – notably formerly victimized groups – to bear witness to their experiences, pursue truth-telling exercises and voice their opinions openly without fear of reprisal.[11] Moreover, officially sanctioned mechanisms and rituals of historical reconstruction are essential to ensure the legitimacy of post-transitional regimes in the eyes of injured parties who may grant forgiveness, for full and official disclosure of past injustices and crimes as well as widespread transmission of such findings are prerequisites for forgiveness. Lastly, the cultivation of vibrant and unrestricted public discourse carries several benefits, as citizens can acquire information about and come to realize the scale and gravity of particular events or systems, as well as discuss and deliberate about the justification for and limits of forgiveness (Bhargava 2000: 54–5; Crocker 1999; Rotberg 2000: 5–6).[12]

Once institutional capacity-building has been advanced, the first aspect of the work of memory upon which transitional societies embark is the establishment of credible and accurate knowledge to produce as comprehensive a record of the past as possible. Aside from exposing unjust structures and systemic policies, exercises in historical reconstitution through legal proceedings or public inquiries are designed to unearth detailed information about specific human rights violations and the circumstances leading up to them (Bass 2000: 302–4; Crocker 1999;

[10] In many situations, multilateral international organizations (the United Nations and regional institutions like the Organization of American States), NGOs (Human Rights Watch, International Center for Transitional Justice, etc.) and international tribunals (such as the International Criminal Court) monitor, unearth and supply evidence of what occurred in the past, thereby contributing to national efforts to recover the truth. See Crocker (2000: 114–18) and Zalaquett (1993: xxvii).

[11] In many South American and Eastern European societies during transitional periods, religious and secular civic associations have been among the principal players supplying evidence of past humanitarian abuses and crimes – evidence which underground networks secretly collected and documented under authoritarian rule (Crocker 2000: 111; Minow 1998: 54; Zalaquett 1993: xxvii).

[12] For instance, the deliberations and final reports of several investigative commissions (in South Africa, Chile, Brazil, Argentina, Australia, and so on) have been the subject of considerable media coverage and public interest. The hearings of the South African Truth and Reconciliation Commission were regularly broadcast on national television and radio, and extensively covered in the press.

Hayner 2001). Frequently, this kind of public investigatory function is of great significance for victims as well as their relatives and friends who, before they can contemplate forgiving, express a need to know what exactly happened and who is responsible (Bhargava 2000: 54–5; Minow 1998: 77; Rotberg 2000: 3). Almost as important is the desire to come to grips with why such things occurred, to explain the causes and consequences of instances of grave injustice, the structural conditions, mechanisms and worldviews that made them possible (ranging from inflammatory speech and systemic racism to police and armed forces brutality, foreign intervention, pervasive corruption and deficient policy prescriptions), as well as the gains derived therefrom (among others, economic status or profit, socio-cultural domination and political power). Correspondingly, fact-finding institutions play a role in the public discernment of responsibility by attempting to clearly identify perpetrators, beneficiaries and bystanders – without falling into the trap of 'victors' justice' through a disregard for due process and fairness.[13]

If the practice of forgiveness is to be feasible, every effort must be made to secure the participation of both parties in the labour of historical reconstruction. On the one hand, survivors, victims and eyewitnesses are commonly the first to come forward and break the silence surrounding, or challenge widespread ignorance of, particular crimes and unjust regimes by publicly sharing their experiences. As explained in Chapter 1, testimonies are indispensable for collecting evidence and informing citizens about the extent, gravity and full impact of certain policies and belief-systems. On the other hand, the varying degrees of success of truth commissions in different societies indicate that the collaboration of those who planned and perpetrated mass human rights violations is important, for disclosure of what they did and knew sets the moral stage for their requests to be forgiven. Because they held decision-making posts, perpetrated or witnessed certain acts, or had access to privileged information regarding the functioning of particular institutions and the roles of various players, those who were 'on the inside' are uniquely positioned to unfurl a web of secrecy and deception; as several cases have shown, their accounts are sometimes the only means to effectively pierce the inner sanctum of a regime and to shed light on the multiple schemes its leaders devised and executed. Hence, they can assist in

[13] While efforts to recover the past must not lose sight of the morally asymmetrical 'big picture' (namely, what side or group bears primary responsibility for human rights abuses), they should not shy away from identifying other, smaller-scale violations that may have been committed (e.g., in the case of resistance movements that mistreat captured enemies).

correcting the historical record and filling out the gaps in the picture of what previously existed and happened.[14]

In projects of historical reconstruction tied to the practice of forgiveness, publicity is vital in marking the end of an epoch of grave human rights abuses by demonstrating to domestic and world audiences that a society or group is embarking upon a process of facing up to and condemning its past. Indeed, the prospect of forgiving others is more likely for former victims and survivors if their dignity and civic equality are publicly recognized, whether by virtue of providing them with opportunities to bear witness to and denounce the suffering to which they were subjected, having ordinary citizens listen to their testimonies and acknowledge their veracity or having such experiences and accounts officially validated by states or international organizations (Bhargava 2000: 51; Borneman 2002: 289; Crocker 1999; 2000: 136; Lefranc 2002: 71–2; Minow 1998: 70–2). At the same time, the exposure of perpetrators, beneficiaries and bystanders to public investigation and to deliberation about and criticism of their actions is symbolically meaningful, because it opens them to scrutiny and confronts them with the reasons they are expected to apologize and ask for forgiveness.

We would be wrong to conclude that fact-finding sums up the labour of historical reconstitution, since the task goes well beyond the discovery and retrieval of an always already existing truth. In fact, the reinterpretation of the past, the creation of valid interpretive knowledge and the supplying of normative meaning to events and facts is equally important given that transitional societies must face not only the challenge of acquiring a reliable collective memory, but also the question of the kind of collective memory and historical narratives that they will adopt. Therefore, citizens and state leaders ethically and politically reframe and resignify public discourse about the past, so that previous ways of thinking and acting are recast in a different light and a different understanding of them can emerge. It matters a great deal, for example, that societal narratives about a certain atrocity shift from its legitimization to its condemnation as a crime against humanity, as well as whether it is integrated into a process of seeking revenge or reconciliation between

[14] The innovative 'truth for amnesty' provision of the South African Truth and Reconciliation Commission is notable in this respect because it disregarded perpetrators' intentions and concentrated instead on the historically reconstructive benefits of their revelations. What mattered was less whether particular persons were motivated to testify in front of the Commission in order to demonstrate genuine repentance or to escape criminal prosecution, and more the complete disclosure of their own participation in the apartheid system and what they knew about its functioning.

former enemies.[15] Stated differently, the act of unearthing and reflecting reality is simultaneously one of socio-political construction of it to make it meaningful for present and future generations. As Crocker has commented in the case of truth commissions, '[i]f [they] are backward-looking, they are so precisely as historical founding projects; they deal with the past not for its own sake but in order to clear the way for a new beginning' (Crocker 2000: 125).

This process of historical world-making, of partly constituting the past through its rereading, aims to generate commensurable interpretative universes where different parties can meet. Forgiveness is contingent upon such an overlapping of perpetrators' and victims' horizons of meaning, to the extent that they agree, at minimum, about the factual record of what occurred, the reasons for and consequences of a specific humanitarian violation or systemic social injustice, and the morality attached to it. This does not imply that absolute unanimity across all sections of domestic or world opinion, or the consecration of a single, orthodox narrative about the past, is a necessary condition for forgiveness. On the contrary, interpretive pluralism and reasonable disagreement are signs of democratic robustness, for citizens ought to retain and exercise their right to dissent as well as to contest official versions of history that risk congealing into new and supposedly self-evident dogmas (Gutman and Thompson 2000). Initially, we can give all truth claims a fair hearing and subject them to public scrutiny and discussion, through which debate and assessment of their accuracy, normative orientation and political effects can be undertaken. This process of public evaluation and sorting out allows us to discover the merits and flaws of various positions, and thus to determine what lies outside the bounds of minimal agreement and reasonable disagreement.[16] Historical fact-finding thus serves to reduce the range of denials, distortions and outright lies about the past that can circulate within the public sphere without being questioned or discredited by most citizens and officials. Such a narrowing-down averts absolute

[15] The work of historical resignification strives to transform the meaning of a massacre in national mythology, in order that its recognition as a collective stain and comprehension of its place within a larger context of genocide, ethnic cleansing or mass violence replace faulty justifications of it as insignificant and necessary to ensure a group's survival or to extract vengeance for ancestral wrongs.

[16] With regards to the 1973 Pinochet *coup d'état* and the subsequent military dictatorship in Chile, for example, Zalaquett comments: 'Adamantly opposite views about the coup still persist, although most Chileans have come to agree to disagree on this issue. However, it is now widely acknowledged in Chile that a distinction must be made between the coup d'état and the human rights violations committed by the military regime. While the inevitability or admissibility of the former could be controvertible, there ought not be two opinions about the utter illegitimacy of the latter.' (Zalaquett 1993: xxiv)

historical relativism and moral neutrality – the idea that all interpretations of the past are equally valid and desirable – and thus struggles against the appearance of an unbridgeable gap between parties, which would make forgiveness impossible; how could, say, a survivor of state torture forgive his or her jailers if they maintain that such activities never occurred or are essentially virtuous? While not guaranteeing *a priori* consensus about the past, the work of memory can create a mutual analytical and normative terrain where reasonable differences of interpretation can be discussed and negotiated in and through the process of forgiving.

And not to be overlooked is the fact that historical reconstitution is a prerequisite for a just practice of forgiveness, one that fairly apportions responsibility for past humanitarian catastrophes and settles on effective sanctions for those found responsible. It is to these matters that we now turn.

Are all guilty, or is anyone responsible?

The public labour of reckoning with the past, whereby members of national and global civil societies become cognizant of what acts were committed and who or what perpetrated and benefited from them, allows a society to combat various kinds of collective amnesia. Yet in itself, it remains but a preliminary step in a practice of forgiveness that encounters a second peril – that of perpetrators, bystanders and beneficiaries of human rights abuses and structural injustices remaining unrepentant. A familiar instance of this tendency originates from wrongdoers' refusal to believe or accept evidence proving the existence of a system or a series of events, or by pleading ignorance about them ('I did not know what happened or the full extent of what was being done'). Worse still are explanatory justifications of the moral legitimacy or political necessity of mass crimes, which perpetrators and beneficiaries may view either as contributing to the greater good, or at least as unfortunate but inevitable means of realizing such a desirable end: to complete a totalitarian 'utopia' (in Cambodia under the Khmer Rouge, in China during the Cultural Revolution), to combat a rival political ideology (in Pinochet's Chile or Suharto's Indonesia), to take revenge for past injuries or to ensure the survival of a group by seeking to exterminate another ('we must kill them before they kill or infect us').

Another pervasive form of unrepentance in transitional settings consists of the escape from personal responsibility, whereby perpetrators and beneficiaries admit what they did and how they gained (and may even retrospectively come to recognize the wrongness of their ways of thinking and acting), yet try to excuse them away and find attenuating circumstances to reiterate their innocence (Murphy and Hampton 1988: 20). In such cases, wrongdoers will shift or deflect personal responsibility in four distinct ways. They may try to scapegoat other persons, often subordinate or superordinate members of an institution or group onto whom all blame supposedly falls (e.g., 'buck-passing' or the 'few bad apples' rationale). Secondly, they may engage in a tactic of bureaucratic diffusion of accountability, according to which they portray themselves as mere cogs in the machine who were following orders from their superiors or obeying the laws, rules and regulations in place at the time, without possessing any decision-making power or knowledge of the consequences of their actions; this is what Arendt (1994 [1965]: 289; 1998 [1958]: 45) and Bauman (1993: 126) after her have termed 'rule of nobody'. In addition, they may use notions of collective guilt to societally dissolve their individual responsibility, by proclaiming that all citizens are equally guilty and thus that no one ought to be singled out. Each person is represented as a victim of a socio-political environment where 'ideological brainwashing', fear and bloodlust were rife, or where respect of human rights was utterly absent (Kiss 2000: 77). Finally, wrongdoers may disingenuously express sorrow for their actions in order to obtain public sympathy and, as a result, escape from or minimize the severity of their punishment; the shedding of 'crocodile tears' may occur in order to strategically assume limited responsibility for their past acts and decisions.

By concentrating on the practice of forgiveness, we can come to understand the labour of apportioning and accepting responsibility that counteracts the dangers of unrepentance. Within societies living in the aftermath of mass injustices, only the building-up of public discourses and cultural rituals designed to perform such labour can overcome deeply engrained routines of blame-shifting and self-deceptive justification. Nevertheless, as indicated above, the idea of collective guilt to which some transitional societies have turned is a non-starter in this respect, owing to its indiscriminate nature and the likely rejection by most citizens of their externally imposed and morally homogenizing identity as 'guilty subjects' (Schaap 2001). As Arendt has tersely stated, '[w]here all are guilty, nobody is' (Arendt 2003 [1968]: 147). In addition to enabling perpetrators and beneficiaries to hide from scrutiny by melting into the crowd, the attribution or assuming of collective guilt circumvents the necessary social task of determining differential degrees of responsibility among domestic and global players. By sanctioning the dubious proposition that human rights abuses are exclusively institutional and societal in character, what is thereby effectively exonerated are specific actors' actions and decisions. Conversely, collective guilt represents a totalizing and absolutist concept that leaves no room for the possibility of individual innocence and performance of the good; it disregards the fact that, in virtually all situations where human rights have been severely violated, certain persons actively resisted or refused to collaborate with an unjust or criminal endeavour (Jaspers 1947; Schaap 2001: 750–2).[17]

Whether nationally or transnationally based, social and political institutions discarding the idea of collective guilt have still faced the problem of how to distribute responsibility justly for grave abuses of human rights. Much confusion has been generated as a result, yet to my mind, the question is most productively tackled by drawing upon a modified version of Jaspers's argument about German guilt in the wake of the Shoah.[18] Accordingly, I want to propose a tripartite taxonomical scheme that distinguishes between the enactment of different roles *vis-à-vis* severe human rights violations:

(1) Criminal responsibility involves perpetrators, those who directly participated in such violations by planning and ordering them, making relevant decisions and/or directly performing actions.
(2) Moral responsibility deals with bystanders, those who were passively complicit and acquiesced or lent their tacit support by deliberately choosing not to know what was occurring (conscious self-deception or justification), who knew but opted not to intervene (indifference to the suffering of others) or should have known by virtue of their structural positions in an oppressive system and their connections to others who knew (implausible denial).
(3) Political responsibility concerns beneficiaries, those who accrued unjust advantages and privileges because of their involuntary membership in a political community whose institutions and leaders perpetrated certain acts in their name (Arendt 2003 [1968]: 149–50); for instance, while they may not themselves have actively participated in the apartheid regime or completely realized its severity, many white South Africans did gain considerably from it socio-economically, politically and culturally.

This analytical model, which the next section will connect to kinds of justice, informs this chapter's conception of the work of forgiveness. Indeed, if the latter is to proceed, existing experiences point to the fact that it is important for parties who are criminally, morally and politically responsible to acknowledge publicly the wrongness of their past acts as well as to condemn them unconditionally, without searching to legitimize

[17] I would add that collective guilt comes perilously close to essentializing claims about the 'evil nature' of specific groups or peoples, such as the idea of 'national character'.

[18] This tripartite model is partly derived from Jaspers's (1947) discussion of different forms of guilt (criminal, moral, political and metaphysical), though I follow Arendt (2003 [1968]) and Schaap (2001) in finding the idea of responsibility more ethically and politically useful than that of guilt.

them *ex post facto* (Hayner 2001: 26–7; Henderson 2002; Murphy and Hampton 1988: 26; Tavuchis 1991: 17). They can assume responsibility either by apologizing for what they did or omitted to do (in the case of perpetrators and bystanders), or if they were beneficiaries, by recognizing the privileges that they derived from an unjust situation or system. In turn, prior to the official granting of forgiveness, national and global civil society groups should be involved in processes of public debate and assessment of wrongdoers' requests for forgiveness.

Despite the importance of ensuring popular participation, numerous problematic understandings of forgiveness and apology employ ideals of expressive authenticity and sincerity drawn from moral psychology to support an intentionalist mode of judgement of demands to be forgiven for mass crimes. The crux of the matter is believed to consist of the discovery of the genuine intentions or motives of those asking for forgiveness, in order to determine whether they are truly sorry and sincere in repenting – that is, whether they are being transparent in divulging the feelings, beliefs and thoughts that lie in their 'heart of hearts'.[19] Intentionalism cannot but gauge such matters by falling back upon formalist criteria. What matters, then, are the visible signs of a contrite wrongdoer's intentions and the virtuosity of his performance, or in other words, whether or not and to what extent this performance is convincing to an audience by virtue of its degree of impression management and ability to externalize and communicate 'appropriate' sentiments effectively (Goffman 1971: 113; Tavuchis 1991). Consequently, rhetorical skill and style are thrust into unwarranted positions of evaluative prominence; given the difficulty of discovering a speaker's true motives and feelings, the authenticity and virtuosity of her performance are likely to be determined by her capacity to utilize words and gestures evoking collectively shared meanings that resonate with her audience. Specific speech formulas ('I am sorry') and narrative patterns (individual tragedy and repudiation of the past), as well as an appropriate facial and corporeal demeanour and disposition (tearfulness, bowing or lowering of the head, a quivering voice, a halting speech, etc.) triggering a network of background understandings, are thus assumed to express sincere remorse, shame and regret.

Intentionalism is a misleading starting-point for actors engaging in the practice of forgiveness, for it cannot satisfactorily address the aforementioned shedding of 'crocodile tears' on the part of those asking for forgiveness, who can mobilize a 'cheap' or 'phony sentimentality' (Arendt

[19] For a somewhat similar critique of a sentiment- and motive-based understanding of forgiveness as 'soulcraft', see Digeser (2001).

1994 [1965]: 251; 2003 [1968]: 148; Schaap 2001) whereby they put across an impression of apparent sorrow for their deeds while being presented with the prospect of impunity (Améry 1995). As for the audience that must decide whether or not to forgive, its task – when translated in intentionalist terms – consists of parsing out disingenuousness from sincerity in apologies and requests to be forgiven, based upon the performative criteria laid out above. Yet in light of show-trials and forced confessions in various settings around the world, neither the state nor civil society institutions ought to be in the Inquisition-like business of trying to read the hearts and souls of others, or of claiming to unmask those who are genuinely and completely sorry from those who are only partially or strategically so.

Hence, as Chapter 3 will also contend for the practice of foresight, the labour of forgiveness is more readily compatible with the principles of global justice when it moves from an intentionalist to a consequentialist framework, in which repentance is ascertained through the content and effects of wrongdoers' and beneficiaries' public rituals and discourses of acknowledging responsibility and making amends for their past deeds. From a consequentialist perspective, judgement draws less on persons' motives or effectiveness of the performance of a role than on how they contribute to rectifying the moral asymmetry constitutive of the relation of forgiveness, by collaborating with historical reconstruction, refraining from obstructing the institutionalization of a domestic and global human rights culture (entrenched in law, treaties and constitutions), and even directly confronting the ills and suffering caused by their actions and decisions. For instance, in certain national truth commissions (in Guatemala and South Africa most notably), perpetrators who testified publicly had to listen to their victims' recounting of experiences of mass abuse and injustice, and answer questions from these victims or their families. Not only do such procedures validate norms of public accountability, but they may also destabilize perpetrators' self-justifications by compelling them to come face-to-face with the lifeworlds of the victims from whom they are asking forgiveness. Furthermore, the publicization of victims' accounts via official institutions and civic associations may also engender a consequentialist logic for bystanders and beneficiaries, who are made aware of the impact of their tacit support for systemic human rights violations and the unjust gains derived from their belonging to particular groups or political communities.

Besides its function in rectifying the historical record, the task of assuming criminal or moral responsibility can assist in advancing rituals of collective ethico-political purification and rebirth. This may occur when perpetrators demand to be forgiven, or when leaders apologize on behalf of the politically responsible citizens whom they represent.[20] Whether originating from a state or an international organization, then, the official recognition of wrongdoing carries symbolic weight in its representing a public repudiation of past injustices, as well as its opening up to a new socio-political order that breaks with the previous system. In instances where official institutions refuse to apologize, ordinary citizens may seek independently to take moral and political responsibility for former deeds committed in their name, thereby incorporating confrontation with past human rights violations into public discourse (e.g., the response of many Australian civil society groups with respect to the issue of the Aboriginal 'stolen generations').

The offering of an apology and consequent request to be forgiven thus mark wrongdoers' willingness simultaneously to admit fault and subject themselves to judgement via the state and both national and global public opinion. In essence, parties taking responsibility for massive human rights abuses are asking those who may forgive them to distinguish doer from deed, so that the collective condemnation of these abuses can still leave enough political and normative space to determine that those who committed them are potentially redeemable – and thus deserving of forgiveness (Margalit 2002: 199–200; Murphy and Hampton 1988: 83–5). Conversely, wrongdoers cannot ask to be forgiven unless they recognize the legitimacy of democratic and fair processes of public deliberation about their demands and, moreover, unless they accept the retributive and restorative sanctions they may have to face as a result (individual punishment, systemic dismantling of a regime, loss of unfairly acquired privileges, etc.). To adopt a consequentialist vantage-point means that efforts to make amends are measured by the effectivity flowing from the taking of responsibility, that is to say, the consequences that perpetrators, bystanders and beneficiaries must bear.

Of course, in transitional situations, wrongdoers may well deny responsibility and remain defiantly unrepentant, a decision that actors engaging in practices of forgiveness must respect if the principle of political dissent is to be entrenched in a new environment of democratic pluralism. What civil society and the state must resist is the temptation to make a coercive response that would compel perpetrators to confess against their will, and thereby to produce apologetic and remorseful subjects at all costs. Instead, societies have turned to the exercise of justice, in a manner that

[20] For example, a politician may apologize, in the name of a nation, to formerly victimized domestic groups or to the citizens of another country, or a representative of the world community may do the same on the latter's behalf for failure to aid populations in need (as was the case with Kofi Annan in the aftermath of the Rwandan genocide).

sanctions those responsible for human rights abuses independently of whether or not they admit as such. Under these circumstances, as we will discuss in the next section, forgiveness remains possible.

The search for justice: neither impunity nor vigilantism

In the conception of the practice of forgiveness presented in this chapter, the reconstruction of the past and of the finding and taking of responsibility are complemented by a third task, that of exercising justice in order to symbolically rectify human rights abuses, sanction those responsible and compensate victims. Correspondingly, national and transnational institutions promoting processes of forgiveness have done so to work through two opposing perils, namely impunity and vigilantism. On the one hand, as survivors of atrocities, NGOs and social movements have indicated, the consequentialist paradigm framing the work of global justice is incompatible with the reality of perpetrators going unpunished. Because it bypasses the act of holding such perpetrators collectively accountable by subjecting them to domestic and international law, criminal impunity makes forgiving difficult, if not impossible and undesirable; the highly questionable nature of unconditional amnesty and blanket immunity becomes particularly striking when considering cases such as those of Pol Pot and the Khmer Rouge leadership in Cambodia, of Pinochet in Chile (Burbach 2003; Lefranc 2002: 43–51) or of Indonesia's Suharto during its occupation of East Timor. Thus, the struggle for global justice must clearly oppose the appropriation of discourses of forgiveness to sanction the whitewashing of individuals and organizations responsible for grave abuses. Another danger stems from the misuse of the logic of forgiveness to support what could be termed institutional impunity, whereby a society takes no measures to dismantle the ideological, political and socio-economic structures that underpinned a previous regime. To ask or demand to be forgiven becomes dubious when the worldviews and beliefs of morally responsible bystanders and the gains of politically responsible beneficiaries are merely reproduced, swept under the rug or remain unchallenged.

On the other hand, the exercise of justice faces what Arendt identifies as the constitutive paradox of radical evil, the fact 'that men are unable to forgive what they cannot punish and that they are unable to punish what has turned out to be unforgivable' (Arendt 1998 [1958]: 241). Accordingly, the practice of forgiveness counterbalances the tendency toward vigilantism, the 'eye for an eye' precept of *lex talionis* that would quickly degenerate into either a state-imposed reign of terror or the wreaking of revenge on former perpetrators by citizens taking matters into their own hands. This is why a non-calculative vision of justice is significant, for it seeks to sanction persons responsible for grave human rights abuses while recognizing the dire consequences of following norms of retributive proportionality – as well as, ultimately, the latter's inability to fully address the scale and intensity of suffering that such abuses have caused (Bass 2000: 304–7; Digeser 2001).

Over the past decade or so, trials and truth commissions around the world have faced these realities in developing notions of justice linked to forgiveness in transitional settings (Bass 2000; Hayner 2001; Minow 1998). Moreover, certain states, international organizations and civic associations in domestic and global civil societies have supported such initiatives, notably by urging the extra-territorial prosecution of those responsible for war crimes and crimes against humanity (e.g., in Belgium and Spain) and the creation of international tribunals (such as the International Criminal Court in The Hague, and the tribunals sponsored by the United Nations for Rwanda and the former Yugoslavia). What is interesting in most of these cases is their consequentialist orientation, the fact that they have generally sought to sanction wrongdoers irrespective of their authentic intentions and of their acknowledgement of responsibility. Furthermore, many progressive civil society groups engaged in the politics of forgiveness have been able to differentiate between the fact that they are not entitled to forgive on behalf of victims and the responsibility to demand justice in their name (Abel 1991: 232).

But, based on these initiatives, what are the outlines of a just labour of forgiveness? I want to propose a dual model that articulates retributive justice for criminal responsibility with restorative justice for moral and political responsibility, in a way that systematizes efforts along these lines in various societies. Rather than portraying these two facets of justice as intrinsically incompatible, this model is designed to tackle the individual and collective dimensions of wrongdoing as well as the symbolic and material aspects of forgiveness; sanctioning holds persons accountable for their actions and signifies collective disapproval of the latter, at the same time as structural redress for past wrongs aims to implement a more just social order. We can thus analyse how different societies' practices of forgiveness fall along a retributive–restorative continuum.

Contrary to what some arguments conflating forgiving with impunity may claim, a just practice of forgiveness is premised upon the criminal prosecution of persons who planned and perpetrated severe human rights violations. Conversely, critics of retributive justice who equate the latter with primal emotions of hatred or revenge fail to recognize that legally sanctioning wrongdoers for grave human rights abuses is legitimate and necessary to hold them accountable, address asymmetrical moral circumstances and remove ill-gotten symbolic and material gains, in addition to performing a host of functions that transcend mere punishment.[21] Indeed, a criminal trial represents the centrepiece of rituals of purification of the body politic via public denunciation of perpetrators' deeds, thereby bolstering the instituting of a new social order that morally distances itself from what preceded it (Borneman 2002: 298; Crocker 1999). Prosecution also tries to establish the principles of equal dignity of human beings and uniform application of domestic and international law; holding wrongdoers accountable affirms an ideal that is far from being realized today yet remains pivotal to the work of global justice, namely that no one is above universal human rights criteria and that blatant disregard for those rights will not be condoned.

The retributive purging of political and military leaders who committed or ordered massive injustices from their posts and the stripping of their honorific titles (which may have previously immunized them from prosecution) can be effective tools in draining their power base. When accompanied by measures such as lifetime bans on holding public office and mechanisms to counter the belief-systems of previous regimes and liquidate their institutional foundations, criminal prosecution can assist forgiveness by taking steps toward preventing the reoccurrence of human rights violations in particular societies. In countries where citizens believe that they are protected against grave abuses, or at least where they believe that those committing acts of this nature will be aggressively prosecuted, groups can forgive more easily.

Retribution is a necessary but not sufficient component of forgiveness, which is why it needs to be combined with restorative justice. Though sometimes muddled and wide-ranging, the latter includes the following elements: '(1) to affirm and restore the dignity of those whose human rights have been violated; (2) to hold perpetrators accountable, emphasizing the harm they have done to individual human beings; and (3) to create social conditions in which human rights will be respected' (Kiss 2000: 79). It is the fourth aspect of restorative justice – namely, its commitment to reconciliation, often at the expense of sanctioning (Kiss 2000: 79) – that can be at odds with a retributive orientation, yet not inherently so. Indeed, states, civil society groups and international organizations in many transitional contexts have attempted to develop arrangements that fall somewhere along the retribution–restoration continuum,

[21] As Hampton puts it: 'Since I have analysed the retributive sentiment as something other than a species of hatred or kind of anger, it is possible, on my analysis, for one to desire retribution and still drop one's resentful, indignant or hateful emotions, and have the change of heart which constitutes forgiveness.' (Murphy and Hampton 1988: 157–8)

albeit with varying degrees of success. For instance, the 'truth for amnesty' formula applied during the hearings of the South African Truth and Reconciliation Commission extended the possibility of individual immunity from criminal prosecution for perpetrators of severe human rights abuses during the apartheid era in order to facilitate processes of historical reconstruction and societal reconciliation, but with strict conditions: those coming forward had to apply for amnesty, with a committee reviewing requests on a case-by-case basis and having the authority to reject them if based on doubtful or illegitimate grounds; during their testimony, witnesses had to fully disclose what they knew and how they were involved in the apartheid regime; and the crimes they committed had to be political in character (that is, serving political ends or motivated by political beliefs, as opposed to deeds committed for personal and/or financial gain).[22]

There is no doubt that, when combined with a weak or non-existent retributive facet, restorative justice can verge on impunity – as critics of the South African situation have convincingly demonstrated. None the less, solely evaluating justice from the narrowly legalist perspective of criminal responsibility does not allow for a proper appreciation of the extra-juridical retributive impact flowing from the restorative requirement of public truth-telling. In fact, as a result of publicly disclosing the positions they occupied and the acts they committed, perpetrators of grave injustices frequently experience socio-cultural shaming and stigmatization within their own societies. Besides the erosion of social capital due to loss of standing and possible ostracism by peers, revelations of participation and complicity with mass crimes can seriously damage their relations with friends and relatives who may not have been previously aware of the extent and seriousness of their crimes (Crocker 2000: 103–4; Ntsebeza 2000: 164). Likewise, restorative measures extend to the fining of wrongdoers to recover ill-gotten gains and compensate victims, and their being compelled to make amends through community service.

The dual model of justice being proposed here is not intended to condone human rights violations by explaining them away as mere

[22] For a more detailed description of the amnesty rules for the South African Truth and Reconciliation Commission, see Boraine (2000: 148–9) and Minow (1998: 55–6, 59). Created in 2002, the East Timorese Commission for Reception, Truth and Reconciliation improved upon its South African predecessor in stipulating an additional condition for amnesty: that perpetrators not only admit and apologize for their crimes, but engage in restorative acts (community service, material or symbolic compensation to victims and their communities) (Hayner 2001: 255–6, 261–2). Therefore, the latter example represents a 'truth and restoration for amnesty' formula.

mistakes attributable to attenuating circumstances; to understand the doer is not to excuse the deed (Murphy and Hampton 1988: 24–5, 40; Jankélévitch 1998 [1967]: 1074–5). However, to be clear, its restorative dimension supports practices of forgiveness that aim gradually to transform post-transitional moral and social relationships between erstwhile victims, on the one hand, and perpetrators, bystanders and beneficiaries, on the other. In the places where it has been implemented, restorative justice feeds off the possibility that repentant wrongdoers are willing to commit not to repeat their crimes and to work to reverse the harm they did and unjust benefits they gained, by either facing legal and socio-cultural sanctions, repudiating their former worldviews or by helping to alleviate the circumstances of subordinate groups over which they previously held sway. At the same time, it depends upon victims' and survivors' readiness to differentiate doer from deed, so that the latter is not considered to sum up all of the former's worth and that a shared humanity between victims and perpetrators is recognized. To forgive and be forgiven flow out of the prospect of this sort of labour of ethical and political recalibration between parties.

Despite being at best only partially achieved in post-transitional societies to date, a restorative principle remains vital to practices of forgiveness that contribute to global justice: the implementation of structural reforms geared to redress wrongs and unjust advantages accrued by those morally and politically responsible for severe human rights violations. Whereas retribution exclusively deals with criminal responsibility on an individual basis, restorative justice can also tackle institutional and collective factors that informed the ways of thinking and acting of bystanders and beneficiaries – factors such as racism and cultural disparagement, political oppression and exclusion, as well as extreme socio-economic deprivation. In other words, a substantive understanding of forgiveness includes measures to redistribute symbolic and material resources that had previously been concentrated in the hands of leaders and supporters of past regimes or unjustly acquired through participation in abhorrent systems of social oppression (slavery, apartheid, etc.), in part through compensation for or correction of illegitimately and coercively acquired resources (e.g., land from indigenous peoples in the Americas and Oceania, and property from interned ethnic communities in the United States and Canada during the Second World War).

As such, national and global civic associations involved in the politics of forgiveness have demanded that states and international organizations implement a variety of restorative policies. These include financial reparations to victims themselves or to their relatives and descendants; provision of free health-care and education to members of stigmatized groups, as well as implementation of affirmative action programmes; restitution of property wrongly appropriated (land, money, art works, etc.), sometimes extending to management of territory, self-government and greater political autonomy (notably for indigenous peoples in New Zealand and Canada); and commemorative monuments and rituals (reburials of victims, memorial days) that affirm the dignity of groups whose identities and cultural traditions had been attacked.[23] Although such policies are meaningful, the prevailing tendency to view them as short-term 'one-offs' that are sufficient in and of themselves is problematic. Instead, I want to argue, these measures represent cumulative steps in a project of distributive justice that works toward a mode of forgiveness dedicated to rectifying systemic patterns and sources of inequality (Crocker 1999). How can forgiveness survive otherwise, if 'business as usual' prevails in post-transitional settings where structural inequalities are simply allowed to reproduce themselves and ongoing atrocities are tolerated? What cases from around the world strongly suggest is that groups are in a position to forgive their former enemies and oppressors once serious attempts are made to correct socio-economic, political and cultural asymmetries that were either at the root of the injustices they suffered or direct outcomes of them.

The dual model of justice presented here simultaneously addresses criminal responsibility via retribution and moral and political responsibility via restitution, thereby linking the possibility of forgiveness to the instituting of a new and just social order. And as we shall see in the next section, only then can the forgiving and forgiven parties ponder the possibility of reconciliation that may ensure their peaceful co-existence in the wake of mass injustices.

[23] For case studies of a range of situations around the world where several kinds of reparations and restitutive measures have been recommended or implemented, see Barkan (2000), Brooks (1999), Hayner (2001: 170–82) and Minow (1998: 100–2). Policy recommendations regarding Aboriginal peoples in Canada and Australia are found in, respectively, Royal Commission on Aboriginal Peoples (1996), available in summary form at www.ainc-inac.gc.ca/ch/rcap/rpt (accessed 21 March 2004), and National Inquiry Into the Separation of Aboriginal and Torres Strait Islander Children from Their Families (1997), available at www.austlii.edu.au/au/special/rsjproject/rsjlibrary/hreoc/stolen (accessed 21 March 2004). For a useful critique of the assimilationist and economically rationalist stances of the Australian state and some civil society groups toward reconciliation, see Short (2003). Regarding the land restitution to the Maori people in New Zealand, notably through the mechanism of the Waitangi Tribunal, see Bourassa and Strong (2000).

Reconciliation: breaking the vicious circle of vengeance

As several precedents indicate, the last and most difficult task of forgiveness consists of reconciliation between victims and perpetrators of severe human rights violations – something that is conditional upon the realization of the other components of the practice of forgiveness (historical reconstruction, attribution and acknowledgement of responsibility, and forms of justice along the retributive–restorative continuum). From the critical substantivist perspective that I am upholding here, the dampening of first-order emotions and reactions of resentment and vengefulness, required for forgiveness (Margalit 2002: 204–5; Murphy and Hampton 1988: 20; Shriver 1995: 8), is the potential outcome of complicated normative and socio-political labour by social actors instead of – as is commonly seen in literature on the subject – the result of a sudden dramatic change of heart on their part or their attaining a state of grace and righteousness.

Accordingly, the work of reconciliation in transitional and post-transitional contexts has encountered a number of similar obstacles. First among these is the aforementioned drive toward collective amnesia, the deliberate forgetting of the past in order to move forward expeditiously after grave injustices have been committed. The discourse of reconciliation thus becomes imbued with an illusion of finitude, whereby certain civic associations and states begin to use it to justify settling accounts with history once and for all. Aggrieved parties are asked not to 'rock the boat' by reopening old wounds and revisiting painful moments that are best left buried in the sands of time (Améry 1995). At the opposite end of the spectrum, a peril exists in the cultivation of an obsessive sense of societal remembrance that imprisons victim and perpetrator groups in the past, to the point that they are neither able nor willing to shift their historically entrenched roles and perspectives. This dominion of the past over the present blinds actors to changing socio-political and normative circumstances and funnels them into established pathological patterns of thought and action, thereby creating a thirst for vengeance without limit or end.[24] Indeed, those holding

[24] Contrary to what some analysts have argued, the problem is not too much collective memory – a mnemonic excess that can be corrected by forgetting – but rather the kind of collective memory that a society fosters. For example, the civil war in the former Yugoslavia was fuelled by the creation and widespread acceptance of a continuous historical narrative that, in addition to being demagogically manipulated to foment ethnic and religious violence, did not distinguish between the distant past, the recent past and the present (Ignatieff 1998). For several groups who perpetrated atrocities there, all incidents and grievances seemed to exist contiguously in temporal terms, regardless of when they may have actually occurred.

themselves hostage to the past are condemned to believe that an evil act can never be overcome and, consequently, that we are in its grip forever (Arendt 1998 [1958]: 237). More often than not, an obsessive memory does nothing more than nurture a vicious circle of revenge, according to which the inflicting of mass suffering by one side in a conflict or unjust system begets a similar or worse response from the other side through the periodic reversal of the positions of victim and perpetrator. The historical record speaks to the fact that from this outlook can only emerge a perpetual and escalating state of enmity, ruled by a primal law of retribution stipulating that 'we' must slaughter members of the group that slaughtered 'us', or subject them to the same sort of subordination that we experienced when 'they' were in power (Minow 1998: 10–11; Morin 2000: 26; Tutu 1999).

One of the most pervasive problems found in societies embarking upon a path of forgiveness originates from the latter's instrumentalization in the name of a form of reconciliation legislated from above, whereby states or international organizations prescribe that formerly victimized groups and individuals must forgive erstwhile perpetrators for the sake of societal unity, nation-building and political stability in a transitional epoch. When participating in the work of global justice, the practice of forgiveness ought not to be conflated with a diktat of pacification which orders victims and survivors to personally forgive and reconcile themselves with wrongdoers, regardless of the sort and effectivity of the ethico-political tasks that the relevant parties may have pursued (Améry 1995; Digeser 2001; Lefranc 2002: 129–33; Murphy and Hampton 1988; Wilson 2001).[25] Put differently, societies trading off historical truth, repentance and justice for reconciliation by establishing a new socio-political order in which unrepentant and unaccountable perpetrators and bystanders remain in power or simply live with impunity are often powder-kegs breeding resentment and grievances that can erupt into open conflict at any point in time. Morally and politically flawed processes of reconciliation, then, not only represent unsound foundations upon which to rebuild societies following large-scale human rights abuses, but also erode the prospects for global justice.

Distinct from this issue, although no less questionable, is a version of reconciliation that sometimes equates it with restoring an original

[25] In fact, as Murphy contends, resentment toward moral injuries is tied to a person's sense of respect for him or herself and, conversely, the willingness to forgive unconditionally and too readily can be an indication of inadequate self-respect (Murphy and Hampton 1988: 16–17). Hence, personal resentment cannot and ought not be legislated away institutionally, and individuals ought not be ordered or socially pressured to overcome it.

condition of socio-political harmony and equality between citizens – a condition that severe injustices eroded, and that forgiveness is supposed to recapture. Conceived in this manner, reconciliation draws upon a retrospective construct of a mythical past in which discord and relations of power are absent. A fictionalized past, however, cannot serve as a model for a transitional present and future where global and national civil society groups must engage with one another in order to confront the possible persistence of historical amnesia, unrepentance and impunity.

To work through these perils, we can take our cue from an Arendtian position suggesting that the practice of reconciliation is better grasped as a process of socio-political constitution than of restoration (Digeser 2001: 67n5; Schaap 2001). At stake is not an idealized return to an earlier state of society, but the instituting of a different socio-political and moral order characterized by the assertion of the human dignity and equal worth of all citizens. In this vein, reconciliation is a form of world-making, of reflexively refounding a society through the adoption of politically and socially constructed conventions and the design of new institutions; what shape this collective rebirth takes, notably whether it will be consistent with principles of global justice, essentially depends upon struggles between actors. When interpreted as a constitutive practice, reconciliation can be better understood as an ongoing process in the cultural and political life of a country or of global civil society, that is to say, a temporary institutional assemblage incessantly recreated through public discourse and action among citizens. Rather than being imbued with finality and invested with the capacity instantly to overcome all of the obstacles that a transitional society faces, mechanisms of reconciliation are part of a perpetual exercise in world-making. As sceptics about the South African Truth and Reconciliation Commission have claimed – to counter the latter's occasionally over-zealous rhetoric and the general population's unrealistic expectations – it did not mark the end-point of reconciliation, but merely a possible beginning toward lasting and structural undoing of a legacy of violence and injustice.

Using this perspective of reconciliation as constitutive of a new social order rather than as the restoration of a mythical golden age, we can grasp how parties involved in it have sought to construct a relationship to history that recognizes the violent and unjust pasts of their societies. In transitional settings, public commemorations of grave human rights abuses can thus serve as a reminder of the importance of continuously working to avoid the deterioration of relations between former enemies. At the same time, reconciliatory forgiveness has the capacity to loosen the past's iron grip on the present, allowing actors to struggle out of the vicious circle of revenge that entrapped them. In this ethical and socio-political labour is found the creative thrust of reconciliation, for although victims and survivors cannot turn the clock back, they can forgive a repentant doer while condemning the deed that he or she committed – or at the very least accept to live peacefully with their erstwhile foes.

Yet, *contra* what many governments assert through strongly communitarian discourses, reconciliation need not suspend or hide socio-political pluralism within post-transitional societies in order to bolster ideals of cultural uniformity or inherent unanimity among citizens (Lefranc 2002: 296–7; Wilson 2001). Instead, a practice of forgiveness that incorporates the prospect of reconciliation can put differences and non-violent disagreement into play via agonistic processes of public deliberation among a variety of positions within civil societies, which can enable the build-up of democratic vibrancy and robustness within previously immiserated public spheres. Accordingly, citizens can learn to forge reconciliatory agreement by expressing diverging opinions, attempting to persuade others of the merits of their positions and negotiating an overlapping consensus that recognizes divergent yet compatible viewpoints. Of course, this kind of public discussion and debate must always take place 'within the bounds of civility' (Gutman and Thompson 2000: 34), as states must guard against it slipping into an incitement to violence while promoting respect of others as civic equals. Furthermore, the labour of reconciliation navigates between the requirements to cultivate a diversity of perspectives and to arrive at a convergence of interpretations about past events; civil society actors may well argue about the share of criminal, moral and political responsibility borne by various sectors of society, but negationisms of the historical record (denying the occurrence of specific events) and legitimations of human rights violations and systemic injustices (what was done in the past was justified by the circumstances, or intended for the greater good) cannot be part of the discourse of reconciliation (Dwyer 1999; Hayner 2001: 162–3). Hence, the latter becomes untenable if the stances of parties involved in the practice of forgiveness violate norms of global justice and universal equality.

In order to shore up a pluralist conception of reconciliatory practices, I want to distinguish between a negative and thinner version of reconciliation, on the one hand, and an affirmative and thicker one, on the other. Much more widespread in transitional settings because more easily attainable, the minimalist version consists of former enemies refraining from armed conflict and violent enmity against each other; peaceful co-existence is thus achieved by adhering to the democratic rule of law and the respect of human rights. Once grave injustices have been overcome, parties can agree to reconcile only to the extent that they achieve a state of benign mutual indifference, a progressive 'rehumanization' of each side in the eyes of the other that prevents any group from being further victimized. Put differently, a society where a thin reconciliation operates is geared toward 'reciprocal civility', the tolerance for others that treats them as civil equals when one is treated as such in return (Gutman and Thompson 2000). While this model is hardly lofty in its ambition, it does mark a significant process of the labour of forgiveness, for the fact that citizens emerging out of situations of systemic violations of human rights are sometimes able to live together without resorting to mass violence is no small feat (Crocker 1999; Digeser 2001: 65; Sampson 2003; Shriver 1995: 8–9).

The merits of a minimalist reconciliation is that it allows for dissensus and critique in transitional contexts, where public officials may seek to impose an unjust settlement, invent an artificially harmonious ideal of political community or expect that former perpetrators will be instantly pardoned regardless of whether or not they have engaged in substantive processes of forgiveness (Bhargava 2000: 60–3; Crocker 2000: 108; Gibney and Roxstrom 2001: 935; Minow 1998: 17, 20; Nagy 2002: 326). Societies can recognize an individual's right to withhold forgiveness personally, notably in instances of calculated and wilful inflicting of mass suffering – with the proviso that such a refusal does not threaten peaceful co-existence (through revenge killings, for example). Indeed, this kind of passive reconciliation, of tolerance for former enemies that makes parties refrain from taking the law into their own hands, is both valuable and transnationally 'enforceable'. International and regional organizations can send peacekeeping troops to prevent the eruption of renewed warfare, whereas global civil society actors can monitor newly created arrangements for possible abuses of power.

Beyond their minimalist incarnations, reconciliatory discourses in transitional societies are frequently animated by affirmative and thicker aspirations whose outcome is a dramatic transformation of the relationship between parties: the conversion of foes to friends, or the befriending and love of former enemies (Arendt 1998 [1958]: 243; Murphy and Hampton 1988: 83–6; Nagy 2002: 328–9; Tutu 1999). If this ideal is unrealistic in the aftermath of massive human rights violations and troubling when elevated to the status of an unconditional good (severed from the attainment of justice) or an institutionally prescribed paramount objective – as has tended to be the case in some national truth and reconciliation commissions (Wilson 2001) – it does help sketch the contours of a process achieving complete moral and social symmetry between forgiving and forgiven actors. Civically and politically, such a process includes the rehabilitation of all members of a society as fully fledged citizens, who are able and willing to collaborate with one another in finding common ground and instituting a new social order (Kiss 2000:

79). In cultural terms, thick reconciliation involves widespread civil society participation in the invention of historical narratives and collective symbols that commemorate past horrors and injustices, pay tribute to victims, celebrate societal rebirth and reimagine a different present and future (Lefranc 2002: 298–9). Yet to be substantive, the reconstitution of society must aim to redress forms of discrimination and socio-economic inequalities resulting from historically entrenched structural injustices (Tutu 1999: 273–4).[26] Put succinctly, then, a maximalist project of reconciliation is characterized by a commitment to cultural recognition and socio-economic redistribution.

As opposed to what many proponents of reconciliation would argue, I do not believe that its thick version is intrinsically superior or more desirable than its thinner counterpart. Rather, the practice-based framework proposed in this chapter assesses reconciliatory situations according to the manner and extent to which actors perform the various tasks comprising the labour of forgiveness, regardless of whether they result in minimal or maximal outcomes. Moreover, though a reconciliatory thickening may occur as groups and individuals repeat relevant patterns of thought and action over time, no automatic movement in this direction exists in societies attempting to overcome a legacy of mass suffering. As examples from around the world demonstrate, the precise variant of reconciliation suited for specific settings cannot be legislated in advance or in a top-down fashion, since it is adapted to established relations of power and socio-cultural realities. Ideally, the cultivation of a vibrant civil society and democratic state equipped with strong representative institutions assists citizens to openly deliberate and negotiate appropriate reconciliatory arrangements – with particular attention to the needs of formerly stigmatized and persecuted groups and the requirements of global justice. Indeed, failure to meet such requirements can be subject to criticism from international organizations and members of global civil society.

Conclusion

The current *leitmotif* of revenge in world affairs ought not obscure the fact that many actors are electing to pursue paths of forgiveness in response to systemic injustices and grave human rights abuses. Nevertheless, established paradigms of interpretation of forgiveness tend to reduce

[26] Financial reparations and major institutional reforms are key recommendations of several official reports on the subject, ranging from the South African and Chilean Truth and Reconciliation Commissions to the aforementioned Canadian Royal Commission on Aboriginal Peoples and the Australian National Inquiry Into the Separation of Aboriginal and Torres Strait Islander Children from Their Families (Hayner 2001: 164–5).

the latter to a legal outcome (juridico-political models) or moral ideal (theologico-philosophical models), thereby neglecting how it represents a mode of social action constituted through dialogical, public and transnational labour. I introduced the notion of the practice of forgiveness to formulate a theory of practice that underscores how the implicated parties enact a set of ethico-political tasks through which an initial situation of moral asymmetry between them can be converted into one of relative socio-political symmetry: historical reconstruction, acknowledgement and attribution of responsibility, exercise of justice and reconciliation.

Accordingly, the chapter considered the first peril encountered by the labour of forgiveness, the belief that societies should forget the past in order to forgive, and offered an alternative according to which investigatory and truth-telling exercises can establish a comprehensive and just record of severe human rights violations in transitional societies. Following these processes of reconstitution of the past come the problems of unrepentance and collective guilt, against which forgiveness can be based upon the tasks of assigning and assuming responsibility for documented wrongdoings. Thus, I proposed a tripartite framework that distinguishes between those who are criminally, morally and politically responsible, while advocating a consequentialist logic of assessment of apology and responsibility-taking. Yet given that wrongdoers can either acknowledge responsibility for their actions or refuse to do so, the possibility of forgiving them is more usefully tied to their being held collectively accountable through the bringing to bear of institutionalized democratic forms of justice that can ward off the prospects of impunity, on the one hand, and vigilantism, on the other. I suggested that the local articulation of elements from both retributive and restorative modes of justice is best suited to these challenges, since it is fully compatible with a practice of forgiveness and can additionally address structural inequalities connected to human rights abuses. The chapter closed by considering how the labour of forgiveness can enable former enemies to distance themselves from patterns of revenge in transitional contexts, via forms of reconciliation understood as acts of creation of a new socio-political order rather than the rediscovery of a supposedly harmonious and unified past. In order to bolster a pluralist model of forgiveness which counters arguments about reconciliatory homogeneity and unanimity, I distinguished between a negative and thin concept of reconciliation (where parties are content with peaceful co-existence) and an affirmative and thick one (where citizens join in a common project of societal reconstruction) – neither concept being intrinsically superior to the other.

To reiterate what has been claimed throughout this chapter, the concept of a mode of ethico-political practice is not intended to promote forgiveness as an all-encompassing and instantaneous solution in the wake of mass suffering. Contrary to much inflated theological and secular rhetoric, I do not believe that forgiveness carries an inherent power to conquer all evil by 'washing away sins' or wiping the historical slate clean. What has been done can never be completely undone, and what has been lost can never be perfectly recovered; to deny this is to fail to appreciate the arduous labour involved in seeking and granting forgiveness. Indeed, even in settings widely hailed as success stories, such as post-apartheid South Africa, there is much evidence to suggest that the perils enumerated here may stubbornly survive – albeit sometimes more feebly than before. Certain citizens, in the name of letting sleeping dogs lie in transitional societies, continue to try to forget a horrific past or to reinterpret it in dubious ways. Others may be unrepentant with respect to their wrongdoings, as well as refuse to accept responsibility or to apologize for the acts they committed, the tacit support they provided or the advantages they derived from systemic injustices. Some humanitarian violations may remain unprosecuted and those responsible for them never held publicly accountable, which may in turn prompt victimized groups and individuals to take the law into their own hands. And last but not least, reconciliation may at best remain superficial and partial, with the threat of renewed, spiralling eruptions of violence hanging over the protagonists and of structural hierarchies being reproduced over time. Hence, no society emerges from grave episodes of human rights abuses and achieves forgiveness overnight, nor do foes suddenly or miraculously become friends.

Going even further, certain commentators have declared that '[f]orgiveness died in the death camps' (Jankélévitch 1986: 50) of Nazi Germany or, one could add, in the killing fields of Cambodia, the former Yugoslavia and Rwanda. Perhaps this is so. Indeed, perhaps this ought to be so when wrongdoers repudiate reciprocal participation in the labour of forgiveness designed to rectify a situation of moral asymmetry. At the same time, we should keep in mind that, however difficult and limited it may be, forgiveness is not doomed to failure since it persists as a source of hope and justice in the face of disastrous legacies and seemingly intractable troubles around the world. For several societies and groups struggling to recover from severe human rights violations, it offers the prospect – sometimes the only prospect – of a better future. Forgiveness, then, amounts to no more and no less than an 'ethical gamble' (Morin 2000: 25). Despite this, as I have tried to show here, societies can stack the odds in their favour by engaging in an ensemble of reciprocal ethico-political tasks that cannot negate forgiveness's essence as a risky and unending endeavour, yet can transform it into a gamble that is eminently worthwhile to take if global justice is to survive.

3 Cautionary tales: on foresight

Introduction

The future appears to be out of favour today, having seemingly become the province of mystics and scientists – a realm into which the rest of us rarely venture. Mere mention of the idea of farsightedness, of trying to understand what may occur in our wake in order to make sense of the here and now, conjures up images of fortune-telling crystal balls and doomsday prophets, or of eccentric pundits equipped with data-crunching supercomputers spewing forth fanciful prognostications about how human beings will eventually live. This curious situation goes back to a founding paradox of early Western modernity, which sought to replace pagan divination and Judaeo-Christian eschatology with its own rational systems of apprehending time. Thus came into being the philosophy of history, according to which human destiny unfolds teleologically by following a knowable and meaningful set of chronological laws leading to a final state of perfection. Condorcet, Kant, Hegel and Marx, to name but a few, are the children of this kind of historicism that expresses an unwavering faith in the Enlightenment's credo of inherent progress over time.

Yet in our post-metaphysical age, where the idea of discovering universal and stable temporal laws has become untenable, the philosophy of history lies in tatters (Heller 1993). What has stepped into the breach is a variety of sciences of governance of the future, ranging from social futurism to risk management. By developing sophisticated deontological procedures and modelling techniques springing out of the venerable traditions of probability and statistical studies, prognosticators convert the future into a series of predictable outcomes extrapolated from present-day trends, or a set of possibilities to be assessed and managed according to their comparative degrees of risk and reward.[1] Although

[1] On the history of such sciences, see Hacking (1990). A widely read futurist manifesto is Toffler (1970). The World Futures Studies Federation promotes research along such lines that is more explicitly critical; see www.wfsf.org (accessed 28 January 2006). On risk management, see Baker and Simon (2002), Haller (2002) and Leiss (2001). Two leading journals in the field are *Risk Analysis* and the *Journal of Risk Research*.

commendable in their advocacy of farsightedness, these scientistic forms of knowledge are hampered by the fact that their longing for surefire predictive models and flawless projections inevitably come up short, hitting up against their grudging realization of historical contingency and the consequent popular incredulity about their claims to truth.

If historicism and scientistic governance provide questionable paradigms through which to contemplate the future, a turn to the conventional political forecasts of the post-Cold War world order hardly offers more succour. Entering the fray, one is rapidly submerged by Fukuyama's (1992) 'end of history', Huntington's (1996) 'clash of civilizations', Kaplan's (2000) 'coming anarchy' or, perhaps most distressing of all, the so-called 'Bush Doctrine' of unilateral pre-emption. For the Left, this array of unpalatable scenarios merely prolongs the sense of hope betrayed and of utopias crushed that could somewhat be held at bay before 1989, but that came crashing down as quickly and unstoppably as the Berlin Wall did in that fateful year.[2] Under such circumstances, is it any wonder that many progressive thinkers dread an unwelcome future, preferring to avert their gaze from it while simultaneously eyeing prospective-minded analysis with equal doses of suspicion and contempt?

But neither evasion nor fatalism will do if the work of global justice is to forge ahead. Some authors have grasped this, reviving hope in large-scale socio-political transformation by sketching out utopian pictures of a just world order.[3] Endeavours like these may well be essential, for they spark ideas about possible and desirable futures that transcend the existing state of affairs and undermine the flawed prognoses of the post-Cold War world order already mentioned; what ought to be and the Blochian 'Not-Yet' remain powerful figures of critique of what is, and inspire us to contemplate how social existence could be organized differently. None the less, this chapter adopts a different tack by exploring how a dystopian-inflected practice of prevention of massive human rights violations, which I am terming a farsighted cosmopolitanism, is becoming one of the key components of the work of global justice. Indeed, if both witnessing and forgiveness are primarily retrospective modes of socio-political labour designed to address past human rights abuses, foresight is geared toward what may come – toward, that is, averting potential suffering to future generations and opposing foreseeable erosions of their socio-economic and civil-political rights through actions or policies taken in the present.

[2] For mostly mournful yet defiant reflections on this state of affairs, written in the immediate aftermath of the collapse of the Eastern bloc, see Blackburn (1991).

[3] Writings with a self-consciously utopian tone include Falk (1995), Hardt and Negri (2000; 2004), Held (2004) and Morin and Kern (1993).

The place of farsighted cosmopolitanism in the work of global justice is growing because one of the notable features of public discourse and socio-political struggles about human rights over the past few decades is their negationist and prospective hue: they are devoted as much to the prevention of human rights crises as to the realization of the good or, in other words, less to what ought to be than what could but must not be (Beck 1992: 49).[4] In the twenty-first century, the lines of political cleavage are being drawn along those of competing dystopian visions. The debates in the lead-up to the 2003 invasion of Iraq provide a vivid illustration of this tendency, as both camps rhetorically invoked incommensurable catastrophic scenarios to justify their positions. And as many analysts have noted, the multinational anti-war protests culminating in the 15 February 2003 marches and rallies on all continents marked the first time that a mass movement could mobilize a substantial number of people dedicated to averting war before hostilities had actually broken out. More generally, given past experiences and awareness of what might plausibly occur in the future, given the cries of 'never again' (the Holocaust, Bhopal, Rwanda, etc.) emanating from different parts of the world, the avoidance of mass suffering is seemingly on everyone's lips and on everyone's conscience. From the United Nations and regional multilateral organizations to states, from non-governmental organizations to transnational social movements, all the way down to concerned citizens, the determination to avert both global injustices and the amplification of existing ones is setting up a new dynamic in world affairs. For several progressive actors in global civil society, allowing past disasters to reoccur and severe human rights abuses to unfold is normatively unbearable and politically debilitating, since they imply callous tolerance of serious harm to future generations. Although such abuses continue virtually unabated owing to the lack of concerted and effective action on the part of states and international organizations, we would be ill-advised to dismiss summarily what a widely circulated and influential report by the International Commission on Intervention and State Sovereignty identifies as the 'responsibility to protect', a consequent burgeoning of a 'culture of prevention' (Evans and Sahnoun 2001: 27) and belief in the possibility of managing humanitarian emergencies (Calhoun 2004: 374–6), which carry major, albeit still poorly understood, implications for a just world order.

[4] Of course, the two objectives are logically interdependent, since critique and opposition to the realization of certain outcomes is premised upon adherence to certain ethico-political ideals (freedom, justice, equality, etc.) – and vice versa. I will return to this point in the last section of the chapter.

Hence, rather than bemoaning the current pre-eminence of a dystopian imaginary, I am claiming that it may be heralding a novel mode of practice of global justice that can be termed preventive foresight. We should not reduce the latter to a formal principle regulating international relations or an ensemble of policy prescriptions for officially sanctioned players on the world stage (states and international organizations), but rather view it as a sort of farsighted labour constituted through social processes whereby numerous associative groups in national and global civil societies are simultaneously creating and putting into practice a sense of responsibility for the future by attempting to anticipate and avoid severe and structurally based injustices and crises. Although these actors engage in farsighted labour with varying degrees of institutional support and access to material and symbolic resources, and despite the fact that they perform it in multiple political and socio-cultural settings, three recurring characteristics hold it together and thereby allow us to identify it as a distinctive mode of practice of global justice: dialogism, publicity and transnationality. While this chapter weaves each of these features into its fabric, let me briefly explain them here in a more sustained fashion.

In the first instance, preventive foresight is an intersubjective or dialogical process of address, recognition and response between two parties in global civil society: the 'warners' who anticipate and initially send out word of forthcoming or possible extreme human rights violations, and the audiences being warned, those who recognize and heed their interlocutors' messages by demanding that governments and/or international organizations take measures to steer away from such crises. Without mutual recognition, the practice of preventive foresight is impossible, for warning signals cannot be picked up and transmitted to an audience, or yet again simply fall on deaf ears.

Secondly, preventive foresight is entwined with the notion of publicity, deriving both its effectiveness and legitimacy from public debate and deliberation among constituencies concerned with and coalescing around struggles to avert specific global injustices (Habermas 1989a [1962]; 1996: 328–87). Hence, the environmental and peace movements, humanitarian NGOs, and other similar globalizing civic associations are becoming significant actors that, despite having little direct decision-making capacity in world affairs, are increasingly involved in public opinion and will formation; they disseminate information and alert citizens about looming catastrophes (in what could be called consciousness-raising and conscience-triggering efforts), lobby states and multilateral organizations from the 'inside' and pressure them from the 'outside', in addition to fostering citizens' participation in debates about how to prevent or stop looming global injustices.

The above remarks point to the third notable trait of preventive foresight, its transnational character. Confirmation of this trend is found in the now commonplace observation that we live in one world, that the scope and impact of severe human rights violations transcend any and all territorial borders. The globalization of such situations, or the fact that their spillover effects cannot be geographically contained, leads to interdependence between the planet's populations. Whether by choice or necessity, we are witnessing greater integration of citizens from far-flung parts of the earth into transnational 'risk communities'.[5] Moreover, on account of dense media and information flows, knowledge of impending crises can instantaneously reach the four corners of the globe – sometimes well before individuals in one locale experience the consequences of a crisis originating in another one. Accordingly, associative groups are aiming to cultivate a globalizing ethos and set of strategies to respond to the manifold future injustices confronting humanity.[6]

An implication of the last point can be teased out. We should not take for granted the existence of global civil society as an already fully established arena for transnational socio-political relations, notably in light of its continued underinstitutionalization. Nor should we simply view it as an organizational complex that is the sum of the varied groups of which it is composed. Instead, I would like to consider how the practice of preventive foresight represents one of the key processes through which the constitution of global civil society is occurring. Social movements, NGOs, diasporic groups and other civic associations are engaging in dialogical, public and transnational forms of ethico-political action that are generating a space 'below' the official and formalized sphere of international relations. The work of preventive foresight consists of forging ties between citizens, contributing to the circulation of flows of claims, images and information across borders, promoting an ethos of farsighted cosmopolitanism, and both forming and mobilizing citizens who debate and struggle against possible catastrophes – all of which create and sustain a global civil society. Furthermore, aside from the fact that the existing institutional architecture of world affairs has achieved what are at best mixed results in averting large-scale human rights violations, global

[5] See Beck (1992; 1999; 2000; 2002), Habermas (2001: 56) and World Commission on Environment and Development (1987). Even regions of the world less prone to 'local' humanitarian disasters on their own soil (e.g., North America, Oceania) are invariably affected by them, notably through increased refugee flows, geopolitical destabilization and diasporic politics.

[6] To be clear, I am not arguing that the transnationalization of prevention bypasses national governments, but rather that it supplements initiatives directed at states with global civically oriented ones.

civil society offers a different route through which we can envisage preventive action.[7] Indeed, over the past few decades, civic associations – rather than states and international organizations – have been the ones to take the initiative in this area, warning citizens and campaigning to have foreseeable global injustices put on the public agenda; official institutions have, for the most part, been content to follow global civil society's lead. Consequently, preventive foresight will first need to consolidate itself in this informal realm before it can 'move up' to become institutionalized as a possible *modus operandi* of a new world order. If the prevention of global injustices is eventually and consistently to trump the assertion of short-term and narrowly defined rationales (national interest, profit, bureaucratic self-preservation, etc.), civic associations must begin by convincing or compelling their official representatives and multilateral organizations to do so.[8]

Because the culture of prevention that is taking shape in global civil society remains itself a work in progress, the argument presented here is poised between empirical and normative dimensions of analysis. It proposes a theory of the practice of preventive foresight based upon concrete struggles and discourses already present in the 'actually existing' sphere of global civil society, while simultaneously advocating the adoption of certain principles that would substantively thicken, and assist in the realization of, a sense of responsibility and care for the future of humankind. I will therefore proceed in three steps, showing how the work of preventive foresight combats objections to it and problems that could invalidate it. The first part of the chapter contends that the development of a public aptitude for early warning about global cataclysms can overcome flawed conceptions of the future's essential inscrutability. This will be followed by a claim that an ethos of farsighted cosmopolitanism – of solidarity that extends to future generations – can supplant the short-term and presentist outlooks that predominate today through appeals to the public's moral imagination and use of reason. In the final section of the chapter, I argue that the commitment of global civil society actors to norms of precaution and transnational justice can hone citizens' faculty of critical judgement against the alarmist abuse or resigned misinterpretation of the dystopian imaginary, thereby opening the way to public deliberation about the social construction of an alternative world order.

[7] On the repeated refusal of US administrations to intervene to avert or stop genocides in the twentieth century, see Power (2002a). On the West's indifference to the HIV/AIDS crisis in sub-Saharan Africa, see Carroll (2003). Regarding the United Nations' bureaucratic inaction in the face of the Rwandan genocide, see Barnett (2002).

[8] For a similar argument regarding cosmopolitan solidarity, see Habermas (1996: 380–2; 2001: 111–12).

But before plunging into an examination of each of these facets, we need to consider the shifting socio-political and cultural climate that gives rise to the practice of concern for the future of humankind, as well as the intellectual frameworks that attempt to account for it.

The cradle of prevention

Cosmopolitan farsightedness may well have a lengthy pedigree, but the factors most responsible for its contemporary prominence can be traced back to the second half of the twentieth century. Societies emerging out of the horrors and devastation of two world conflicts came to recognize that three specific dangers needed to be averted at all costs: wars of aggression; genocide and crimes against humanity; and nuclear armageddon. Responses from within the official channels of the international system countered the first two of these perils: the charter giving birth to the United Nations, which prioritized the principles of state sovereignty, peace and security (in replacement of its ill-fated predecessor, the League of Nations); the signing of the Universal Declaration of Human Rights; and the UN Convention on the Prevention and Punishment of the Crime of Genocide. However, the onset and escalation of the Cold War, characterized by a seemingly intractable East–West confrontation that paralyzed the United Nations while encouraging a nuclear arms race, largely rendered official institutions ineffective. This stalemate explains the formation of nuclear disarmament movements in the 1950s, which was spurred on by the terrifying realization that human beings had devised the means for their own annihilation and that the two geopolitical blocs were pursuing an 'exterminist' systemic logic (the balance of terror, or mutually assured destruction).[9] Human survival could no longer be entrusted to governments or multilateral institutions; ordinary citizens had to organize themselves to tackle such policies head-on. Beginning in the 1970s, another threat came to light, that of planetary ecological ruin brought about by an industrialism that mercilessly depleted the earth's resources and polluted the environment at an unsustainable pace. Landmark and widely debated reports, notably those from the Club of Rome (Meadows *et al.* 1972) and the Brundtland Commission (World Commission on Environment and Development 1987), galvanized sections of public opinion and created socio-cultural conditions that were favourable to the expansion of the environmental movement.

[9] On exterminationism, see Thompson (1985). Regarding the movements themselves, see Smith (1965) and Wittner (1993; 1997).

Since the end of the Cold War, growing discursive and institutional attention to the imperative to prevent mass suffering is not translating into systematic efforts to actually do so in world affairs; after Rwanda came Darfur, and the tackling of the HIV/AIDS pandemic in sub-Saharan Africa and Asia has been half-hearted at best. However, these failures should not completely obscure certain encouraging signs at the level of global governance. The dissolution of the bipolar stalemate between East and West potentially opened the door to greater interstate coordination and multilateral collaboration, perhaps most significantly at the United Nations Security Council.[10] The creation of supranational judicial institutions (e.g., the International Criminal Tribunal for the former Yugoslavia and the International Criminal Court) are also signal achievements, for, though primarily designed to prosecute past crimes against humanity, they may well have a latent deterrent effect against the carrying out of mass atrocities in the future. The Rome Treaty establishing the International Criminal Court is itself part of an expanding infrastructure of multinational conferences and agreements that has come into being over the past decade or so. Most frequently under the auspices of the United Nations, governments and NGOs have participated in large-scale summits, often resulting in agreements or declarations incorporating strong preventive language – albeit still without enforceability; for instance, the Kyoto Protocol on climate change, the Declaration on the Responsibilities of the Present Generations Towards Future Generations, and the United Nations General Assembly's adoption in principle of the responsibility to protect populations from crimes against humanity.[11] Furthermore, in the last few years, the rise of important transnational humanitarian, feminist, peace, environmental and social justice struggles has given rise to alternative summits (most prominently, the World Social Forum), where activists and representatives from NGOs and social movements are joining forces to demand that formal institutions take preventive action against violations of socio-economic and civil-political rights, or indeed cease to pursue policies generating such violations. Hence, cosmopolitan foresight is but the latest tendency of globalization from below.

What other factors account for the recently enhanced standing of preventive foresight? As indicated in Chapter 1, we should take into

[10] It remains to be seen whether the Bush administration's current stance of aggressive unilateralism will permanently compromise such prospects.

[11] See, respectively, the following websites: //unfccc.int (accessed 7 November 2003); www.unesco.org/cpp/uk/declarations/generations.pdf (accessed 7 November 2003); www.responsibilitytoprotect.org (accessed 22 January 2006). The agreement to adopt the responsibility to protect is found in the United Nations 2005 World Summit outcome document, which is available at the latter website.

consideration the host of initiatives to bear witness to and institutionalize the collective memory of some of the last century's major instances of human rights violations, which stand for many citizens as paradigmatic instances and highly charged signifiers of the dire consequences of a lack of farsightedness. Remembrance of past atrocities has galvanized some sectors of public opinion in national and global civil societies, making the international community's failure to act in spite of prior warning of upcoming crises (Rwanda, Darfur, the HIV/AIDS pandemic) appear particularly callous. If nothing else, the United Nations and its member-states are being pressured and shamed to admit that they could have done, and could still do, more to avoid such situations and that they need to take steps in this direction. Also playing a role in thrusting preventive foresight to the forefront of world affairs is the appearance of new perils to human rights and the resurgence of 'older' ones. For the most part kept in check or bottled up during the Cold War, virulent forms of ethno-racial nationalism and religious fundamentalism have reasserted themselves in ways that are now all too familiar: civil warfare, genocide and 'ethnic cleansing'. And if mutually assured destruction is not much of a threat anymore, other forces have come to fill the vacuum, namely climate change, AIDS and other diseases spreading across the world (BSE, SARS, etc.), as well as grinding poverty. 'World risk society' is alive and well (Beck 1999).[12]

At the beginning of this chapter, I alluded to the fact that the transition toward a dystopian 'emergency' or 'catastrophic' imaginary in the North Atlantic region has partly been responsible for the renewed concern for farsightedness (Calhoun 2004; Sontag 1966).[13] Instead of implying despondency or fear, this trend assists notions of historical contingency and fallibilism to gain traction against their determinist and absolutist counterparts in a manner that nurtures foresight (Beck 1992; Brown

[12] I would insist more strongly than does Beck that the globalization of risks does not imply an equal distribution of them across the world. Regardless of socio-economic position or geographical location, all persons share some perils more or less evenly, yet the degree of exposure to many risks varies greatly within and between societies. The principal dividing lines follow the global North–South axis as well as gender, class and ethnic hierarchies, with vulnerable and subordinate segments of the world's populations being comparatively overexposed to transnational crises. Thus, the redistribution of future dangers is an important component of a politics of global justice.

[13] For a discussion of the role of dystopias in modern thought, see Kumar (1987). Feenberg (1995; 1999) convincingly demonstrates that dystopianism was central to New Left political struggles and social movements opposed to technocratic rationality and power, as emblematized in Marcuse's diagnoses of a 'one-dimensional man' and a 'totally administered society', as well as Foucault's 'carceral archipelago'.

2001: 1–6; Heller 1993).[14] Once we recognize that the future is uncertain and that any course of action produces both unintended and unexpected consequences, the responsibility to face up to potential disasters and intervene before they strike (when 'things are not going according to plan') becomes irrefutable. From another perspective, negationism lies at the core of politics in global civil society, with each social movement mobilizing constituents by deploying its own dystopia: for environmentalism, it is 'Frankenfoods' and a lifeless planet; for Western feminism, totalitarian patriarchy of the sort depicted in Atwood's (1985) *Handmaid's Tale*; for the alternative globalization movement, McWorld and a global neoliberal oligarchy; for the peace movement, a mushroom cloud enveloping the earth; and so forth. Dystopianism is acting as a catalyst for public debate and a spur to action, inviting citizens to engage in the labour of preventive foresight.

How has academic literature addressed this potential sea-change in world affairs? For heuristic purposes, we can distinguish among three approaches to the question. The first of these is the body of work within political philosophy known as just-war theory, which has sought to develop universal criteria through which can be assessed the rights and duties of governments to wage armed conflict against other states. In the past decade or so, these debates have mainly been framed in terms of humanitarian intervention, a rubric that was given renewed urgency as a result of 'bystanding' during the 1994 Rwandan genocide, as well as by the 1999 NATO bombing campaign in Kosovo and the 2003 invasion of Iraq. In light of the central organizing principle of the Westphalian system, state sovereignty, can military intervention in the affairs of a particular country be justified if mass atrocities against civilians might occur (or are occurring)? If so, under what conditions and according to what procedures is it legitimate?[15] Though crucial, such queries are mostly

[14] This acknowledgement of contingency has also tempered the kinds of utopias now being formulated, which tend to eschew what had been a deeply engrained, intransigent perfectionism and absolutism in favour of fallibilism and self-critique.

[15] The contemporary *locus classicus* on just-war theory is Walzer (1992). With regard to interventionism, see several contributions to Archibugi (2003), as well as Bartholomew and Breakspear (2004), Bradol (2004), Chandler (2003), Chomsky (1999), Cohen (2004), Doyle (2001), Evans and Sahnoun (2001), Gowan (2003), Habermas (1999; 2003), Ignatieff (2001; 2002; 2003a; 2003b), Kennedy (2004), Kouchner and Bettati (1987), Luban (2002), Pieterse (1997), Rieff (2002), Teeple (2004), Walzer (1992; 2002a; 2002b; 2003; 2004), Weiss and Hubert (2001), Wheeler (2000) and Zanetti (2001). For an interesting discussion of the positions and dilemmas of prominent US 'liberal hawks' preceding the invasion of Iraq, see Packer (2002) Despite the fact that a detailed analysis of debates regarding humanitarian intervention, such as that provided in Kurasawa (2006), is beyond the scope of this chapter, I can none the less outline a typology of three sets of oppositions which structure debates in the literature on the topic:

framed from within the official sphere of international governance, concentrating on states' and multilateral organizations' institutional and procedural aspects while overlooking the role of participants in global civil society and that of the social processes undergirding preventive action.

Public policy research, the second identifiable paradigm discussing global prevention, has been more open to informal dimensions of transnational politics, for it frequently analyses the interaction between official and unofficial actors in forestalling armed conflict between or within nation-states. It thus acknowledges that NGOs can assist governments and international institutions in the pursuit of preventive diplomacy, assistance that can range from the implementation of measures such as economic sanctions and trade inducements to the brokering of peace between warring parties.[16] Yet the strategic and practical orientation of public policy research results in an undertheorization of the ethical and socio-cultural anchors of farsightedness in relation to global justice. Moreover, policy proposals rarely give global civil society its due or value it for its own sake, being primarily interested in how NGOs can insert themselves into existing institutional decision-making channels; associative networks become appendages to their more formal counterparts.

Beck's well-known concept of 'risk society' represents the third way of interpreting the renewed preoccupation with prevention (Beck 1992; 1999). The risk society thesis has the merit of highlighting the recent expansion of collective reflexivity, that is to say, the increasing public awareness of the numerous dangers facing humankind and ordinary citizens' questioning of the institutions producing, and experts managing, these dangers. Likewise, it usefully identifies the reordering of political action in relation to a consciousness of catastrophe resolutely oriented to

(1) muscular interventionism (the defence of human rights anywhere in the world, by arms if necessary, is required) versus neo-realism (state sovereignty is the cornerstone of the international system, protecting weaker states against stronger ones) and neo-imperialism (humanitarian rhetoric is a pretext for the extension of Western global hegemony);
(2) intentionalism (the reasons guiding interventionism must be valid and justified) versus consequentialism (intervention must result in better circumstances for the affected civilian population than the situation that it is meant to resolve);
(3) absolutism (all interventions must conform to formal requirements and the rule of international law, both of which must be applied consistently) versus pragmatism (such litmus-tests cannot always be satisfied, and exceptions to them are warranted under certain circumstances).

Of course, the positions of individual authors demonstrate frequent overlap between these different categories by mixing and matching arguments from opposed viewpoints.

[16] See Evans and Sahnoun (2001), Kuper (1985), Rotberg (1996) and Weiss and Hubert (2001).

the future. Nevertheless, it does not sufficiently formulate the principles that should guide the public assessment of risks and socially constructed visions of the future, nor fully ponder how, apart from reacting to imposed crises, participants in global civil society can affirmatively nurture a politics of preventive foresight grounded in a sense of responsibility for temporally distant others.

All in all, then, although insights from the principal philosophical, public policy and sociological frameworks dealing with the question of global prevention will be incorporated in the following pages, the three approaches skirt over much of what is revealing about struggles to avert gross human rights abuses as forms of farsighted cosmopolitanism. Hence, I want to put forth a theory of ethico-political practice, a reconstruction of the dialogical, public and transnational labour of preventive foresight that articulates the socio-political processes underpinning it to the normative ideals that should steer and assist in substantively thickening it as it becomes an increasingly important component of the work of global justice. Let us thus turn to the first component of the work of preventive foresight, the creation of a capacity for early warning that attempts to counter a belief in the utter inscrutability of the future.

The aptitude for early warning

When engaging in the practice of preventive foresight, the first obstacle that actors in global civil society encounter is deep-seated doubt about the value of the exercise itself. According to certain so-called 'postmodern' lines of thinking, the aforementioned crisis of conventional paradigms of historical analysis signifies that it is pointless, and perhaps even harmful, to strive for farsightedness. If, *contra* historicist teleology, time has no intrinsic meaning, direction or end-point to be discovered through human reason and if, *contra* scientistic futurism, prospective trends cannot be predicted without error, then the abyss of chronological inscrutability opens up at our feet. The future is unknowable, an outcome of chance circumstances that cannot be mastered. Therefore, rather than embarking upon grandiose yet ultimately futile speculation about what may occur, we should adopt a strong pragmatism that abandons itself to the twists and turns of history; let us be content to formulate *ad hoc* responses to global injustices as they arise.

While this argument has the merit of underscoring the fallibilistic nature of all predictive schemes, it conflates the necessary recognition of the contingency of history with unwarranted assertions about the latter's total opacity and indeterminacy. Acknowledging the fact that the future cannot be known with absolute certainty and that predictions are imperfect does not imply abandoning efforts to understand what is brewing on the horizon and prepare for massive human rights abuses and structural crises already coming into their own. In fact, the incorporation of fallibilistic and contingent perspectives into the labour of preventive foresight means that we can remain ever more vigilant for warning signs of disaster, while also improving the effectiveness of this practice of farsightedness to respond and attempt to avert unintended or unexpected consequences and developments (a point to which I will return in the final section of this chapter). In addition, from a normative point of view, accepting historical contingency and the self-limiting labour of farsightedness places the responsibility to prevent mass suffering squarely on the shoulders of present generations. The future no longer appears to be a metaphysical creature of destiny or the cunning of reason, nor can it be sloughed off to pure chance. It becomes, instead, a social construct shaped by decisions in the present – including, of course, deciding to try to anticipate and prepare for possible and avoidable sources of harm to our successors.

Buoyed by a sense of both analytical contingency and ethical responsibility toward the future, the idea of early warning is making its way within certain progressive circles of global civil society. Despite the fact that not all large-scale and systemic human rights violations can be predicted in advance, the multiplication of independent sources of knowledge and sophistication of detection mechanisms enables anticipation of many of them before it is too late. Indeed, in recent years, the capacity for early warning has dramatically increased, in no small part because of the impressive number of NGOs for which prevention is an integral part of their mandate.[17] Spread across the world, these organizations are often the first to detect signs of trouble, to dispatch investigative or fact-finding missions, as well as to analyse, and warn the world about, upcoming dangers; to wit, the lead role of aid and relief groups regarding the HIV/AIDS crisis in sub-Saharan Africa (frequently months or even years before Western governments or multilateral institutions followed suit). Thus, a loosely knit network of watchdog groups, composed of local and outside experts and activists, is acquiring finely tuned antennae to pinpoint indicators of forthcoming or already unfolding crises (Feil 2002: 449; Gutman 2002: 455).

[17] Virtually all major environmental and humanitarian NGOs include early warning and prevention in their stated objectives (Evans and Sahnoun 2001; Rotberg 1996). Two of the better-known organizations specifically devoted to disaster prevention are the International Crisis Group (www.intl-crisis-group.org) and the Center for the Prevention of Genocide (www.genocideprevention.org).

The meaning of facts about global injustices is never a given, as it must be socially constructed through processes of interpretive assessment. Accordingly, social movements, NGOs and other unofficial 'early warners' situate particular signs of trouble into larger catastrophic patterns, piecing such signs together into chains of events whose outcomes become discernible. It is only when trends are positioned into socio-cultural contexts that they become significant as indicators of danger.[18] Going a step further, I would add that the identification of potential human rights abuses is not sufficient for early warning to proceed. Findings must be coded, that is to say, invested with symbolic meanings that are likely to address their intended audiences' existing concerns about the future or successfully establish new sets of preoccupations for them. Since citizens do not necessarily or immediately recognize the importance of a particular event or tendency, its implications need to be demonstrated ('this is why you should care'). Civic associations can thus work to transform the HIV/AIDS epidemic from a remote possibility to an irreversible and grave threat to human survival, and genocide from an isolated aberration in remote places to an affront to universal moral equality.[19] Succinctly put, symbolic and interpretive means prepare the terrain for public recognition of warnings.

Global civil society's growing ability to invest preventive messages with public significance is part and parcel of an 'advocacy revolution' (Ignatieff 2001).[20] Threatened populations and allied organizations situated in the affected zones or dispersed across the planet are acting as early warning beacons that publicize perils, educate citizens about them and appeal for action on the part of states and multilateral institutions. Advocates have devised a host of 'naming and shaming' strategies and high-profile protest campaigns to this effect, notably the staging of elaborate and highly

[18] For instance, the melting of polar ice caps and the stirring of ethnic hostilities by political leaders are not particularly significant in and of themselves, yet they are now widely read as warning signals of the possibility of climate change and genocide, respectively. In this and the next paragraph, the analysis partly draws from Alexander (2003). For a typology of early indicators of conflict, see Forum on Early Warning and Early Response, *Conflict Analysis and Response Definition* (London: FEWER, 2001); available at www.fewer.org/res/70.pdf (accessed 19 December 2003).

[19] 'Genocide' and 'weapons of mass destruction' are prime examples of words that have acquired an intensely stigmatic meaning, from which they can draw public attention and provoke moral outrage. Cultural coding is therefore never politically or normatively neutral. As I contend in the final section of this chapter, citizens must publicly deliberate about such interpretive strategies and scenarios regarding the future in order to determine their analytical plausibility, political effects and normative foundations.

[20] More generally, see Barber (2003), Beck (1999), Habermas (1996; 2001) and Rotberg (1996).

publicized events (including press conferences, petitions, mass marches, boycotts, and boldly spectacular stunts that denounce the reckless pursuit of profit, bureaucratic inertia or the preponderance of vital national interests in world affairs).[21] Despite being incapable of stopping or averting most global injustices, this advocacy revolution is having some 'trickle-down' and 'trickle-up' effects: it is establishing audiences of constituents and ordinary citizens conversant with some of the great challenges and tragedies facing humanity, as well as putting pressure on official institutions to be proactive in their long-term planning and shorter-term responses.

None of this would be possible without the existence of global media, whose speed of circulation and range of coverage make it possible for reports of an unfolding or upcoming crisis in any part of the world to reach viewers or readers in all others almost instantaneously. Notwithstanding the highly selective character of what the media deems newsworthy and both state and commercial influence on the content of what is broadcast, warnings are being disseminated and circulating around the globe. Carrying out acts of mass violence in secrecy (Tiananmen Square, East Timor, Chechnya, Darfur, etc.) is more difficult, since few things escape from the satellite camera's gaze, the cellular telephone's speaker or the notebook computer's keyboard. In this respect, if the Internet is not the democratizing panacea whose advent technological determinists have been heralding for years, it remains an important device through which citizens and activists can communicate with one another, as well as share and spread information.[22] And if media interest most often comes during or after a crisis rather than preceding it, the broadcast of shocking images and testimonies can nevertheless shame governments and international organizations into taking steps to stop further harm to human beings; the 'CNN effect' or its BBC counterpart, to which we should now add the 'Al-Jazeera effect', makes its presence felt in some instances. Even more promising is the possibility that the threat of media exposure may dissuade individuals and groups

[21] For a discussion of legal and public pressure innovations with respect to human rights, see Ignatieff (2001: 10–12). On boycotts, see Beck (1999: 40–7). Over the years, Greenpeace has gained public notoriety and media exposure by performing risk-taking or highly visible actions, such as the unfurling of banners on famous public monuments, confrontations with whaling ships at sea, efforts to interfere with the testing of nuclear weapons and the destruction of genetically modified test crops.

[22] There is no doubt that the Internet is playing a vital role in the rise of 'subaltern counter-publics', such as independent media and the alternative globalization movement discussed in Chapter 5, with websites containing information about possible dangers that frequently contest official risk assessments. The phrase 'subaltern counter-publics' is taken from Fraser (1997: 69–98).

from enacting genocidal plans or reckless gambles with our future (Gutman 2002).[23]

Being dialogically based, the labour of preventive foresight can only function effectively if and when addressees within global civil society listen to forewarnings. The confluence of several aforementioned factors is making this process of public recognition more likely today, not least of which is the dystopian inflection of the *Zeitgeist* that produces a socio-cultural space where awareness of potential human rights abuses is present. Through a variety of channels, victimized groups and advocates for various causes have become skilled at communicating their warning messages to wider audiences, which are themselves coalescing around and debating certain problems (Chechnya, Darfur, HIV/AIDS, etc.). As Beck argues, one of the defining traits of 'reflexive modernization' is a healthy public scepticism toward and acknowledgement of the fallibility of official expertise in risk assessment, whether originating from governmental or private sources (politicians, technocrats, pundits, corporate spokespersons, etc.) (Beck 1992: 29–32). After Bhopal, Rwanda and Iraq, official scenarios are being carefully scrutinized and vigorously contested in national and global public spheres, whose progressive members are frequently offering alternative narratives that emphasize preventive foresight from within a perspective of cosmopolitan farsightedness. Hence, in a world where early warnings of several major human rights violations are readily available, or at least where dangers can be reasonably anticipated, pleading ignorance or utter helplessness to anticipate what may come in the future becomes much less plausible.

Cultivating a farsighted cosmopolitanism

In the previous section, I described how participants in global civil society have developed the capacity to produce, disseminate and receive warning signals regarding upcoming global injustices. What we have not attended to so far is a serious peril that challenges the labour of preventive foresight, namely, the possibility that audiences may not be willing to listen to such warnings and may prefer recklessness or insouciance toward the future to farsightedness. Indeed, modern societies are imbued with shortsightedness, a 'temporal myopia' that encourages most persons to live in a self-referentially presentist world where they screen out anything that is

[23] The traditions of documentary film-making and investigative journalism that survive at the edge of novelty-driven and reactive commercial news media thus perform an essential public service by taking up the tasks of warning audiences about forthcoming human rights crises and explaining their potential repercussions.

not of the moment and thus perceived to exist outside of the bounds of the here and now (Bindé 2001). The commercial media, advertising and entertainment industries are powerful forces in this respect, cultivating a 'tyranny of real time' (Virilio 1997 [1995]: 18–19) that itself feeds a societal addiction to the 'live' and the immediate for their own sake. Critics have insisted upon the consequential erosion of collective memory, yet the impact upon farsightedness is no less dire.

The infamous quip attributed to Madame de Pompadour, '*après nous, le déluge*' (after us, the flood), perfectly captures an acute manifestation of presentism, namely, callousness about the future. Two closely related tendencies underlie it: the belief that we should strictly concern ourselves with whether our actions, or lack thereof, have deleterious consequences visible to us in the short to medium term (temporally limited responsibility); and sheer indifference toward the plight of those who will come after us (generational self-centredness). Substantively, the two are not much different from one another in that they both shift the costs and risks of current decisions onto our descendants. 'The crisis of the future is a measure of the deficiency of our societies, incapable as they are of assessing what is involved in relationships with others', Bindé writes. 'This temporal myopia brings into play the same processes of denial of others as social shortsightedness. The absence of solidarity in time between generations merely reproduces selfishness in space within the same generation.' (Bindé 2001: 93) Thus, to the NIMBY ('not-in-my-backyard') politics of the last few decades can be added 'not-in-my-lifetime' or 'not-to-my-children' logics. For members of privileged groups in the North Atlantic region, massive human rights violations are something that others who are socio-economically, geographically and temporally distant will have to worry about and tackle.

The variations along these lines are numerous. One is the oft-stated conceit that prevention is a luxury that we can scarcely afford or is unwarranted in the first place. Some discourses thus attempt to legitimize procrastination by minimizing the urgency or gravity of potential global injustices. Why squander time, energy and resources to anticipate and thwart what are, after all, only hypothetical dangers (Burkhalter 2002: 445)? Why act today when, in any case, others will do so in the future? We should limit ourselves to reacting to events if and when they occur. A 'bad faith' version of this argument goes even further by seeking to discredit, reject or deny knowledge of evidence pointing to upcoming crises. We now enter into the domain of blatant negligence and 'culpable ignorance' (Haller 2002: 152–5),[24] as manifest in apathy toward climate change or

[24] Regarding how this applies to genocides in the 1990s, see Power (2002a).

the genocides in Rwanda and Darfur. At another level, instrumental-strategic forms of thought and action, so pervasive by virtue of their institutional embodiments in the state and the market, are rarely compatible with the demands of farsightedness. The calculation of the most technically efficient means to attain a particular bureaucratic or corporate objective, and the subsequent relentless pursuit of it, necessarily exclude broader questions of long-term prospects or negative side-effects. What matters is that profits or national self-interest be maximized with the least effort and as rapidly as possible.

What can be done in the face of these authoritative sources of short-sightedness? With its championing of universal solidarity, cosmopolitanism provides certain answers. In a manner that global civil society participants have been quick to embrace, cosmopolitans make the case that we have a duty of care for others that transcends the conventional bonds of nationality or shared socio-cultural attributes (gender, class, ethnicity, religion, etc.) to include all persons, and this by virtue of our common humanity. While it is conceivable that the universalism of this responsibility could be enlarged to apply to future generations, advocates of cosmopolitanism have thus far neglected to make the case for such a move. To my mind, however, a vibrant culture of prevention requires a farsighted cosmopolitanism, a chrono-cosmopolitics that extends solidarity along both temporal (or generational) and spatial (or geographical-cum-cultural) axes. In other words, 'intergenerational solidarity' must become an essential component of any project of global justice that takes seriously the idea of defending and advancing the human rights of human beings who will live in our wake, just as we do for those who are among us today (Bindé 2001: 111; Jonas 1984: 40–2).

For a farsighted cosmopolitanism to take root in global civil society, actors within it can adopt a thicker regulative principle of concern for the future than the one currently in vogue (which amounts to little more than an afterthought of the nondescript 'don't forget later generations' ilk). Hans Jonas's 'imperative of responsibility' is valuable here, for it suggests a relationship to the future consonant with the work of farsightedness and the construction of global justice (Jonas 1984). Jonas's consequentialism breaks with the presentist assumptions embedded in the intentionalist tradition of Western ethics. In brief, intentionalism can be explained by referring to its best-known formulation, the Kantian categorical imperative according to which the moral worth of a deed depends upon whether the *a priori* 'principle of the will' or 'volition' of the person performing it – that is, his or her intention – should become a universal law (Kant 1949 [1785]: 17–19). For intentionalists, *ex post facto* evaluation of the outcomes or effects of an act, and of whether they correspond to the initial intention, is peripheral to moral judgement. We find a variant of this logic in Weber's discussion of the 'ethic of absolute ends', that 'passionate devotion to a cause' which elevates the realization of a vision of the world above all other considerations; conviction and passion without the restraint of caution and prudence are intensely presentist.[25]

By contrast, consequentialism takes a cue from Weber's 'ethic of responsibility', which stipulates that we must carefully ponder the potential impact of our actions and be prepared to assume responsibility for them – even for the incidence of unexpected and unintended results. Neither the contingency of outcomes nor the retrospective nature of certain moral judgements exempts an act from normative evaluation. On the contrary, consequentialism reconnects what intentionalism prefers to keep distinct: the moral worth of ends partly depends upon the means selected to attain them (and vice versa), whereas the degree of correspondence between intentions and results is crucial. At the same time, Jonas goes further than Weber in breaking with presentism by favouring an 'ethic of long-range responsibility' that refuses to accept the future's indeterminacy in stoic resignation, gesturing instead toward a practice of farsighted preparation for crises that could occur (Jonas 1984: 21–2). From a consequentialist perspective, then, intergenerational solidarity would consist of striving to prevent our endeavours causing large-scale human suffering and damage to the natural world over time. Jonas reformulates the categorical imperative along these lines: '[a]ct so that the effects of your action are compatible with the permanence of genuine human life', or '[a]ct so that the effects of your action are not destructive of the future possibility of such life' (Jonas 1984: 11).[26] What we find here is a substantive and future-oriented ethos on the basis of which associative groups can engage in the labour of farsightedness and the work of global justice.

Having suggested a way to thicken the normative foundations of farsighted cosmopolitanism, I would now like to discuss the sociocultural strategies that progressive global civil society participants have begun to employ, and can continue to utilize, in order to create a sense of intergenerational solidarity. Both the moral imagination and reason represent triggers of cosmopolitan farsightedness that have entered public discourse in a variety of settings with the objective of combating

[25] For Weber's discussion of the ethic of ultimate ends and the ethic of responsibility, see Weber (1946 [1921]: 115–27).

[26] See also Jonas (1984: 38–42). Such ideas are similar to the ones adopted in Articles 3 and 4 of the UNESCO Declaration on the Responsibilities of the Present Generations Towards Future Generations; see www.unesco.org/cpp/uk/declarations/generations.pdf (accessed 7 November 2003).

presentist myopias.[27] The first of these catalysts appeals to us to ponder carefully our epoch's legacy, to imagine the kind of world we will be leaving for future generations; what will social life be like if today's potential mass human rights violations become tomorrow's realities? Left dystopianism performs just this role of confrontation with hypothetically catastrophic futures, for whether through novelistic, cinematic or other means, it can conjure up visions of global crises in order to spark reflection and inspire resistance (Jonas 1984).[28] By way of thick description, dystopian tales call upon audiences' moral imagination so as to plunge them into their descendants' lifeworlds. Catastrophic narratives about the future draw readers and viewers in, encouraging them to identify with the plight of, or transpose themselves into, the positions of fictional protagonists.

Progressive NGOs and social movements active in global civil society have drawn upon the moral imagination in similar ways, introducing dystopian scenarios less as prophecies than as rhetorical devices that act as 'wake-up calls' (say, about an ecologically dead planet, widespread famines or global devastation wrought by HIV/AIDS). Dystopias are thrust into public spaces to jolt citizens out of their complacency while awakening their sense of concern for those who will follow them. Negationist tropes are intended to foster public deliberation about the potential cataclysms facing humankind, the means of addressing them, as well as the unintended and unexpected consequences flowing from present-day trends. Because they help us imagine the strengths and weaknesses of different positions toward the future of the social and the stakes at play within each of them, dystopias have the additional merit of crystallizing many of the great issues of the day. Amplifying and extrapolating what could be the long-term consequences of current tendencies, public debate can act to clarify the future's seeming opaqueness. Likewise, the fostering of a dystopian moral imagination has a specifically critical function: the disquiet it provokes about the prospects of later generations is designed to make us radically put into question the 'self-evidentness' of the existing social order.[29] If we imagine ourselves in the

[27] On the importance of the moral imagination for solidarity with others, see Laqueur (2001) and Rorty (1989; 1998a). As noted in Chapter 1, Rorty nevertheless unjustifiably privileges the roles of moral sentiments without properly considering how the faculty of rational judgement must also come into play.

[28] However, I would argue that Jonas's concept of a 'heuristics of fear' goes too far in searching to evoke and rely upon negative sentiments that unscrupulous demagogues or opportunists can easily manipulate. Dystopian scenarios should provoke concern, rather than fear, in order to trigger reasonable public discussion and debate.

[29] On this point with respect to science fiction more generally, see Jameson (1982).

place of subsequent generations, the taken-for-granted or normalized shortsightedness of our institutionalized ways of thinking and acting becomes problematic. Indifference toward the future is neither necessary nor inevitable, but rather a socio-cultural construct that can be challenged through the labour of preventive foresight if we are to cease tolerating foreseeable global injustices.

In addition to the moral imagination, the appeal to reason constitutes a trigger for intergenerational solidarity, given that the idea of gambling with humanity's future or failing to minimize its possible sources of suffering is logically unsustainable. Here, a Rawlsian contractualist thought-experiment can be a means through which to demonstrate the soundness of farsighted cosmopolitanism, since actual deliberation between current and future generations is obviously impossible. If, in the original position, persons were to operate behind a chronological veil of ignorance that would preclude them from knowing the generation to which they belong, it is reasonable to expect them to devise a global social order characterized by a fair distribution of the burdens of potential human rights abuses over time – or, even better, one that aims to eliminate the prospects of such abuses altogether. Conversely, it is unreasonable to expect contractual parties to agree to a situation where these burdens would expand over time and thereby be transferred from one generation to the next, as a presentist position would do. 'The life of a people', Rawls (1971: 289) writes, 'is conceived as a scheme of cooperation spread out in historical time. It is to be governed by the same conception of justice that regulates the cooperation of contemporaries. No generation has stronger claims than any other.'[30] I would add that it is only through the practice of preventive foresight that the translation and application of this norm of cross-generational fairness to our existing predicament becomes possible.

Quite aside from this contractualist justification, actors in global civil society are putting forth a number of arguments countering temporal myopia on rational grounds. Concisely put, they have made the case that no generation, and no part of the world, is immune from global injustices. Complacency and parochialism are deeply flawed, for even if we earn a temporary reprieve, our children and grandchildren will likely not

[30] From a cosmopolitan perspective, 'humankind' should replace 'people' in the above quotation, since Rawls's understanding is too bound up with the nation-state and, as a result, spatially and culturally particularistic. For confirmation of this, see Rawls (1999). For an incisive critique, see Pogge (1994). On the generational component of the original position, see Rawls (1971: 137, 284–9).

be so fortunate unless steps are taken today. Similarly, it might be possible to minimize or contain to faraway places the risks and harms of neglect in the short term, although the parrying of an eventual blowback or spillover effect is improbable. As argued in the previous section, all but the smallest and most isolated of crises rapidly become globalized on account of the existence of transnational circuits of ideas, images, people and commodities. Regardless of where we live, our descendants will increasingly be subjected to the impact of environmental degradation, the spread of epidemics, gross North–South socio-economic inequalities, refugee flows, as well as civil war and genocide (Calhoun 2004: 378). What may have previously appeared to be temporally and spatially remote risks now 'come home to roost' in ever faster cycles.

Progressive global civil society participants have vigorously argued that procrastination makes little sense, and this for four principal reasons: it places little value on the lives of potential victims of human rights violations; it exponentially raises the costs of eventual action in the future; it reduces the choice of preventive options; and it erodes the latter's effectiveness. With the foreclosing of long-range alternatives, later generations may be left with a single option, namely, that of reacting to global injustices as they arise in order to try to curtail devastation and suffering whose severity and scope could be unprecedented. We need only think of how gradually more difficult it becomes to control the HIV/AIDS pandemic, let alone reverse it, or to halt mass atrocities or famines once they are under way. The practice of preventive foresight is grounded in the opposite logic, according to which deciding to work through perils today greatly enhances both the subsequent room for manoeuvre and the chances of success in averting crises. The creed regarding the unaffordable or unnecessary character of prevention can be turned on its head, since we cannot afford not to engage in preventive labour. Moreover, despite its limited success in seriously impacting decisions by governments and multilateral bodies, farsighted cosmopolitanism is not as remote or idealistic a prospect as it appears to sceptics; as Falk (2000: 29) writes, '[g]lobal justice between temporal communities, however, actually seems to be increasing, as evidenced by various expressions of greater sensitivity to past injustices and future dangers'. With mixed results, global and national civil society groups are attempting to entrench a new generational self-conception, according to which we view ourselves as the provisional caretakers of our planetary commons. Out of a sense of responsibility for the well-being of those who will follow us, struggles for global justice in the here and now become that more pressing.

Toward an autonomous future

Up to this point, we have seen how the practice of preventive foresight challenges presumptions about the inscrutability of the future and indifference toward it, with transnational socio-political relations nurturing a culture and infrastructure of prevention from below. None the less, unless and until it is substantively 'filled in', the argument is vulnerable to misappropriation or capture, in that farsightedness is not intrinsically emancipatory. Therefore, this section proposes to specify normative criteria and participatory procedures through which citizens can determine the legitimacy and effectiveness of competing preventive measures in order to move closer to a just world order through processes of public debate and deliberation.

Foremost among the possible distortions of farsightedness is alarmism, the manufacture of unwarranted and unfounded doomsday scenarios. State, civil society and market institutions may seek to produce a culture of fear, or manipulate an already existing one, by deliberately stretching interpretations of reality beyond the limits of the plausible so as to exaggerate various risks and prospects of impending catastrophes, or yet again by intentionally promoting certain prognoses over others for instrumental purposes. Accordingly, regressive dystopias can operate as Trojan horses, advancing political agendas or commercial interests that would otherwise be susceptible to greater public scrutiny and opposition – not to mention those that undermine the work of global justice. Instances of this kind of manipulation of the dystopian imaginary are plentiful: the invasion of Iraq in the name of terrorism and the imminent threat of use of 'weapons of mass destruction',[31] the severe curtailing of American civil liberties amidst fears of a collapse of 'homeland security', the neoliberal dismantling of the welfare state and public services in the global North and South as the only remedy for ideologically constructed fiscal crises, the neoconservative expansion of policing and incarceration due to supposedly spiralling crime waves, and so on and so forth. Alarmism socially constructs and culturally codes the future in particular ways, thereby inserting the resulting viewpoints into conventional or newly created crisis narratives, belief structures and rhetorical conventions. As much as alarmist ideas beget a culture of fear, the reverse is no less true.

[31] Habermas convincingly states: 'Apart from the difficulty of the lack of evidence, the Bush Doctrine doesn't even offer a plausible explanation for the *preventative* use of military force. The violence of the kind of global terrorism – 'war in peacetime' – escapes the categories of state warfare. It cannot justify the necessity of revising and loosening the strict clause that regulates states' self-defense in international law, and by no means in favor of permitting an anticipated *military* self-defense.' (Habermas 2003: 367–8)

If fearmongering is a misappropriation of preventive foresight, resignation about the future represents a problematic outgrowth of the popular acknowledgement of global injustices. Some believe that the world to come is so uncertain and dangerous that we should not attempt to modify the course of history; the future will look after itself for better or worse, regardless of what we do or wish. One version of this argument consists of a complacent optimism perceiving the future as fated to be better than either the past or the present. Frequently accompanying it is a self-deluding denial of what is plausible ('the world will not be so bad after all'), or a naïvely Panglossian pragmatism ('things will work themselves out in spite of everything, because humankind always finds ways to survive').[32] Much more common, however, is the opposite reaction, a fatalistic pessimism that is reconciled to the idea that the future will be necessarily worse than what preceded it. This is sustained by a tragic conception of history according to which humanity is doomed to decay, or a cyclical one where pathological repetition of the mistakes of the past is the norm.

On top of providing dubious assessments of what is to come, alarmism and resignation would, if widely accepted, undermine a viable practice of preventive foresight. Indeed, both of them effectively encourage public disengagement from deliberation about scenarios for the future, which would appear to be too fraught with danger, pointless or unnecessary for ordinary citizens. The resulting 'depublicization' of debate would leave dominant groups and institutions (governments, markets, etc.) in charge of sorting out the future for the rest of us. How, then, can a participatory process of prevention from below, advancing the work of global justice, emerge? The answer lies in cultivating a public capacity for critical judgement and deliberation, so that participants in global and national civil societies subject all claims about potential gross human rights abuses to examination, evaluation and contestation. Two concepts are particularly well suited to these tasks: the precautionary principle, and the vision of a just world order.

Salient in discussions of environmental and techno-scientific risks, the precautionary principle can be applied to posit prudence and vigilance as deontological counterweights to the multiplication and intensification of situations of socio-economic and civil-political distress in the contemporary world. From a precautionary standpoint, the lack of absolute certainty about a serious, irreversible and plausible global injustice should

[32] There is also a technologically determinist variant of this line of thinking, which believes that humankind will be able to discover techno-scientific solutions to global injustices. 'Necessity is the mother of invention', goes the proverb.

not deter us from erring on the side of caution and taking reasonable measures to address it (Callon *et al.* 2001: 263–308; Ewald 2002; Haller 2002: 99–113).[33] Consequently, the instrumental-strategic orientation to action can be balanced by a two-part injunction: act prudently (that is, in a manner that aims to avoid mass human suffering and ecological damage), and do no harm (that is, in a manner that does not worsen the existing state of affairs or move us closer to a crisis). Kant's (1991a [1784]: 54) bold cry of '*Sapere aude*!' comes face-to-face with Jonas's (1984: 204) humble pleas of 'Beware!' and 'Preserve!' Built into any precautionary stance is a participatory and reflexive concept of 'measured action', which stipulates that groups or institutions should only take decisions about following a particular course of action after extensive public input, deliberation and informed consideration of the range of options and their probable effects.[34] This kind of participatory reflexivity forthrightly acknowledges the fallibility of decision-making processes about the future, notably because of the existence of unexpected and unintended consequences. As such, measured action is an intersubjective practice that is always subject to revision through decisional feedback loops incorporating factors that may emerge out of a subsequent broadening of collective horizons: better arguments, new evidence, unforeseen or inadvertent side-effects, shifting public opinion, etc. Additionally, precaution's self-limiting character allows us to advocate turning away from certain possibilities if they are likely to introduce large-scale risks without proper steering mechanisms to control or alleviate them – including the endangering of human survival, the creation of potentially greater problems than the ones targeted by the original plan, or plausible increases of extreme human rights violations.

The second normative concept assisting global civil society in its discussions of, and discernment among, rival dystopian scenarios is a comprehensive vision of a just world order. Indeed, the project of constructing global justice can calibrate the injunction to precaution, to the extent that the pursuit of the latter must be consistent with the realization of the former. In implementing the precautionary principle, civic associations present at national and transnational scales can simultaneously promote universal socio-economic and civil-political rights; conversely, the labour of cosmopolitan farsightedness is incompatible with forms of action that

[33] As Ewald points out, the precautionary principle is entrenched in Article 15 of the United Nations' 1992 Rio Declaration on Environment and Development. See www.un.org/esa/sustdev/documents/agenda21/english (accessed 27 November 2003).

[34] For an excellent discussion of the concept of measured action, to which I am indebted in this paragraph, see Callon *et al.* (2001: 263–308).

would result in eroding the human rights of populations simply in the name of precaution.

Thus, through an articulation of precautionary and global justice norms, I want to propose a general template to guide public evaluation of varying dystopian scenarios in order to assist progressive global civil society groups and citizens to determine whether they should oppose or support preventive action. Three sets of considerations, each of which combines intentionalist and consequentialist elements, are particularly appropriate for this task. Notwithstanding the fact that these three dimensions overlap and interweave in practice, it remains useful to distinguish among them for heuristic purposes:

(1) *Analytical*: Is a particular dystopian scenario plausible according to credible knowledge of the past, the present and the future? What evidence substantiates it?
(2) *Ethical*: What values and principles underpin it? Does it strengthen or erode the labour of preventive foresight, and specifically the principles of precaution and global justice?
(3) *Political*: By whom is it adopted or rejected, in whose interests and through what institutions? What effects does this have and, in particular, to what kind of future is it likely to contribute?

For instance, I have advocated elsewhere a stance of 'weak interventionism' that would enable progressive global civil society elements to urge multilateral organizations to commit to military intervention in order to prevent or halt crimes against humanity under certain circumstances (Rwanda, Darfur, etc.), yet would also allow such elements to oppose the abusive instrumentalization of the use of force to advance the interests of Western states in situations such as Iraq (Kurasawa 2006).[35] In the case of humanitarian intervention, then, further specification of the categories above produces the following typology:

(1) Analytical appraisal of the humanitarian crisis:
    (a) *kind and scale*: Does it involve a large-scale loss of life (through genocide, ethnic cleansing, famine, etc.)?
    (b) *timing*: Is it imminent or ongoing, rather than in the past or merely potential?
    (c) *evidence*: Is information about it valid, does such information come from credible sources and has it been substantiated by independent observers?

[35] For an enlightening analysis of why the invasion of Iraq was not a legitimate humanitarian intervention, see Ken Roth's report on behalf of Human Rights Watch, which is available at www.hrw.org/wr2k4/3.htm (accessed 18 February 2005).

(2) Socio-political assessment of the military action:
   (a) *intentionalism*: Is its primary objective to prevent or put an end to large-scale dying and suffering, and what other interests are at play?
   (b) *decision-making*: Is it called for and approved by progressive national and global civil society groups (Human Rights Watch, ActionAid, etc.), and has it been subject to democratic processes of public debate and deliberation within nation-states participating in it?
   (c) *appropriateness*: Are the means to be used proportional to the situation, and will only the minimal amount of force necessary to remedy it be employed?
   (d) *consequentialism*: Is it likely to be effective in improving the predicament of victimized populations in the short term (rather than worsening it), and is it designed to minimize unintended and unforeseen consequences in the medium to long term?[36]

By applying these criteria to the critique of misuses of farsightedness, civic associations can argue that alarmism, for one, thrives by demagogically appealing to societal fears that can neither be substantiated nor correlated with plausible representations of reality. Further, fearmongering aims to conserve questionable aspects of the status quo (say, regarding the weakness of environmental regulations) or to dangerously reshape domestic and global socio-political orders (in the case of the Bush administration's belligerent unilateralism and doctrine of pre-emptive warfare) in order to consolidate the positions of dominant groups and institutions.[37] Similarly, resignation does not fare well when subjected to these evaluative categories. The naïvely optimistic conceits according to which 'the world will not be so bad after all' and 'it will all work itself out in the end' beg the question: for whom will this be the case? Although some privileged fractions of future generations will probably experience comparatively fewer risks and might suffer less from global injustices, most will not

[36] This model draws in part from the series of conditions for military intervention laid out by the International Commission on Intervention and State Sovereignty: the scale of the humanitarian crisis (just cause), the right intention or purpose, multilateral authority, last resort, proportional means and reasonable prospects of success. See Evans and Sahnoun (2001: xii, 32–7) and Weiss and Hubert (2001: 140–3). None the less, I differ from the Commission in stressing the incorporation of considerations of global justice in any evaluation of humanitarian intervention.

[37] In this respect, we can best combat terrorism through multilateral non-military means, such as collaboration and information-sharing between national law-enforcement and intelligence agencies, the prosecution of suspects in international courts of law and the promotion of 'preventive democracy'. For an elaboration of the latter idea, see Barber (2003).

be so fortunate. Moreover, keeping in mind the sobering lessons of the past century cannot but make us wary about humankind's supposedly unlimited ability for problem-solving or the discovery of solutions in time to avert all possible crises. In fact, the historical track-record of last-minute, technical 'quick-fixes' is hardly reassuring, and what's more, most of the serious human rights violations that we face today demand complex and sustained strategies of planning, coordination and execution over the long run (e.g., extreme poverty, HIV/AIDS, genocide and civil war). For its part, fatalism's conceit that humankind is doomed from the outset puts off any attempt to minimize risks for our successors, essentially condemning them to face global injustices unprepared. An *a priori* pessimism is also unsustainable given the fact that preventive action can have appreciable beneficial effects, notably in averting or stopping mass slaughter and death through warfare, famine or disease.

The framework proposed above should not be restricted to the critique of misappropriations of farsightedness, since it can equally support the reconstructive components of the practice of preventive foresight by fostering democratic discussion and debate about a future that human beings would freely self-determine. One way to understand this is to borrow Foucault's (1984) Nietzschean metaphor of genealogy and invert it. By contrast to his investigations that trace back forgotten or marginalized modes of thinking and acting in order to elaborate histories of the present, genealogies of the future perform a farsighted mapping out of the possible ways of organizing social life. They are, in other words, interventions into the present intended to facilitate participation on the part of the progressive elements of global civil society in shaping the field of possibilities of what is to come. Once a process of filtering out of competing and contrasting dystopian visions occurs on the basis of their analytical credibility, ethical commitments, and political underpinnings and consequences, groups and individuals can ponder the remaining legitimate scenarios in their genealogical mappings of the future. Of course, much of this depends upon civic associations undertaking complex and difficult processes of public education, in order to give ordinary citizens access to information about future risks of human rights abuses and heighten their capacity to make sense of and assess such information. While many of the evidentiary facts and arguments can be highly technical and frequently distorted by commercial media channels – thereby rendering them difficult to grasp by laypersons – NGOs and social movements are having some impact upon the democratization of expert knowledges via public information campaigns and widely distributed reports.

Hence, the first task consists of addressing the present-day causes of eventual global injustices, to ensure that the paths we decide upon do not contract the range of options available to our successors (Jonas 1984: 41–2). Just as importantly, the labour of genealogically inspired farsightedness can assist in acknowledging that the future is an entirely human creation instead of the product of metaphysical and extra-social forces (God, nature, destiny, etc.), as well as begin to reflect upon and publicly deliberate about the kind of legacy we want to leave for those who will follow us. Participants in global civil society can then take – and in certain instances have already taken – a further step by committing themselves to socio-political struggles to forge a world order that, aside from not jeopardizing human and environmental survival, is designed to rectify the sources of transnational injustices that will continue to inflict needless suffering upon future generations if left unchallenged.

Conclusion

In recent years, the rise of a dystopian imaginary has accompanied damning assessments and widespread recognition of the international community's repeated failures to intervene adequately in a number of largely preventable human rights disasters (from the genocides in Rwanda, East Timor and Darfur to the spiralling HIV/AIDS pandemic in parts of sub-Saharan Africa and Asia). Social movements, NGOs, diasporic groups and concerned citizens are not mincing words in their criticisms of the United Nations system and its member-states, thus beginning to shift the discursive and moral terrain in world affairs. As a result, for increasing swaths of global public opinion, as well as for some heads of government and international organizations, what has been exposed is the callousness implicit in disregarding the future. The *realpolitik* of national self-interest and the neoliberal logic of the market will continue to assert themselves, yet demands for, and expectations of, farsightedness are also forging ahead. While governments, multilateral institutions and transnational corporations are not likely to instantly modify the presentist assumptions underlying their methods of operation or worldviews, they are being closely monitored to assess how and why they decide to take action (or, as is more often the case, refuse to do so), as well as sometimes held publicly accountable for egregious instances of shortsightedness. What may seem like a modest or insignificant development at first glance would have been unimaginable even a few decades ago, indicating somewhat improved prospects for farsighted cosmopolitanism.

Does this mean that before long we can expect all impending global injustices to be addressed comprehensively? Apart from the unabashed assertion of national and economic interests, at least two other structural factors make such an outcome unlikely within the existing world order. In the first place, because of the decentralized institutional design of global civil society, there exist few coordination mechanisms among its different participants and no single clearing-house for the collection, processing and analysis of information about possible human rights abuses – information that could then be transmitted to the general public, governments or international organizations (Evans and Sahnoun 2001: 21; Rotberg 1996). Currently, warnings may not always reach these addressees, or get lost on the way in the clamour of multiple campaigns and messages emanating from NGOs, social movements, victim groups and concerned citizens.

The second problem is one of asymmetrical leverage between the official and unofficial spheres of global politics: despite mounting evidence that states and multilateral institutions are responding to preventive claims and requests, progressive groups within global civil society are deprived of direct decisional power. They have made important advances in gaining lobbying influence over, and access to, decision-making bodies, but their main tool is still the mobilization of public opinion to pressure or convince these bodies to act. Hence, these groups do not have the capacity to ensure the translation of demands for prevention from below into action from above (especially around issues of implementation, regulation and enforcement).

These two limits pose serious obstacles to a practice of preventive foresight unless meaningful institutional reforms of the global system are put into place. For example, democratic reforms of the United Nations could establish a Global Peoples' Assembly or a similar world parliamentary body with decision-making power surrounding questions of humanitarian intervention (Falk and Strauss 2003). Because it would include representatives from national and global civil societies, this kind of body would be more open to popular input and oversight, as well as capable of serving as an arena where claims about unfolding and upcoming global injustices could be assessed and debated within strict time-frames; advocacy groups (human rights NGOs, social movements, diasporic communities, etc.) could put forth demands for action and have them publicized, deliberated over and acted upon if deemed to be legitimate. At the same time, and in lieu of a major overhaul of the regime of international governance, it would be a mistake to underestimate or simply dismiss the impact of the web of treaties, summits, judicial innovations, grassroots 'naming and shaming' tactics and protest movements that have come to form, in recent years, a vast preventive infrastructure. I have argued that this dynamic is itself constitutive of global civil society and can thus best be appreciated when observed 'from below'. Unofficial actors are engaging in dialogical, public and transnational struggles to avert global injustices, accordingly cultivating a farsighted and dystopian-inspired form of social action oriented toward the future.

The chapter further aimed to demonstrate that the labour of preventive foresight is composed of three sets of practices striving to overcome difficulties that define our era's predicament. Participants in global civil society are engaged in developing an early warning capacity about upcoming crises by collecting evidence, disseminating it and labouring to have it publicly recognized. This sort of farsightedness responds to the contingent nature of the future without succumbing to the conviction that it is absolutely unknowable and indecipherable. Transnational associative groups are also nurturing intergenerational solidarity, a sense of care for those who will follow in our wake. I suggested that, to adequately combat the presentist and shortsighted indifference toward the future that is typical in the contemporary world, a more explicitly farsighted cosmopolitanism needs to take root within global civil society. Normative thickening of this ideal could be accomplished via the long-term consequentialism of Jonas's imperative of responsibility, a prospect whose traces we can already find in growing appeals to the moral imagination and reason to activate our concern for later generations. The last section contended that the labour of preventive foresight can parry its possible alarmist misappropriation or the unintended inducement of resignation by advocating a process of public deliberation that articulates the principles of precaution and global justice. A farsighted politics can function through the public use of reason and honing of the capacity for critical judgement, whereby citizens put themselves in a position to debate, evaluate and challenge varying dystopian narratives about the future in order to determine which are more analytically plausible, ethically desirable and politically effective in bringing about a world order that is less perilous yet more just for our descendants. Many fora, ranging from local and face-to-face meetings to transnational and highly mediated discursive networks, are sowing the seeds of such a practice of future-oriented participatory democracy.

None of this is to disavow the international community's lamentable record of achievement in avoiding foreseeable human rights crises over the last decades, nor to minimize the difficulties of implementing the kinds of global institutional reforms described above and the perils of historical contingency, presentist indifference toward the future, or alarmism and resignation. To my mind, however, this is all the more reason to pay attention to the practice of cosmopolitan foresight in global civil society, through which associative groups can build up the latter's coordination mechanisms and institutional leverage, cultivate and mobilize public opinion in distant parts of the world, as well as try to compel political leaders and national and transnational governance structures to implement certain policies. While seeking to prevent egregious human rights violations either from worsening or, better yet, from occurring in the first place, these sorts of initiatives can and must remain consistent with a vision of a just world order.[38] Furthermore, the labour of farsightedness supports a social constructivist view of the future, according to which we are the creators of the field of possibilities within which our successors will dwell. The current socio-political order, with all of its short-term biases, is neither natural nor necessary. Accordingly, informed public participation in deliberative processes makes a socially self-instituting future possible, through the involvement of groups and individuals active in national and transnational civil societies; prevention is a public practice, and a public responsibility.

To believe otherwise is to leave the path clear for a series of alternatives that heteronomously compromise the well-being of those who will come after us. We would thereby effectively abandon the future to the vagaries of history ('let it unfold as it may'), the technocratic or instrumental will of official institutions ('let others decide for us') or gambles about the time-lags of existing risks ('let our progeny deal with their realization'). But as I have tried to show here, this will not and cannot be accepted. Re-engaging in autonomous preventive struggles, then, is most likely to sustain an emancipatory politics. A farsighted cosmopolitanism that aims to avert massive human rights abuses while working toward the realization of precaution and global justice represents a compelling ethico-political project, for we will not inherit a better future. It must be made, starting with us, in the here and now. In our day and age, no less than any of the four other modes of practice discussed in this book, preventive foresight stands as a key component of the work of global justice.

[38] As Power (2002b: 264) argues in the case of genocide prevention: 'Because it is unlikely that Western leaders will have the vision to recognize that they endanger their countries' long-term vital national interests by allowing genocide, the most realistic hope for combating it lies in the rest of us creating short-term political costs for those who do nothing.'

4 The stranger's keeper: on aid

> Overcoming poverty is not a gesture of charity. It is an act of justice. It is the protection of a fundamental human right, the right to dignity and a decent life. (Nelson Mandela in Bedell 2005: 64)

> Humanitarian action is more than a technical exercise aimed at nourishing or healing a population defined as 'in need'; it is a moral endeavor based on solidarity with other members of humanity. (Terry 2002: 244)

> Our lives matter. The five million people in South Africa with HIV matter, and the millions of people throughout the world already infected with HIV matter. So it is not simply a question of cold statistics we are putting to you, but a question of valuing every person's life equally. Just because we are poor, just because we are black, just because we live in environments and continents that are far from you does not mean that our lives should be valued any less. (Achmat 2003: xv)[1]

Introduction

To be one's sister's or brother's keeper: a seemingly innocuous yet potentially ethically infinite injunction to help others, especially when they find themselves in situations of extreme vulnerability. Perhaps to tame its prescriptive weight, most of us have chosen to interpret it in a restricted fashion by applying it primarily, or even exclusively, to members of fairly circumscribed and proximate moral communities. Indeed, the requirement to ensure the well-being of those with whom we share bonds of intimacy or familiarity (family or community members, friends, etc.) – or at least of preventing harm to them – finds its negation in the commonly accepted tendency to ignore the suffering of socially or geographically distant persons and groups, toward whom we feel little or no obligation to lend assistance. Over the past two centuries, discourses of nationalism and republicanism have expanded the limits of such moral

[1] Zachie Achmat is the chairperson of the Treatment Action Campaign in South Africa.

communities beyond those of familiarity or immediacy by claiming that we must meet the needs of our fellow citizens, with whom we apparently share a sense of cultural identity and belonging anchored in a similar set of socio-historical experiences, beliefs and rituals. Accordingly, what has come into being is a sense of national solidarity, of brotherhood and sisterhood institutionalized via citizenship (with its conception of rights and duties accorded to all members of a nation-state) and the welfare state (with its programmes designed to meet the basic needs of citizens).[2]

Yet what if, rather than conceiving of the task of helping others as affectively, culturally or territorially circumscribed, we imagine it to be without bounds? Such an idea is hardly novel, its origins dating back to the longstanding universalism of a variety of religious worldviews ('we are all God's children or creation') as well as certain civilizations' humanist perspectives (ranging from certain strands of European Marxism to the African concept of *ubuntu*); Western humanitarianism, for one, takes shape out of the Judaeo-Christian ideal of charity and the Enlightenment concern for the welfare and happiness of humankind through the development of its rational faculties. However, the contemporary rise of discourses of cosmopolitanism and struggles for global justice, with their attendant universal conception of human rights, has revived the notion of aid to distant others in the Euro-American world. Lest I be misunderstood, this is not to claim that closeness and similarity – whether perceived or actual, or yet again emotional, socio-cultural or spatial – are fading as forces in the constitution of moral reciprocity today, but rather that the process is complicated by a consciousness within some sectors of global civil society of the significance of concern for others beyond local and national borders. Progressive civic associations are demanding that the imperative to assist persons in need be applied to all of the world's population, including those segments experiencing large-scale and intense suffering as a result of severe poverty, chronic disease, famine and war. For an increasing number of advocates of socio-economic rights beyond borders, we are becoming remote strangers' keepers no less than those of our sisters or brothers; better yet, strangers are being redefined as sisters and brothers who cannot be left in

[2] See Ignatieff (1984) and Marshall (1950). The dismantling of the welfare state in Europe and North America that began under Thatcher and Reagan has accelerated in the age of global neoliberalism, seriously endangering the socio-economically redistributive capacities of national governments by reviving a socially Darwinian logic of individual responsibility and 'self-reliance'. As this chapter and the next contend, what becomes urgent in this context is not only opposition to the further erosion of nationally based programmes and mechanisms of progressive reallocation of resources, but the cultivation of transnational practices of aid and solidarity.

harm's way while those able to help remain bystanders (Beitz 1999; Corbridge 1993; Singer 2002).

The question, then, becomes that of reconceptualizing the practice of humanitarian aid as a socio-economic aspect of the work of global justice that intersects with the latter's civil-political dimensions discussed in the previous chapters. Yet this threatens to introduce as many problems as it may resolve, given that the historical record of Western 'assistance' to impoverished regions of the world is a dubious one. Harkening back to colonialism, claims of helping people in the global South have often been little more than the 'white man's burden', the rhetoric of a civilizing mission serving as a pretext to establish, reproduce and legitimate Euro-American economic, political and cultural imperialism.[3] Witness the ambiguous standing of the project of development today, which became the main Western paradigm of long-term and sustained foreign aid in the second half of the twentieth century, but is now regularly assailed for its numerous failures and counter-productive outcomes. Despite the fact that some critical understandings of development are compatible with global justice,[4] the flawed modernizing and technocratic versions of it remain dominant in official policy circles and among Western decision-makers.[5] As a result, the legacy of development is the production of a vast system of governance over the global South via international financial institutions (the World Bank, the International Monetary Fund and their regional counterparts).

Critics of this development-as-modernization discourse have convincingly pointed out that it smacks of neo-colonialism because of its socio-cultural chauvinism toward South American, African and Asian societies, which must supposedly emulate the Northern path to growth in order to shed their 'underdeveloped' status. For its part, foreign aid has remained small – a minuscule proportion of even the largest donor countries' GDP – and has often been tied to a host of conditions designed to promote donor nations' geopolitical and economic interests (ActionAid 2005a).[6]

[3] The most recent rendition of this line of thinking is to be found in the Bush administration's neoconservative 'democratic providentialism' (Ignatieff 2004), its justification for warfare and military intervention in the Arab world being framed in the language of spreading liberty and democracy.

[4] Progressive Western NGOs, multilateral organizations and scholars using the idiom of development have made significant contributions to the realization of universal human rights by advocating transnational poverty reduction and wealth redistribution, as well as the establishment of parity with civil society actors in the global South.

[5] The founding work of modernization theory is Rostow's *Stages of Economic Growth* (Rostow 1960).

[6] In an excellent report, ActionAid demonstrates that real government aid to poor countries (that is, money directly available for poverty reduction on the ground) amounted to only 0.1% of donor countries' gross national incomes (GNI) in 2003, far below official aid figures that place it at 0.25% of GNI and even worse when compared to the United

Championing policies of export-oriented and foreign investment-fuelled growth, modernization theory was applied to supply Western countries and transnational corporations with affordable and abundant supplies of raw materials and labour, while leaving the vast majority of populations in the global South in a state of abject poverty. Once modernization was coupled to neoliberalism, the results became plain to see: many countries entered into massive debt traps, compromising their domestic productive capacities and privatizing an already fragile public service infrastructure. Consequently, structural inequalities and the North–South socio-economic gap have widened since the end of the Second World War (ATTAC 2004; Bello 2002a; Escobar 1995a; 1995b; Sachs 1992; Sheth 1987).

Certain writers have claimed that even international emergency relief, which represents the 'purest' form of humanitarian assistance, has lost its way. If it saves lives in the short run, relief work may inadvertently delay the search for long-term solutions to several of the problems plaguing the global South by getting local governments and their leaders 'off the hook'; domestic political factors (e.g., the denial of citizens' civil and political rights, democratic unaccountability, or the pursuit of civil war against particular ethnic or religious groups) and socio-economic policies (e.g., privatization and regressive distributive arrangements) most responsible for generating mass crises may thus never be properly addressed. And many NGOs are now part of a well-oiled, bureaucratic 'disaster relief industry' (de Waal 1997) that devotes as much time and energy pursuing its strategic organizational interests (fundraising and public relations) as it does providing assistance to those in need. Likewise, it is an industry that, over the past decade or so, has willingly compromised its decisional and financial independence, to the point that it risks becoming an informal branch of certain Western nation-states' foreign policies, a partner in the activities of transnational corporations and a technocratic participant in the implementation of international financial institutions' neoliberal programmes (de Waal 1997; Kennedy 2004; Rieff 2002; Terry 2002; Weissman 2004).[7]

Nations' target of 0.7% of GNI. At least 61% of overseas development assistance is 'phantom aid' disbursed for a variety of purposes other than direct poverty reduction: overpriced services from international consultants (referred to as 'technical assistance'), debt relief (that is double-counted as aid), excessive administrative overhead, the tied purchase of goods or services from firms located in donor countries, and so on. Further, only one-third of overseas development assistance goes to sub-Saharan Africa (ActionAid 2005a: 17–28). I would like to thank Lucy Baker for drawing my attention to this report.

[7] Of course, this is not to say that all humanitarian action should be condemned. Terry (2002: 240–5) proposes a useful framework to assess it, based on three criteria. Firstly, what is the intention lying behind aid? Assisting victims of catastrophes who are in need is the only acceptable motive; military aid to armed forces or political aid to prop up political regimes cannot be justified in humanitarian terms. Secondly, what are the means and methods used? While easing the suffering of victims is fundamental, it cannot be pursued by any means

Perhaps most tellingly, neither development nor international relief work constitutes an effective mechanism of global reallocation of material resources. Both rely excessively on the self-conceived benevolence of individual Euro-American donors and countries that can freely choose (or, most often, refuse) to extend a helping hand, simultaneously leaving intact the transnational system that lies at the root of the global South's perpetual impoverishment and subordination. While necessary, even debt cancellation for the most fiscally compromised countries does little to address the underlying structural factors or the system of global neoliberal capitalism that lie at the root of world poverty. However, the more autarchic and isolationist denunciations of aid, which declare that the latter should be entirely abandoned because it is inherently harmful, are themselves unsound. They completely ignore the fact that citizens and governments of Euro-American states have a responsibility and capacity to alleviate the suffering of their fellow human beings and to allow them to cultivate and exercise their capabilities.[8] In addition, since transnational corporations, intergovernmental organizations and rich countries will continue to be heavily involved in Africa, Asia and South America, it behoves groups and individuals concerned with the universal realization of socio-economic rights to pose alternatives to the hegemony of modernizing neoliberalism. Surely, then, the issue confronting us is not whether we should assist distant others, but rather the possibility of shifting the discourse and practice of aid from charity and development toward global justice and human solidarity.[9]

This is precisely what progressive global civil society actors have begun doing in the last few years, by framing the idea of helping distant others not as a matter of patronizing charity or self-aggrandizing generosity, but rather of ceasing to violate the socio-economic rights of the most

necessary (such as the killing of civilians or the participation of relief agencies in military interventions). Thirdly, what are the consequences of international aid, including the unintended ones? One must evaluate whether it actually and substantially helps victims or merely strengthens dubious political regimes, and whether assistance is delivered competently (that is, in a manner that meets the needs of the population).

[8] In this chapter and throughout the book, I use the framework of human rights rather than that of capabilities proposed by Sen and Nussbaum, since the former is more readily amenable to my argument about civil-political and socio-economic dimensions of modes of practice of global justice. Nevertheless, I occasionally borrow from the capabilities approach because of its thicker understanding of the normative and affirmative aspects of human flourishing – in other words, of what we can do and what kinds of lives we can live when the full spectrum of human rights are realized.

[9] I am indebted to Seyla Benhabib for this formulation. See also Farmer (2003: 153–9). A telling indication of this discursive shift can be found in the Make Poverty History campaign, whose manifesto states that '[e]nding poverty is not about charity, it's about justice' (Bedell 2005: 8); during the Live 8 concert in London on 2 July 2005, one of the official slogans was 'From Charity to Justice'.

vulnerable populations whose very subsistence is at stake (most notably women and the poor) as well as opposing the reproduction of the systemic inequalities that sustain such a predicament. When viewed in this way, the practice of aid is simply the concretization of a human entitlement to having one's basic needs met and to have opportunities to develop one's capacities. Assistance represents a small step in this direction, a minimal form of restitution for historical injustices and a way to oppose forms of global structural violence (unfair international trading regimes, neoliberal marginalization and extraction of primary resources without adequate compensation to local populations) that effectively created or heavily contribute to conditions of famine, homelessness, chronic illness and insecure living experienced by many citizens around the planet. Helping others can be done as an expression of ethical responsibility and political struggle in the work of establishing a just world order.[10]

Throughout this chapter, then, I want to explore the implications of interpreting aid as a mode of practice of global justice, in order to move away from its common rendition as an abstract ideal of rescue of persons in distress or a technocratically defined, problem-solving activity of financial support to the underprivileged or their governments. Instead, we can think of aid as a form of normative and political labour that implicates both those helping and those being helped in substantiating the latter's socio-economic rights, while simultaneously struggling against the conditions which cause and sustain vulnerability for vast sections of humankind. By thinking of the labour of aid, we can grasp how it is constituted through the enactment of three sets of tasks and the confrontation with related perils. As such, I want to propose a tripartite model of the practice of helping others that corresponds to the different sections of the chapter. Firstly, at an interpersonal level, aid may generate and amplify status asymmetries between the party lending assistance and the one receiving it, a tendency that civic associations can counter by fostering relations of symmetrical reciprocity. Secondly, if functioning within the confines of the current world order, the work of assistance can contribute to the formation of substantively egalitarian North–South cooperation (including greater recognition of cultural pluralism) and thereby guard against its potential instrumentalization as a mechanism of economic domination and moral regulation over vast regions of the global South. Thirdly, the labour of helping others can include struggles for the structural

[10] Several thinkers have made a case that the moral responsibility to alleviate world poverty lies squarely, or primarily, with citizens of powerful and rich countries, whose governments have devised the existing world system and who disproportionately benefit from it (Crocker 1991; Farmer 2003; Pogge 2001b; 2002a; 2002b; Singer 2002).

transformation of the established system of socio-economic and spatial segregation that produces abuses of the human rights of the poor and women. Put differently, when explicitly framed by the project of global justice, the practice of aid combines the work of recognition (the development of an ethos of response to suffering) with that of redistribution (tackling the fundamental causes of the North–South divide).

Like other modes of practice of global justice, aid is defined by three features. It is a dialogical process aimed at achieving reciprocity between two parties, the donors and the recipients, who must negotiate an asymmetrical relationship that simultaneously implicates material and symbolic hierarchies, on the one hand, and moral equality, on the other. The practice of aid is also indelibly public in that it requires the creation of mechanisms through which recipients democratically participate in debate and decisions about the implementation of assistance directed their way, as well as of national and global spaces where citizens can be informed about humanitarian crises and structural violence, and where public opinion can be mobilized to pressure states and international organizations to act. And, as should be clear by now, the practice of helping strangers is becoming transnationalized, since growing acknowledgement of the borderless character of disastrous situations and systemic injustices draws on a budding sense of responsibility for others beyond the confines of familiarity or territory. At the same time, it tries to challenge the institutionalization of global relations of power that foster grave deprivation and suffering around the planet.

In putting forward a theory of practice of aid, I want to redirect, update and push in a cosmopolitan direction Benhabib's (1992) argument about the possibility of articulating an ethic of care toward concrete others and an ethic of justice applied to generalized others.[11] The first approach is most fully elaborated in the feminist ethic-of-care literature, which has foregrounded the central role of an orientation to others for a subject's self-identity and moral development, as well as the possibility of cultivating a normative stance based on the duty to respond to others' needs (Gilligan 1982; Noddings 1984; Ruddick 1989; Tronto 1993). However, for the most part, this body of literature implicitly or explicitly operates with a maternal model of social relations that has not adequately dealt with the question of material and symbolic asymmetries between care-givers and care-recipients. In addition, it veers toward a moral parochialism that fails to address the globalization of the obligation and

[11] I am referring to the so-called 'care/justice debate' that pitted Gilligan and feminist theorists of care on one side against Kohlberg and Rawls's justice paradigm on the other in the 1980s.

opportunity to lend assistance (which can apply to individuals and groups who are unfamiliar or live far away). Hence the significance of writings on global justice, which have made a case for an egalitarian universalism that simultaneously recognizes cultural pluralism and the realization of substantive socio-economic rights for all human beings, regardless of where they may live (Beitz 1999; Benatar *et al.* 2003; De Greiff and Cronin 2002; Habermas 2001 [1998]; Held 2004; Pogge 2001a; 2002a; 2002b; Singer 2002). But before we discuss the three components of the practice of aid and how they intersect with an ethic of care and one of global justice, they should be contextualized by referring to the global HIV/AIDS pandemic.

The scourge of HIV/AIDS

As the first truly global pandemic (Barnett and Whiteside 2002), there is little doubt that HIV/AIDS represents one of the most pressing crises facing humankind in the twenty-first century. To appreciate the scale and gravity of the situation, however, certain facts bear reiteration. An estimated 39.5 million people worldwide were living with HIV at the end of 2006 – more than a fourfold increase since 1990. In the worst affected countries of southern Africa, such as Botswana, Namibia and Swaziland, between one-quarter and one-third of the adult population is living with HIV/AIDS (with women being disproportionately affected), and life expectancy has declined by as much as thirty-five years relative to its duration without the pandemic. If the crisis is most dire in sub-Saharan Africa as a whole, where an estimated 24.7 million people are infected, it is by no means confined to that continent; in fact, it is rapidly spreading in South and South-East Asia (approximately 7.8 million infected persons at the end of 2006), its next frontier being the population centres of China, India and Russia.[12] Aggravating this trend is the fact that, despite a recent expansion of treatment accessibility, only 20 per cent of those needing anti-retroviral medication (ARVs) to treat AIDS had access to them by the end of 2005 (UNAIDS/WHO 2006a).[13]

[12] See UNAIDS/WHO (2004a; 2004b; 2006a; 2006b) and UNDP (2003: 8, 41, 43). For more information on the rapidly expanding HIV/AIDS crisis in Asia, see ActionAid (2005b) and UNAIDS/WHO (2005a).

[13] The World Health Organization (WHO) and UNAIDS adopted a '3 by 5 Plan', which aimed to provide ARV treatment to 3 million people in low- and middle-income countries by the end of 2005, yet reached only 1.3 million persons. Though a dramatic improvement over the situation that reigned prior to the Plan's implementation – in 2001, only 240,000 people were receiving ARV treatment in these countries – it still falls considerably short of the initial objective (UNAIDS/WHO 2005b; 2006a).

Despite this situation, the HIV/AIDS pandemic has caused far less sustained disquiet from Northern governments or their citizens, and received less media coverage, than more 'spectacular' and 'instantaneous' global catastrophes that have become well publicized in the Euro-American world (terrorism, genocide, natural disasters, etc.) – albeit much more attention than other major deadly diseases that continue to ravage the global South, such as malaria and tuberculosis. None the less, though still being belated and inadequate, a mobilization of civic associations and intergovernmental organizations is occurring. Transnational HIV/AIDS activism has been on the rise (Seckinelgin 2002; Wolfe 2003), high-profile figures have taken up the cause of people living with the pandemic and societies devastated by it, and the United Nations has created a dedicated agency to address the epidemic (UNAIDS) as well as assuming a coordination role for international financial resources through the Global Fund to Fight AIDS, Tuberculosis, and Malaria.[14] The seriousness of the problem was acknowledged in the United Nations' Millennium Development Compact, the centrepiece of a global agenda for change that was ratified by 189 countries in 2000, though without yet producing concerted action on the part of Western governments or substantial clamour by Euro-American public opinion for such action.

From the perspective of the work of global justice, what is interesting is that progressive global civil society actors are employing the HIV/AIDS crisis as a bridgehead to stress anew the massive and longstanding problems of poverty and ill health among much of the world's population, the oft-neglected socio-economic dimension of human rights (Benatar *et al.* 2003; Mann 1997; O'Neill 2002; Pogge 2002c; Wolfe 2003). As Stephen Lewis (the former UN Secretary-General's Special Envoy for HIV/AIDS in Africa) contends, the tepid international reaction to the HIV/AIDS pandemic is nothing less than a crime against humanity, the widespread and ongoing failure to assist AIDS sufferers marking one of the most egregious global injustices of our time[15] and exposing the functioning of a neoliberal economic order which subsumes basic human welfare to the workings of the market. Most illustrative of this tendency are the strategies of multinational pharmaceutical conglomerates that oligopolistically produce, sell and distribute ARVs. With the latter being treated as

[14] Between 1986 and 1996, the UN ran the Global Program on AIDS within the World Health Organization, which was replaced by the current Joint United Nations Programme on HIV/AIDS (UNAIDS) (Poku 2002b).

[15] 'The [HIV/AIDS] pandemic cannot be allowed to continue, and those who watch it unfold with a kind of pathological equanimity must be held to account. There may yet come a day when we have peacetime tribunals to deal with this particular version of crimes against humanity.' (Lewis 2003)

profit-generating commodities rather than life-saving drugs, we have witnessed a wide gap in access to them; as a result, HIV/AIDS has generally become a manageable fact of life in rich countries, whereas it commonly represents a death-sentence in their poorer counterparts. Therefore, seriously confronting the pandemic requires taking steps to restructure the established world order to ensure a meaningful reallocation of material resources. In such a vision, health-care is a global public good and an indelible human right, with universality and parity of access to it being substantively realized.

To grasp better how the idea of aid as a mode of practice of global justice can help us engage with the HIV/AIDS pandemic differently, we should now turn to the three-part framework of the tasks and perils that compose it by starting with the labour of negotiating status asymmetries between those who provide assistance and those who receive it.

Status asymmetries and the possibility of reciprocity

When examining the ethico-political labour of assistance, the first peril that providers and recipients encounter is the creation and preservation of status asymmetries between the two parties. Persons living with HIV/AIDS in the global South find themselves in a multiplicity of subordinate positions relative to Euro-American aid workers and medical staff since, quite aside from obvious differences in health and illness, major symbolic and material inequalities can become manifest in their social interactions. Routinely, those being helped are cognitively disadvantaged by virtue of possessing less comprehensive, or less scientifically validated, understandings of HIV/AIDS (its causes and effects, its scope, rates of transmission, available and effective treatments, and so on). Because of such perceived or actual knowledge hierarchies, those considering themselves expert helpers may discount experientially grounded and local, community-based modes of comprehension of HIV/AIDS as irrelevant or insignificant. In turn, lingering colonial prejudices and civilizational chauvinism toward non-Western peoples – according to which the latter are considered to be members of inferior or 'backward' socio-cultural groups – can result in persons affected by HIV/AIDS in the global South being portrayed and treated as pathological, incompetent subjects who are incapable of grasping their predicament and, thus, what is in their best interests. Furthermore, recipients of aid enduring severe socio-economic deprivation must rely on those assisting them not only to supply them with appropriate pharmaceutically based treatments, but to meet their basic needs for food and shelter.

When combined, physiological, material and symbolic vulnerability can trigger paternalistic processes of infantilization that portray people living with HIV/AIDS as passive and helpless beings (Sontag 1990). Indeed, the more patronizing aspects of scientific, medical and development discourses actively participate in the construction and attribution of victimization to those affected by the epidemic. If some unscrupulous NGOs appropriate and exploit media-transmitted images of abject suffering for fundraising or publicity purposes, it should equally be remembered that the generalized representational tendency toward victimizing others actively undermines their dignity. Appearing to the Western public and aid workers strictly as sick and pitiful individuals requiring mercy, people living with HIV/AIDS can easily be stripped of respect for the breadth and complexity of their existences as well as of acknowledgement of their capabilities. In other words, the process of reducing persons to victims in the name of helping them constitutes a 'status injustice' (Fraser 2003) that deprives them of autonomous agency, their right to be respected and to participate fully in decisions about how they should be assisted. When it is always already presumed that Euro-American providers of aid know best, the belief in their moral superiority thrives.

Still at the level of the intersubjective dangers involved in the practice of aid, the flip side of victimization is the behaviourist and neoliberal discourse of individualizing 'responsibilization', which often amounts to blaming those living with HIV/AIDS in the global South for having contracted it in the first place – rather than, as we shall see in the next section, attempting to understand the structural forces and relations of power that determine the range of decision-making opportunities available to vulnerable segments of the population. Visible in popular policy prescriptions such as ABC ('abstinence, being faithful, and condoms') and VCT (voluntary counselling and testing for those who are HIV-positive), the neoliberal logic of responsibility portrays subjects as rationalist, calculating and self-interested consumers who must make the right choices in the marketplace of sexual risk.[16] According to proponents of this point of view, the transmission of HIV is strictly the outcome of taking wrongheaded yet conscious and fully informed decisions, themselves fostered by pathologized belief-systems and habits that condone reckless or hedonistic sexual conduct; simplistically and erroneously, the pandemic can thereby be reduced to a matter of 'loose morals', 'risky or irrational behaviour' and sexual promiscuity (Irwin *et al.* 2003: 20–1; Seckinelgin 2003: 422). Although programmes of public education

[16] I owe this formulation to Barry D. Adam.

about the prevention of HIV/AIDS are vital, their more conservative variants can be seamlessly integrated with discursive technologies of disciplining of subjects, which function to mould and modify a person's ways of thinking and acting toward what certain Euro-American governments and NGOs deem morally and sexually acceptable, or indeed desirable (e.g., the nuclear family and patriarchal societal organization, monogamous heterosexual marriages and sexual abstinence). 'Responsibilizing' those living with HIV/AIDS in places ravaged by it can make providers of aid believe that they are entitled to divide populations into deserving and undeserving recipients, the former being the 'innocent' who inadvertently become HIV-positive (through birth, sexual assault or blood transfusions, for instance) and the latter being the 'blameworthy' who allegedly do so knowingly – and, not coincidentally, are predominantly members of socially marginalized and stigmatized groups (gay men and female sex workers, for instance).

In contrast to the lack of agency that victimization grants individuals, 'responsibilization' contains a surfeit of it. If the first operates through a structurally deterministic attribution of passivity, the second creates a voluntarist understanding of agency through which persons are viewed as having access to a full range of behavioural choices and identical opportunities to bring such choices to fruition. Ultimately, this kind of individualized and excessive notion of the agent is abstracted from existing structural relations of power in specific socio-cultural settings, where exist an uneven distribution of material and symbolic resources as well as mechanisms of exclusion and domination that constrain the array of available options for many members of societies severely affected by HIV/AIDS (Farmer 2003: 40; Seckinelgin 2003: 422). For instance, gender- and class-based subordination restrict the field of possible action for poor women in the face of the crisis; they thus become a group with a much higher probability of being exposed to it, since they may be coerced or compelled to engage in unsafe sexual practices – not because of deliberate 'irresponsible' conduct, but rather because of socio-economic, cultural and physical subjugation.

Having contemplated the victimizing and 'responsibilizing' effects of intersubjective status asymmetries, how can we conceive of a practice of aid that enables us to level them off? The approaches of certain progressive NGOs assisting people living with HIV/AIDS in the global South (such as Health Alliance International, Partners in Health, ActionAid and Médecins Sans Frontières) are instructive, for they strive to negotiate the tension between, on the one hand, the various hierarchical relations involving providers and recipients and, on the other, their moral symmetry. What these organizations are attempting, then, is to institutionalize an ethic of care for and with concrete others, informed by the principle of reciprocity and the universal entitlement to dignity via the realization of substantive socio-economic rights.

More precisely, a practice of aid connected to global justice becomes possible when providers of assistance are radically open, attentive and responsive to the potential for difference in recipients – that is to say, when the former decentre their own worldviews to learn about and engage with the particularities of the latter's experiences in a relationship of care (Noddings 1984; Tronto 1993). This is not to say that emergency relief workers and medical staff can fit perfectly into the shoes of persons living with HIV/AIDS, nor that such an immaculate transposition is even desirable. Indeed, such a belief would merely represent a denial of the experiential, socio-economic and cultural gaps between the two groups, at which point it becomes all too easy to assume that helpers already know how the vulnerable feel or what they undergo without actually pursuing the dialogical labour of listening and interpretation out of which understanding emerges. Instead, the task consists of enlarging one's horizons through empathy, by coming to acknowledge the specific situations of those requiring aid and seeing them as subjects with beliefs and practices that may not be familiar, yet whose basic dignity must be respected. Seriously engaging with others in this way begins with the realization of a shared condition of human vulnerability, which can be fuelled by the exercise of the helpers' moral imagination in contemplating a reversal of roles with those being helped. In other words, it can be based on a variant of the golden rule: since providers of aid may themselves be in need of assistance in the future, would they want to be treated as they are treating those with HIV/AIDS today? But use of the moral imagination is not enough, since some aid workers and medical staff are also aware of the need to gain knowledge about the political, cultural and socio-economic circumstances of those they are assisting, and thus of the structural obstacles and often precarious existences that produce their positions of vulnerability. Out of openness and attentiveness to the lived realities of concrete others can spring an appreciation of how their situations are simultaneously proximate to and remote from those of providers of aid, as well as of the necessary intersubjective labour thereby involved.

As certain progressive practitioners and thinkers of emergency relief work have noted, what they try to establish is a 'humanitarian space' (Terry 2002: 242) that concretizes an ethos of struggle against want and response to the hitherto unmet basic needs of distant strangers. Beyond bonds of nationality, religion, gender, class, culture, ethnicity and sexuality, ethical primacy falls upon the responsibility to relieve the suffering of any and all human beings. Consequently, it is fruitful to conceive of helping those living with HIV/AIDS as the first step in fulfilling an unconditional responsibility to oppose the abuses of their socio-economic rights (including the right to health), performed without any 'strings attached'; *contra* the missionary philosophy and that of a number of Christian-based NGOs, aid is not provided to recipients in exchange for work on their souls or the opportunity to modify their behaviour. Perhaps most importantly of all, it ought not engender processes of civilizational or religious conversion and cultural assimilation that would seek to Westernize the mores and beliefs of peoples in the global South, for the embrace of cultural pluralism is paramount if assistance is to fit into the work of global justice.

Aiding others can respect their dignity if it concurrently recognizes their equal standing as autonomous moral agents, who possess valid life experiences and are both capable of and entitled to express their needs and grasp their situations. Hence, the objective of the labour of assistance is to achieve a 'parity of social status' (Fraser 2003: 29) between the two parties, who can exist in a relationship of mutuality geared toward levelling off symbolic inequalities. By helping persons living with HIV/AIDS gain a better understanding of their condition while attempting to achieve relative parity in social relations, aid can participate in enhancing the capacity of individuals and groups to make informed decisions about their predicaments – and thereby enhance their autonomy (Gadamer 1996: 136–7; Seckinelgin 2002: 109). Put slightly differently, addressing at the interpersonal level the suffering of those ravaged by the pandemic can expand the range of options available to them, in order for them to cultivate their capabilities in ways that they value and create lives that they find meaningful (Benatar *et al.* 2003: 122–4; Crocker 1992; Nussbaum 1992; 2002b; Sen 1999).

Aid and the construction of egalitarian cooperation

As I mentioned in this chapter's introduction, a practice of aid promoting substantive socio-economic rights must supplement an intersubjective ethic of care for concrete others with an ethic of global justice toward generalized others, in order to participate in the redistribution of material and symbolic resources along the North–South axis and the recognition of the importance of preserving and promoting a multiplicity of ways of life in the world. However, against this stands the danger that Western actors can exploit the need for assistance to consolidate economic, political and cultural hegemony over the global South – something that many mainstream portions of the NGO sector dealing with HIV/AIDS (heretofore termed the 'AIDS industry') have either failed to recognize or in which they have willingly been complicit.

Given how aid policies regarding the pandemic are frequently incorporated into broader development schemata, many of the warnings about neoliberal modernization mentioned earlier are relevant here. Aside from the fact that it commodifies the human right to health and education through the imposition of 'user fees' and excessive prices for ARVs – a point to which we shall return in the following section – the promotion of neoliberalism in countries ravaged by HIV/AIDS has accentuated their dependence upon a global marketplace whose imperative of profit maximization contradicts principles of freedom from want and the meeting of basic needs. Since international funding for HIV/AIDS programmes in these countries is often conditional upon their implementing 'structural adjustment' reforms that reorient their economies toward export-driven growth, their populations are exposed to the vagaries of a system in which their subsistence is never ensured. Indeed, the international trading system is characterized by fluctuating and generally low prices for primary commodities, barriers to the entry of such commodities to Europe and North America, as well as subsidies to large-scale 'agribusinesses' that gain a stranglehold over smaller producers in poorer parts of the world. Foreign aid to stem the HIV/AIDS epidemic is also frequently tied to the carrying out of a privatization agenda, leaving entire industries in the global South, as well as formerly public assets, open to takeover or control by transnational corporations (ActionAid 2005a: 36–9). Nation-states opting for ARV-based treatment programmes, which were until very recently prohibitively expensive, entered into a vicious circle of borrowing and indebtedness requiring further rounds of 'structural adjustment'. Hence, when humanitarian NGOs ignore such realities or become integrated into the machinery through which states and international financial institutions implement neoliberalism, their involvement in the HIV/AIDS crisis directly or indirectly contributes to the reproduction (and in some instances, the exacerbation) of mass poverty and suffering in the worst-affected regions.

In addition, the AIDS industry can participate in the formation of a vast apparatus of Western governance over the global South. Because the domestic priorities of poor countries are increasingly determined by the need to conform to the tenets of economic neoliberalism, accountability is being displaced from national populations to external organizations (such as international financial institutions and Euro-American governments). What's more, even in Southern nations with democratically elected governments, structural adjustment programmes contain numerous mechanisms of outside monitoring and oversight that apply leverage through a variety of fiscal performance criteria and 'carrots and sticks': extension of external debt repayment and loan schemes, tied or conditional funding for HIV/AIDS programmes, foreign investment risk and return ratings, and so on. On a different level, the AIDS industry can use its control over scientific and medical knowledge about the epidemic as an effective means to exercise power, for institutionally validated discourses about preventing the spread of HIV/AIDS and treating it mostly emanate from the North Atlantic region. On account of the inconsistent diffusion of research findings, limited educational resources in the poorer parts of the planet and a 'brain drain' to Europe and North America, many countries devastated by the pandemic find themselves unable to develop a critical mass of domestic expertise and have no option but to rely on external goodwill. In this global scientific division of labour, the deployment and operationalization of uniform models to deal with HIV/AIDS rarely take into consideration local conditions or needs, let alone meaningful input from citizens about strategies to stem the pandemic's tide.

Not to be overlooked is the collective dimension of a phenomenon explained in the previous section, namely that helping those affected by HIV/AIDS can serve as a pretext to entrench forms of cultural neo-imperialism via the application of techniques of moral and sexual regulation – this time targeting not only the individual, but entire socio-cultural lifeworlds. When coupled to moral conservatism, this culturalizing logic pinpoints the pandemic's roots in certain supposedly 'hypersexualized' societies, with the reining in of what is believed to be a rampant and unrestrained promiscuity becoming the principal strategy in the fight against the spread of the pandemic; in the aforementioned ABC policy, the use of condoms takes a back seat to abstinence and the need to be faithful. Needless to say, this sort of intervention freely draws upon disparaging images of the non-Western world, with Christian fundamentalist doctrine maligning belief-systems and modes of behaviour that it then perceives as ripe for remaking.[17]

What is occurring in such instances is a promulgation of the conviction that all societies ought to conform to a particular vision of sexual and cultural life, built around the credos of pre-marital abstinence and compulsory, heterosexual monogamy (Epstein 2005; Matthews 1988;

[17] Dubious claims about the HIV/AIDS crisis in sub-Saharan Africa being a consequence of 'over-sexualization' closely resemble the 'gay lifestyle' arguments integral to the North American AIDS panic during the 1980s. In each instance, members of a subordinate group that has historically encountered high levels of prejudice are deemed responsible for their own plight because sharing stereotypically depicted, biologically essentialized, and stigmatized identity attributes.

Seckinelgin 2003: 423).[18] The morally conservative orientation of such thinking becomes clear when we consider a number of factors: the disproportionate rhetorical and financial weight it places upon the prevention of HIV/AIDS through abstinence (at the expense of treatment for persons already having contracted it); conversely, the undermining of women's reproductive rights and family planning programmes in the global South; and the neglect of gender inequality and female socio-economic subordination. Thus, the discourse of moral displacement leaves unaddressed, or may even accentuate, systemic problems at the core of the HIV/AIDS pandemic, which are themselves grounded in relations of power as well as uneven access to symbolic and material resources.

To be in a position to undermine tendencies toward economic and cultural domination, the practice of aid can fall under the umbrella of a project of global justice devoted to generalized others. As certain progressive civic associations understand, the act of helping persons in need stems from an ethics beyond borders that asserts the universal moral equality of human beings and seeks to protect all against systemic injustices that violate their socio-economic rights. Such violations are plain to see in the case of the HIV/AIDS crisis, for extreme material deprivation and structural violence combine to create a vastly uneven North–South distribution of rates of infection across the planet. This is also the case within several African, Asian and South American societies, where living conditions barely meeting subsistence levels and gender subordination give many women little option but to engage in 'high risk' sexual activities in order to survive and support their dependants; starkly stated, dying of AIDS becomes a temporally and statistically remote prospect when compared to the certainty of starvation or sexual violence (Irwin *et al.* 2003: 19–39; UNAIDS/WHO 2004a: 9–12). This is what the labour of assistance to distant strangers can help to rectify. In and of itself, of course, the work of NGOs helping those living with HIV/AIDS cannot be a substitute for well-designed, long-range domestic programmes to tackle the pandemic, nor should it represent an escape-valve by means of which certain governments shirk responsibility for their own disastrous actions (civil war, corruption, etc.). Nevertheless, as conceptualized in this chapter, the practice of aid can improve the welfare of populations made to suffer by

[18] Resistance to such ideas lies behind the Brazilian government's decision, in May 2005, to decline $40 million in funding from the United States for its AIDS programmes; the Bush administration and Republican-controlled Congress had demanded that Brazilian recipients of these grants sign a pledge condemning prostitution (Phillips and Moffett 2005). I would like to thank Sean Hosein and Lorna Weir for drawing my attention to this fact.

states unable or unwilling to provide their citizens with adequate financial and medical resources in the face of the crisis.

In a more affirmative vein, the labour of assistance can promote the socio-economic rights of subordinate groups by contributing to the realization of substantive principles of human equality (through the reallocation of material and symbolic resources across the world) and freedom (the capacity for persons to exercise their capabilities). As such, progressive actors evolving in the field of HIV/AIDS claim that those living with it are – no less than any other human being – rights-bearing persons and groups entitled to a wide range of choices about the kinds of lives and paths to self-fulfilment they value. To put it bluntly, no one ought be placed in a position where the only available options are hunger or unprotected sex.

We will see in the next section that such a conception of global justice can be engendered through struggles to restructure the current world order, so that the goal of meeting the basic socio-economic needs of all human beings can trump the instrumental logic of capitalist profit or bureaucratic rationality; for instance, the framing of health as a human right is meant to counter the vision of powerful global forces (from multinational pharmaceutical corporations to certain government-based aid agencies and international financial institutions) who treat it as a commodity. Nevertheless, pending these structural transformations, it is still possible for progressive groups to establish egalitarian models of North–South collaboration that can help HIV/AIDS sufferers. Conventionally, the multilateral institutions (UNAIDS, WHO, etc.) and Euro-American governmental aid agencies (e.g., USAIDS, CIDA) that compose the AIDS industry have favoured top-down organizational models characterized by vertical integration as well as centralized fiscal and decisional authority, in such a way that relations of clientelism are forged, with states and civil society groups reduced to the status of subcontracted parties. Yet initiatives such as those developed by ActionAid, Partners in Health and Health Alliance International demonstrate that effective and participatory alternatives can thrive if Western NGOs take seriously notions of reciprocal cooperation with, and grassroots empowerment of, their local counterparts in the global South.[19]

[19] For ActionAid, see www.actionaid.org/309/about_us.html (accessed 4 July 2005). For Partners in Health, see Farmer (2003) and Kidder (2003), as well as www.pih.org/whoweare/vision.html; it has also published a useful *Guide to the Community-Based Treatment of HIV/AIDS in Resource-Poor Settings*, which is available at www.pih.org/library/aids/PIH_HIV_Handbook_Bangkok_edition.pdf (accessed 4 July 2005). For Health Alliance International, see http://depts.washington.edu/haiuw/docs/history.htm (accessed 4 July 2005).

In some cases, community-based prevention and treatment projects are built around horizontal networks of local health-care centres, in which foreign and domestic workers enjoy organizational and decisional parity while local needs are given priority over the strategic objectives of external funders. In turn, these initiatives are premised upon a practice of aid that supports the enrichment of civil societies and public spheres in under-resourced regions of the world, so that civic associations representing and defending the interests of persons affected by HIV/AIDS can be major players in democratic will- and opinion-formation about how to respond to the pandemic and hold those lending assistance accountable for the kind and extent of the aid they provide (ActionAid 2005a: 44–8; Seckinelgin 2003: 423). The inclusion of marginalized groups (such as women, the poor and rural inhabitants) is particularly important in informing public debate and discussion, for their voices are rarely heard around these issues despite the fact that they are the ones most directly affected by them. None of these measures ensures the success of treatment and prevention campaigns, which are subject to a host of complex forces, but they operate against the formation of relations of domination between parties.

The labour of aid to distant strangers described above can also begin from the principle of recognition of cultural pluralism. While criticizing perspectives that threaten the norm of moral equality of all human beings – and thus avoiding an absolute relativism that condones socio-cultural chauvinism and ethnocentrism – participatory North–South partnerships can acknowledge the existence of multiple ways of being human and modes of organizing social life (Benhabib 1992: 153; 2002: 38–9). Egalitarian forms of collaboration thrive on intercultural dialogue and deliberation among parties viewing each other as peers existing in a relation of symmetry, and striving to construct zones of agreement and mutual interest. In addition, what can occur is a levelling of the established knowledge hierarchies between providers and recipients of aid via a democratization of expertise and skills relevant to the HIV/AIDS crisis, through the training of local community leaders and health-care workers as well as the development of extensive public education campaigns addressed to the general public (particularly vulnerable and 'at risk' groups). In turn, such measures can promote informed participation by a wide array of citizens in public discussion and decision-making, in an attempt to secure the direct involvement of those living with HIV/AIDS in governance and policy questions: strategies for prevention of the pandemic's spread, allocation and use of socio-economic resources to combat it and design and implementation of the kinds of programmes to treat the ill (Irwin *et al.* 2003: 61–2). This is precisely what social movements mobilizing around the HIV/AIDS crisis (such as the Treatment Action Campaign in South Africa and ACT UP in the Western world) have tried to make possible, by defending the right of affected persons to have input into and a say about how they are helped, or at least try to hold governmental aid agencies, NGOs, states and international organizations accountable to the populations they are serving.[20]

But ultimately, if it is to advance the work of global justice, the practice of aid must support substantial changes to the existing world order – changes that could themselves eventually alleviate the need for transnational assistance for HIV/AIDS by building up the capacity of sub-Saharan Africa, South-East Asia and other severely hit regions to stem the tide of the pandemic.

Global apartheid or structural transformation of the world order?

Up to this point in the chapter, I have discussed how the parties involved in the practice of transnational aid can encounter intersubjective and institutional patterns of domination immanent to the relationship of assistance itself, and must thereby respond by aiming to foster reciprocity and egalitarian partnerships striving to reallocate material and symbolic resources and to recognize cultural pluralism. However, to be effective, the work of helping distant others cannot be confined to such 'internal' matters, for it must also tackle the systemic foundations of the established global economic order whose very functioning impedes the capacity to relieve the suffering of those living with HIV/AIDS and violates their universal right to health and well-being. Without much hyperbole, then, one can describe the current world situation with regards to the pandemic as one of spatio-political and socio-economic apartheid.

As discussed in various chapters of this book, the prevalence of geographically and culturally circumscribed understandings of responsibility for and empathy toward others represents a serious peril for the project of global justice – not least in the case of the labour of aid. In fact, despite some recent shifts in public opinion and official announcements, the degree of indifference to the ravages brought about by the HIV/AIDS crisis in sub-Saharan Africa and South Asia still remains remarkably high among political leaders and ordinary citizens in the North Atlantic region. For many, since the pandemic has largely been contained in the West due to prevention programmes and the wide availability of pharmaceutical

[20] On the role of US AIDS activists in shaping scientific research on the condition, see Epstein (1996).

treatment, it has become a remote reality with little impact on their everyday lives, or merely the latest of a seemingly endless list of intractable problems besetting the global South. And in the cold calculus of *real-politik*, helping HIV-positive foreigners is placed well outside of most powerful states' restrictive definitions of their national self-interest. Accordingly, the appropriate strategy becomes one of containment of the HIV/AIDS pandemic to the global South, limiting its spread in regions with high rates of infection yet, just as importantly, minimizing the possibility of massive spillover into Europe, North America and Oceania (through, for instance, restrictive and discriminatory immigration policies designed to screen out persons with HIV/AIDS). Containment results in the building of two worlds: Northern fortresses with low infection rates and widely available treatment that make HIV/AIDS manageable; and vast zones in the global South where the pandemic runs rampant, resources to treat it are scarce and millions infected by it die preventably because they go untreated.

Side by side with the spatio-political aspect of this global HIV/AIDS apartheid stands its violation of socio-economic rights, which is every bit as meaningful. The distribution of suffering caused by the pandemic is far from being random or spread evenly across the world's social fabric, instead reflecting existing power differentials within and between nation-states. As mentioned earlier, the most socially marginal groups in the global South have considerably higher rates of infection, mortality and serious illness resulting from AIDS than their privileged counterparts; it is no coincidence that women and the rural poor in sub-Saharan Africa and South Asia – the two most precarious groups in the two poorest regions of the world – have been hardest hit (Farmer 2003). Hence, the labour of transnational aid cannot overlook the intimate links between the HIV/AIDS pandemic, on the one hand, and gendered, racialized and class-based distributional injustices at the level of material and symbolic resources, on the other.

In this regard, one of the major contributing factors is the deployment of neoliberal orthodoxy in the global South. As mentioned in the last section, international financial institutions (the World Bank, the International Monetary Fund and regional development banks) and Western governments routinely demand that heavily indebted countries undertake structural adjustment programmes and embark upon strict debt-servicing schedules in order to qualify for international aid and further loans. However meaningful they may be in the short term, recent demands to cancel the external debt of the poorest countries do little in and of themselves to challenge neoliberalism's entrenchment in the current world order or the functioning of structural adjustment policies designed to reduce the size and share of the state sector in national economies, in order to expose the latter to the 'market discipline' and 'efficiency' of capitalist profit-seeking and foreign competition.[21] Among the first casualties of this kind of shock treatment is the public health infrastructure of poor countries, which must be drastically scaled back to repay loans, make room for the growth of the private sector and follow rigid prescriptions regarding the necessary privatization of existing governmental assets. Accordingly, by eroding the institutional capacity of many nation-states to respond to the HIV/AIDS pandemic at the very time that their populations are being hit the hardest, neoliberalism has only worsened the crisis – and is thus an indirect structural cause of the latter (Lewis 2005: 5–6).

Particularly in sub-Saharan Africa, the cuts in public expenditure on already precarious health-care systems have had ruinous effects, whether in terms of the maintenance of hospital- and clinical-based facilities, the retention and training of medical personnel or the state's capacity to subsidize pharmaceutical treatment for its citizens living with HIV/AIDS (Lurie *et al.* 2003; Poku 2002a).[22] The selling of government-owned infrastructure and the consequent shrinking of the public sector, not to mention the imposition of 'user fees', dramatically amplify already existing inequities in the access, delivery and outcomes of health-care for those affected by the crisis, since an individual's ability to pay is the overwhelming determinant of such factors in a privatized system. Despite the fact that NGOs are attempting to fill the gap by offering health-care services previously provided by the state, their resources remain inadequate in the face of the enormity of the task at hand. In fact, the clear-cut substitution of Euro-American NGOs for the public sector merely serves to dismantle and privatize the latter while converting such organizations into simple service-delivery entities and ignoring the task of building solid local health-care systems in countries reeling from the HIV/AIDS pandemic (Farmer 2003: 244).

[21] The International Monetary Fund's much-maligned 'Structural Adjustment Facility' was initially replaced by the 'Enhanced Structural Adjustment Facility' (1996–9), and more recently by the 'Poverty Reduction and Growth Facility' and the 'Heavily Indebted Poor Countries Initiative'. The change of labels indicates the IMF's attempt to implement modest reforms in response to severe criticisms of its programmes, but the general neoliberal framework remains the same – as do the devastating consequences of its policies in the global South (Bello 2002a: 80–3; Poku 2002a).

[22] In the worst-affected African countries, up to 40 per cent of government revenues are used for foreign debt servicing – a much higher share than that devoted to health-care (Poku 2002a: 538–9). This is where debt cancellation can have its most visible and serious impact.

Another striking facet of socio-economic apartheid concerns blatant planetary allocative injustices in the opportunities for treatment, with medicine and clinical care overwhelmingly remaining the preserve of those living in Northern countries or of wealthier pockets of Southern populations. Already existing global and national relations of power are being amplified along gender, class and ethno-racial lines, to the point that new forms of inequality are emerging among persons and groups receiving qualitatively and quantitatively different levels and kinds of care. For most inhabitants of the global South, the operationalization of health-care into a commodity restricts access to treatment for HIV/AIDS and consequently violates their universal human right to health.[23] The commodification of health-care means that access to ARVs and medical aid becomes a privilege conditional upon a superordinate socio-economic status, that is to say, something granted exclusively to citizens who have the ability to purchase it. From the economically rationalist perspective that animates neoliberal sectors of the AIDS industry, the calculus translates into treatment for the pandemic being deemed cost-effective in the North Atlantic region but supposedly too expensive and inefficient in sub-Saharan Africa, Asia and South America; there, according to some, only prevention programmes are affordable, whereas care for those already infected is understood as a costly burden that cannot be borne. As Seckinelgin (2002: 127) puts it, this amounts to believing in 'drugs for us, condoms for you'.

Despite already being part of one of the largest and most lucrative industries in the world, the transnational pharmaceutical corporations that manufacture, distribute and sell the cocktail of 'brand name' ARV drugs have been content to treat the latter as yet another source of profit, to be made available at the highest cost that the market can bear.[24] Though some progress has recently been made in this area, Big Pharma drags its feet as access to its products is fiscally impossible for millions of people living with AIDS. As the United Nations Development Programme's 2003 *Human Development Report* explains, '[i]n poor countries it is basically impossible to pay international prices for life-saving medicines – and almost criminal to expect poor people to do so' (UNDP 2003: 8).

[23] Paul Farmer has put it starkly: 'We thus find ourselves at a crossroads: health care can be considered a commodity to be sold, or it can be considered a basic human right. It cannot comfortably be considered both of these at the same time. This, I believe, is the great drama of medicine at the start of this century. And this is the choice before all people of faith and good will in these dangerous times.' (Farmer 2003: 175)

[24] These corporations are often collectively designated as 'Big Pharma', in reference to their size and oligopolistic character. They are to be distinguished from generic drug manufacturers that sell lower-cost 'copies' of 'brand name' drugs once patents on the latter have expired or are not enforced.

Virtually undeterred, however, the pharmaceutical industry has employed three main strategies to maximize ARVs' profitability. Firstly, it has relied on and aggressively enforced intellectual property rights and patent protections for its 'brand name' products, using both national and international trade regulations (under the World Trade Organization and its predecessor, the General Agreement on Tariffs and Trade) to prevent the production and sale of lower-cost generic drugs (Cullet 2003; Poku 2002b).[25] In addition, Big Pharma has lobbied and threatened to sue governments in the global South that import generic ARVs produced in countries refusing to enforce patent protections for AIDS medication (such as India, Brazil and Thailand). The third tactic consists of switching between two differential pricing strategies, one where ARV medication is sold more cheaply in the North than the South and the other (known as 'preferential or 'humanitarian' pricing) where the opposite is true. If the latter strategy is certainly preferable to the former, it nevertheless enables the pharmaceutical industry to maximize profitability and secure market shares. Indeed, the preferential price for patented drugs often remains above the cost of manufacturing them (even when research and development costs are factored in), while also making them more competitive against lower-cost but lesser known generic equivalents (Petchevsky 2003: 108–9). For its part, so-called 'humanitarian pricing' represents an effective public relations exercise for Big Pharma, partially blunting the tide of criticism coming from HIV/AIDS activists about profiting from the pandemic. Moreover, 'humanitarian pricing' undermines the possibility that governments and international bodies (notably the World Health Organization) will pursue alternative drug policies or seek to impose price controls or price uniformity for ARVs. Therefore, the pharmaceutical industry can retain its self-regulated status, setting its own manufacturing, distribution and pricing policies according to market conditions while ensuring hefty returns to shareholders.

In sum, then, vast socio-economic inequities in access to medicines create a situation of *de facto* global segregation, with restricted access to treatment condemning many in the poorest regions of the world to die needlessly and helplessly. The neoliberal commodification of health-care instrumentalizes distant strangers, who are treated as mere sources of profit or, in instances where they are unable to pay for treatment, expendable persons. Consequently, progressive groups lending assistance can

[25] The Uruguay Round of multilateral trade negotiations (1986–94) includes a pioneering agreement on trade-related intellectual property rights (TRIPS), which Big Pharma can use to bring a legal claim against national governments that do not enforce pharmaceutical patent protections or turn a blind eye to violations of such patents (Joseph 2003: 429–31).

engage with these forms of spatio-political and socio-economic apartheid, not only by helping those in need but also by working toward a restructuring of the current world order. Stated differently, the labour of aid is not simply a problem-solving exercise that would intervene to 'save' generalized others while leaving intact the underlying factors that place human beings in conditions of acute vulnerability; in an equally significant way, it involves socio-political struggles to substantially change the existing world system. As many civic associations have claimed, material and symbolic deprivation is at the heart of the HIV/AIDS pandemic and can only be tackled by challenging a host of systemic injustices: the failure or refusal of certain governments in the global South to prioritize the basic needs of their citizens; the unwillingness of Northern countries to provide adequate help to such states and to protect and promote the socio-economic rights of all human beings; international financial institutions' imposition of debilitating neoliberal regimes in heavily indebted nations; and the commodification of health-care by the pharmaceutical industry.

In the face of such forces, what is being done to direct the practice of aid in a structurally transformative direction? Progressive global civil society actors are advancing two sorts of relevant arguments. Drawing upon the perspective of global justice, the first discourse is primarily normative in its underscoring of a sense of responsibility toward other human beings. Its most succinct rendition is found in the egalitarian universalism at the heart of the humanitarian imperative: to alleviate the suffering of any and all persons on the sole basis of need, and to aim to help those in distress to the greatest extent possible whenever and wherever necessary. From this vantage-point, not only do Euro-American states and citizens disproportionately benefit from the current global economic system, but they also have the political and financial clout to substantially reform it along more equitable lines – and thereby considerably lessen the devastation of the HIV/AIDS crisis in the global South. The second set of arguments is of a more pragmatic nature, since it points to the reality of transnational interdependence in an increasingly borderless world, no part of which can be sealed off from the others. The pandemic is present in the four corners of the planet and will likely continue to spread with the intensification of migration and travel flows in the twenty-first century unless drastic changes occur.[26] It may well have subsided in the West due to the wide availability of ARVs and extensive prevention campaigns, yet the gradual increases in infection rates in Western Europe and North

[26] Scott A. Wolfe, the Director of Global Health Policy for the International Association of Physicians in AIDS Care, has declared that 'if we want to slow the spread of HIV and halt its devastation anywhere, we must commit to do so *everywhere*' (Wolfe 2003: 37).

America over the past few years is a clear indication that the pandemic's ravages in sub-Saharan Africa and South-East Asia will not spare any region. All fortresses are porous in our globalized age.

The case for health as a fundamental human right and for health-care as a global public good joins these normative and pragmatic strands of thought. Groups such as the People's Health Movement have concretized them by underscoring the principles of universality and parity of access, according to which all human beings are entitled to the same quality and kind of assistance.[27] Consequently, the humanitarian logic of helping those in need is being reframed as a struggle against global injustice, for failing to care for those living with HIV/AIDS clearly infringes upon their socio-economic rights. Because rampant privatization programmes and commercialization of health services are incommensurable with the substantiation of such rights, the labour of aid can therefore support and defend the existence of comprehensive public health-care systems in the countries ravaged by the pandemic. Measures along these lines include increased funding for and a build-up of the organizational capacity of public infrastructure and personnel (including hiring and training of health-care workers and involvement of ordinary citizens), as well as systematic national and local, community-based health-care strategies emphasizing priority of access and effective outcomes for subordinate groups (e.g., women and the poor) (Sen and Grown 1987).

Similarly, the very notion of helping distant others is being redefined by global campaigns that demand treatment for those living with HIV/AIDS as a basic right, and a corresponding understanding of ARVs as primary goods that should be freely (or at least affordably) available anywhere in the world. This rendition of the connection between health-care and global justice is one of the lasting legacies of an alliance of civil society groups formed in response to a 1997 lawsuit filed by the Pharmaceutical Manufacturers Association of South Africa – representing a consortium of transnational drug corporations – against the South African government, which was introducing legislation that challenged full patent protection for 'brand name' ARVs and supposedly weakened intellectual property rights (the Medicines and Related Substances Control Act). Domestic and transnational social movements and NGOs were able to draw considerable attention to the case, which became somewhat of a *cause célèbre* that awoke some segments of public opinion to the absurdity of a situation where a hugely profitable industry was blocking potentially

[27] The People's Health Movement was founded in 2000 with a People's Health Assembly in Bangladesh. See www.phmovement.org (accessed 14 January 2005). Its charter is also reprinted in Hong (2004: 37–41).

life-saving products from reaching millions of poor citizens burdened with AIDS.[28]

In recent years, certain global civil society actors have realized that helping people with HIV/AIDS requires confronting the pharmaceutical sector's hold over health-care, notably in terms of its aggressively oligopolistic tactic of setting up and enforcing intellectual property rights for ARVs; patent protection transforms AIDS into a leading cause of mortality for countless millions in the global South. The promotion of widespread manufacturing and distribution of generic drugs to treat AIDS is foremost among several strategies that are currently being employed to undermine an unjust intellectual property regime. Echoing the organization's famed 'Silence = Death' campaigns of the 1980s in the West, ACT UP's Paris branch has adopted the slogans 'Copy = Life' and 'Copy = Right' to drive the point home: yearly treatment through a generic ARV cocktail (from a firm such as Cipla in India) can cost as little as $150, by contrast to up to $10,000 for its patented equivalent.[29] Other policies include parallel importation, that is, a national government's purchase of ARVs in a third country where they are available at a lower price and reselling of them to its citizens – a way to counter Big Pharma's differential pricing campaigns by exploiting loopholes and inconsistencies in the world market for medication. Countries such as India, South Africa and Brazil have also experimented with compulsory licensing, whereby states order a pharmaceutical corporation holding a patent for a particular ARV to license a public agency or a local generic manufacturer to

[28] The organizations most active in opposing the lawsuit were the South African-based Treatment Action Campaign (www.tac.org.za), ACT UP (with activists in the United States protesting at some of Big Pharma's headquarters) and Médecins Sans Frontières (which organized a 'Drop the Case' petition that collected 285,000 signatures in 130 countries). Demonstrations of various kinds were held in over thirty cities around the world, and Kofi Annan, Secretary-General of the United Nations, became involved in the case. Faced with such public and official opposition, the Pharmaceutical Manufacturers Association voluntarily withdrew its lawsuit in 2001. See Davis and Fort (2004: 150–2), Irwin *et al.* (2003: 125–7), Rivière (2004: 47–8) and Seckinelgin (2002: 128–9). Several civic associations have sustained campaigns for universal access to ARVs: aside from the already mentioned Treatment Action Campaign and Médecins Sans Frontières' Campaign for Access to Essential Medicines (www.accessmed-msf.org, accessed 4 July 2005), these include the Health Global Access Project (www.healthgap.org, accessed 4 July 2005), the Consumer Project on Technology (www.cptech.org, accessed 4 July 2005) and ACT UP-Paris (www.actupparis.org, accessed 4 July 2005). See Sell and Prakash (2004) and Thomas (2002).

[29] The argument that the inflated price for patented drugs is necessary to recover the high research and development costs for such products incurred by Big Pharma holds little credence in most instances. A high proportion of pharmaceutical research and development is actually done in government and university laboratories at public expense, and, moreover, marketing budgets for a particular drug are often two to three times higher than those for research and development of it (Joseph 2003: 433).

produce and sell the drug.[30] The most far-reaching proposals centre around the development of an alternative, not-for-profit pharmaceutical sector dedicated to the most urgent and serious epidemics, such as tuberculosis, malaria and, of course, HIV/AIDS. Médecins Sans Frontières' Drugs for Neglected Diseases Initiative, and the emerging collaboration between researchers working for generic drug corporations in South America, Africa and Asia, have sown the seeds of this kind of conception of medication for the public good.

All of these initiatives seek to shift the logic of assisting people with HIV/AIDS in the global South away from a narrow and short-term calculus of profitability and cost-effectiveness. Normative appeals underline the moral dubiousness of governmental apathy and resistance on the part of Big Pharma, the kind of structural violence that Stephen Lewis has equated with mass murder through willing neglect and complacency (Lewis 2001; 2003; 2005). However, even more pragmatically directed arguments demonstrate that the actual economic costs of providing treatment for those living with HIV/AIDS are modest, especially when considered in the context of the full range of consequences flowing from the pandemic being left untreated in severely affected areas: the decimation of the labour force (notably for skilled and professional jobs), political instability, forced mass migrations of populations, the worsening of the situation of women, and the tearing away of the social fabric because of the loss of entire generations and the resulting creation of millions of orphans.[31] In other words, whether stated in ethical or realist terms, the Euro-American world cannot afford not to offer treatment to those living with HIV/AIDS.

This is to say, then, that civic associations pursuing the work of aid beyond borders are increasingly connecting the HIV/AIDS crisis to the North–South divide; NGOs and social movements have sought to engage the Western public by highlighting such connections and thereby drawing attention to questions of global justice and socio-economic redistribution. In essence, it has become clear to many that the root social causes of the pandemic can only be seriously addressed if and when we undertake

[30] The door to parallel importation and compulsory licensing is open because of the World Trade Organization's 2001 Doha Ministerial Declaration on Intellectual Property Rights and Public Health, which recognizes TRIPS exceptions in the name of protecting public health and granting universal access to treatment.

[31] The Brazilian experiment is instructive, since the country's federal government has adopted a policy of distributing ARVs through a publicly funded, non-profit programme that has yielded net savings – the costs incurred being lower than those associated with the medical care of patients without access to treatment. Moreover, the programme has reduced the incidences of both HIV infections and AIDS-related deaths (Davis and Fort 2004: 153; Irwin *et al.* 2003: 76–7; Petchevsky 2003: 94–104).

to overhaul the world order comprehensively. As such, what such groups are demanding is the incorporation of major redistributive mechanisms benefiting vulnerable populations in the global South, while promoting democratic oversight of transnational corporations that maximize profits at the expense of human welfare, as well as of states that unquestionably sacrifice their citizens' well-being in the name of obeying neoliberal orthodoxy. To oppose privatization programmes that erode the infrastructural capacities of national and local health-care systems, then, civic associations are reasserting the fundamental socio-economic right to health.

Yet breaking longstanding cycles of chronic poverty and subjugation requires a host of other measures to reconfigure the global economic system, such as reorienting the policies of international financial institutions away from structural adjustment programmes and foreign debt repayment. Under current arrangements, many poor nation-states pay more in debt servicing than they receive in foreign aid; not coincidentally, these are often the countries most ravaged by HIV/AIDS. Furthermore, what is needed is to move closer to a solidaristic economy by harnessing collective and individual capabilities to secure material well-being through a number of means: support for collectively-owned and democratically run production units geared toward meeting the needs of citizens (such as cooperatives and self-managed factories); fair trade that ensures just prices for African, Asian and South American primary commodities and manufactured products at the same time as it establishes the conditions for living wages for workers; and the advancement of women's rights, as well as their socio-economic empowerment and cultural status. By viewing the HIV/AIDS crisis as intertwined with global socio-economic injustices in this manner, the practice of transnational aid can tackle both simultaneously.

Conclusion

I opened the chapter by reflecting on the ethical and socio-political implications of the globalization of the principle of being one's sister's or brother's keeper. Best exemplified today by certain forms of humanitarian aid, a boundless duty to help distant strangers is informing the work of global justice in vital ways. In a world that is becoming ever more integrated at some levels and where, more importantly, the socio-economic resources to end extreme material deprivation are readily available, the plight of the disadvantaged everywhere cannot but represent a shared responsibility. Conversely, to remain indifferent to this plight in the upcoming years would represent an acute failure of both the moral imagination and political will.

In spite of this potential sense of concern for others, assisting populations in the global South is by no means a straightforward proposition. The paradigm of developmentalist modernization, as well as vast segments of the 'disaster relief industry', have made what are, at best, limited contributions to the situation of persons in distress, and certainly very little to secure their socio-economic rights in the long term. Hence, we can conceptualize aid as a form of social action, a mode of ethico-political practice that helps vulnerable human beings extract themselves from their immediate life-threatening predicaments, while at the same time aiming to remove the structural injustices that produce conditions of severe poverty, discrimination and transmission of epidemics in many of the world's societies. I have suggested that the practice of helping others is composed of three sets of tasks, the enactment of which allows progressive members of global civil society to confront a host of perils constitutive of the field of humanitarian action. In the first instance, the practice of aid can foster social relations of symmetrical reciprocity to offset donors' tendencies to establish interpersonal dynamics based on status differentials. Secondly, when operating within the confines of the existing world order, the labour of assisting those in need can take place under the aegis of egalitarian and collaborative North–South partnerships dedicated to achieving socio-economically redistributive and culturally pluralistic outcomes – thereby undermining the instrumentalization of transnational assistance to assert fiscal and moral control over non-Western territories and peoples. Finally, to be effective, the labour of aid can pursue initiatives that operate beyond or outside the confines of the established capitalist order in asserting the universal right to health and material well-being, so as to alter radically the neoliberal logic of profitability that produces and sustains systemic spatial and socio-economic segregation.

No less than other modes of practice of global justice considered in this book, lending assistance to distant strangers represents an arduous form of ethical and socio-political labour. Undoubtedly, in the case of the HIV/AIDS crisis, the interpersonal and structural obstacles are daunting, to which must be added the fact that the pandemic has already ravaged entire societies and its transmission rates are worrisome in several regions of the world. Nevertheless, as I have argued throughout the chapter, recognition of the difficulties of the tasks constituting the practice of transnational aid cannot and need not foster despondency; possibilities to improve dramatically the situation of those living with HIV/AIDS already exist and others are being created through forms of struggle that articulate the ethic of care with that of justice. Moreover, if Western public opinion and political determination are still seriously lagging behind the scope of the disaster, pressure from global civil society groups is having some impact in pushing Euro-American states and intergovernmental organizations to tackle this scourge across borders, however inadequately and half-heartedly this has hitherto been done. Concerted action is urgent in order to end mass violations of the human rights of persons whose subsistence and survival are being threatened by acute poverty and ill health. If the ideals of humanitarianism are to mean anything, and if the practice of aid is to carry forth struggles for global justice, they must contribute to stopping the preventable deaths of millions in the global South and eliminating the structural conditions that generate such a catastrophe. Moving from an ethos of charity to one of justice, and from a politics of pity to one of solidarity beyond borders, begins here.

5 Cosmopolitanism from below: on solidarity

For solidarity, because it partakes of reason, and hence of generality, is able to comprehend a multitude conceptually, not only the multitude of a class or a nation or a people, but eventually all mankind.

(Arendt 1963: 88)

Introduction

The final mode of practice of global justice to be considered in this book is solidarity, for, as the previous chapters suggest, it constitutes the ground into which progressive global civil society actors are anchoring other forms of struggle for universal civil-political and socio-economic rights. Apart from the fact that the weaving of ties of mutuality across borders is required for the labour of bearing witness, forgiveness, foresight and aid to be viable, cosmopolitan solidarity stands as the culmination of the work of global justice; beyond the commonplace calls for a planetary consciousness lies a more robust and radical sense of cosmopolitan responsibility for the substantive realization of human rights and opposition to structural injustices in all parts of the world. Indeed, the unprecedented coupling of transnational economic integration and cultural diversity – a coupling for which the term 'globalization' often comes to stand as shorthand – has prompted many prominent figures to call for a new cosmopolitanism or internationalism among the world's peoples.[1] However, the advent of an extreme form of neoliberalism that exacerbates already glaring domestic and global disparities in wealth distribution as well as of a 'clash of fundamentalisms' pitting co-constitutive and Manichean brands of religious extremism to one another (Ali 2002) clearly indicate that a progressive cosmopolitan world order is far from being a necessary outcome of globalizing tendencies.

[1] See Beck (1999: 1–18; 2005; 2006), Bourdieu (1998; 2001), Derrida (1994; 2001), Gilroy (2005), Habermas (2001; 2003) and Habermas and Derrida (2003).

Hence, in order to contribute to the work of global justice, the labour of cosmopolitan solidarity should consist of devising ways of living together that reconcile the ideals of equality and difference, by challenging the deeply entrenched assumption that a sense of togetherness and an egalitarian socio-economic order requires cultural homogeneity, or, conversely, that the acknowledgement of cultural alterity necessarily erodes the social fabric and leads to uneven treatment (Touraine 1997). In other words, it is a matter of directing solidaristic practices toward a coherent articulation of transnational political action aimed at redistribution and recognition (Fraser 1997; Fraser and Honneth 2003).

Of course, solidarity itself is hardly a novel concern. It has existed at the heart of sociological reflection since the latter's disciplinary inception in the middle of the nineteenth century, when European thinkers began to be seriously preoccupied by the potentially corrosive impact upon social cohesion of the transition from the medieval to the modern epoch. For many of sociology's 'founding fathers' (Comte, Tönnies, Spencer, Durkheim, etc.), the 'dual revolution' (Hobsbawm 1977 [1966]) giving birth to modernity in Europe eroded the traditional institutional and ideological sources of social integration. How could bonds of mutual responsibility and communal belonging, as well as shared ways of thinking and acting, be sustained in light of accelerating and seemingly irreversible processes of role differentiation, formalization and complexification of social life, individuation and normative pluralization – and this over what were often vast territorial units? Needless to say, the search for answers has kept sociologists and assorted human scientists busy for the better part of the subsequent century-and-a-half.[2] Yet the worrisome ambiguity of our current situation, which lurches between the belligerent reassertion of

[2] While a comprehensive analysis of the sociological literature on solidarity is beyond the scope of this chapter, I should none the less mention its principal mechanisms and associated intellectual traditions:

(a) *community* (*Gemeinschaft* for Tönnies, mechanical solidarity for Durkheim): similarity due to what are viewed as either socio-culturally constructed or primordial attributes and identities (civic vs ethnic nationalism, race vs ethnicity, sex vs gender, etc.);
(b) *functional interdependence* (organic solidarity for Durkheim, systemic integration for Parsons and Luhmann): differentiation and complementarity of roles and functions, most frequently exemplified by cooperation stemming from the social division of labour;
(c) *structural ascription* (class for the later Marx, standpoint theory): identical locations within the social system reproduced by established structures and institutions, such as 'objective' positions within capitalist relations of production;
(d) *socialization* (*Gesellschaft* for Tönnies, the state and intermediate bodies for Durkheim): inculcation and regulation of common beliefs, values and practices through various social institutions (e.g., education, law, family, media) and ideologies (nationalism, socialism, etc.);

ethnic nationalisms and religious tribalisms, on the one hand, and the unfulfilled promise of a more just world order, on the other, supplies the impetus to ask: how, exactly, can the work of global justice foster a sense of solidarity without bounds? Although sub- and supra-national attachments have existed in various forms and to different extents over time, the widespread recognition of the phenomenon of globalization puts into question the implicitly national frames of reference within which most conventional explanations of social solidarity operate.[3]

At one level, the intensification and multiplication of global flows (of capital, commodities, images, ideas, people, etc.) makes it easier to contemplate types of belonging and mutual responsibility extending beyond territorially- or identity-bound communities. Capitalism's relentless amalgamation of the world's regions into a single marketplace and production site widens the North–South socio-economic gulf, but also sows the seeds of a planetary consciousness among some progressive segments of global civil society, which are arguing for a wider realization of humankind's common plight and a duty of care for culturally and spatially distant others. Furthermore, globalized communication and media infrastructure, diasporic communities and continued mass migration are making multiculturalism a ubiquitous, albeit contested, reality in most parts of the world, thereby confronting many peoples with other ways of being and thinking. At another level, the forces of neoliberalism are mercilessly advancing, privatizing and commodifying much of what is in their reach and accordingly threatening the very existence of public spheres in several societies. This gradual loss of the commons and of a sense of the collective good feeds a pathological, instrumentalist hyper-individualism that

(e) *micro-interaction* (symbolic interactionism, ethnomethodology): forging and reinforcing of social bonds through intersubjective relations in everyday life, including habitual or routinized patterns of behaviour and the transmission of background assumptions, symbols and meanings;

(f) *self-identification* (class consciousness for the earlier Marx and Lukács, the subject for Touraine): an action-theoretical conception, according to which commonalities are generated by the self-conscious regroupment of individuals into socio-political groups and movements organized to confront shared sources of subordination and to advance mutual interests.

For a fuller discussion of solidarity on which the above account draws, see Bayertz (1999), Calhoun (2002: 288–90) and Crow (2002). With its argument about solidarity being a mode of practice and the significance of solidaristic labour, my own position is closest to the 'self-identification' paradigm, although others will sometimes be used throughout this chapter.

[3] My point is not that solidarity has only existed within the framework of the nation-state; historically – and to this day – city-states, sub-national regions, continents, supra-national empires, universalist ideologies (religions, political doctrines, etc.) and collective identities (gender, ethnicity, etc.) have also inspired a sense of togetherness. However, sociologists and other social scientists have generally neglected these other loci of solidarity, primarily employing an understanding of society (and thus of solidarity) that is nationally bounded.

reduces citizens to generic consumers caught in the circuits of global capital.

Enter cosmopolitanism, which, with its long and distinguished pedigree, has recently resurfaced in order to address some of the dynamics noted here. Whether in its normative guise as a universalist moral ideal whereby human beings should primarily understand themselves as citizens of the world respectful of and conversant with a multiplicity of ways of life, or as an institutional project concerned with devising a vibrant body of international law and transferring sovereignty 'upward' to institutions of global governance, cosmopolitan discourses are undoubtedly valuable. The egalitarian universalism defended by progressive versions of cosmopolitanism envisages cutting across and joining together transnational struggles for the right to cultural difference and distributive justice, producing a vision of all of humankind's incorporation into a pluralist yet just world order. Moreover, cosmopolitanism valiantly strives to eschew the pitfalls of both communitarianism and liberal individualism, by rejecting the former's culturally homogenizing and exclusionary (or in-group/out-group) tendencies as well as the latter's monadic and abstract vision of social life. Nevertheless, much of this potential remains unfulfilled because, as I will contend in the first section of this chapter, cosmopolitans' distrust of dense localized social relations – which they equate too readily with the primordialism of ethno-nationalism and other 'pre-political' identities – causes them to adopt an excessively formalist and thin conception of the socio-political dimensions of collective existence (Calhoun 2002; 2003). Accordingly, this socially minimalist position from above transforms solidarity into a matter of 'trickle-down' integration of the world's citizens by virtue of their adherence to a common political culture composed of universal principles (participatory democracy, human rights, etc.) entrenched in international law and global institutions. Obviously, this sort of project is unobjectionable in and of itself, but it represents only one dimension of cosmopolitan solidarity.

Therefore, instead of being solely (or even principally) viewed as a normative ideal or legal-institutional project from above, cosmopolitan solidarity is, just as importantly, a transnational mode of practice whereby actors construct bonds of mutual commitment and reciprocity across borders through public discourse and socio-political struggle. The crux of the matter lies in grasping the labour of creating and enacting solidarity, the performance of normatively, aesthetically and politically oriented forms of social action that thicken cosmopolitanism from below. As a mode of practice, cosmopolitan solidarity engages in socio-political tasks that confront three distinct sets of perils: cultural homogenization, political fragmentation and social thinness. Correspondingly, the second section of the chapter will problematize the culturally assimilationist stance of many proponents of egalitarian universalism, according to which solidarity depends upon a difference-blind or difference-transcending unity around a single core identity; to the contrary, I will contend, the recognition of cultural pluralism is becoming a *sine qua non* for establishing viable solidaristic ties without bounds and from below. At the same time, as the third section of the chapter will aim to demonstrate, there is no necessary trade-off between such cultural recognition and the forging of political affinities between groups and persons from different parts of the world. By honing in on the discursively mediated forging of intersections and commonalities between such actors, we can grasp the networked or web-like character of the kind of cosmopolitan solidarity that may be emerging today. The various strands of the chapter will converge in its final part, where I will question the supposition that a culturally pluralist and politically decentred model of solidaristic cosmopolitanism can and should aspire to nothing more than a socially thin and formalist global consensus. This is to neglect the publicly dialogical and creative qualities of certain transnational political and aesthetic practices, through which ordinary citizens and some progressive civic associations active on the world stage can gradually cultivate and negotiate robust relations of mutuality.

In order to help conceptualize and illustrate the argument presented here, I will refer to the alternative globalization movement (hereafter AGM), which began to enter public consciousness around the world with events such as the 1994 Zapatista rebellion in the Chiapas region of Mexico and the 1999 Seattle protests that contributed to the collapse of World Trade Organization negotiations, and gained more visibility with the launch of the World Social Forum in 2001 and the 2003 protests against the US-led invasion of Iraq.[4] To be clear, my intent is not to

[4] I use the designation 'alternative globalization movement' instead of the better-known 'anti-globalization' tag, for it is clear that the AGM is not opposed to globalization *per se*, but rather to the narrowly economistic neoliberal version of it grounded in market fundamentalism – the credo of free trade and the open circulation of capital, goods and services which, even if taken on its own terms, is more rhetoric than reality in a world economy where OECD governments regularly proclaim their faith in open markets while selectively applying the doctrine itself (by, for instance, subsidizing domestic producers and erecting trade barriers against imports from poorer countries while aggressively pressuring such countries to eliminate their own subsidies and protectionist policies). Furthermore, the AGM has an explicitly global outlook. This is so in terms of the multinational composition of its member-groups, the kinds of causes and strategies they espouse, as well as the means of communication they employ (albeit with sub-Saharan African civil society groups and issues being underrepresented). For the AGM, then, an

champion the AGM or to make the case that it perfectly embodies or realizes cosmopolitan solidarity, nor even that it completely overcomes the three sets of perils noted above; it is much too diverse and amorphous an entity, regrouping under its vast umbrella groups ranging from world federalists to economic and cultural protectionists with widely different stances toward cosmopolitan principles, to sustain such claims. None the less, it is good to think with segments of the AGM that – in attempting to respond to these perils and invent a different form of global solidaristic politics – assist in the theoretical reconceptualization of the labour of cosmopolitanism from below. And to add another caveat, the following pages are not intended as a full-blown political sociology or social movement analysis of the AGM, something that would require a different order of demonstration, evidentiary methodology, and evaluation of the participants (their claims, objectives, resources, successes, etc.).[5] Instead, the AGM serves as a springboard to analyse how certain forms of public discourse and socio-political struggle can fuel cosmopolitan solidarity. Bonds of mutual responsibility with distant others cannot be inherited or presumed as given in a post-traditional and multicultural world, and they cannot be solely legislated or prescribed from above on the basis of normative principles or institutional arrangements; they must be made through the pursuit of obstacle-laden tasks that are integral to the work of global justice.

The limits of cosmopolitanism from above

Before examining in greater detail existing approaches to cosmopolitan solidarity, we need briefly to consider why the topic has become so prominent in recent years. Indeed, this development marks a response to historical tragedy and a globalized present, for three principal factors have put into question excessively nation-state-centric understandings of solidaristic ties: ethical dubiousness, political erosion and sociological

alternative and substantive project of globalization widens the application of the idea of freedom of movement across borders to include people, ideas and information (e.g., the Sans-papiers movement in France and the No One Is Illegal organization, both of which defend the rights of undocumented immigrants in the North). An alternative globalization also entails fair trade, global distributive justice, recognition of cultural diversity, participatory democracy, peace and environmental sustainability. See Graeber (2002: 62–5) and Klein (2002: 76–84).

[5] For a sophisticated examination of the AGM that partly draws from political opportunity theory in social movement analysis, see Tarrow (2005). For 'insider' accounts of the AGM, see Brecher *et al.* (2000), Cockburn and St. Clair (2000), Goodman (2002), Graeber (2002), Klein (2002), Notes from Nowhere (2003) and Starr (2000). For organizational analyses of the World Social Forum, the principal institutional manifestation of the AGM, see Hardt (2002), Mertes (2002), Pianta (2003) and Schönleitner (2003).

inadequacy. In the first instance, cosmopolitans have made the case that a sense of togetherness and mutual responsibility based upon socio-cultural similarity or shared territoriality can promote a moral parochialism that does not extend rights and duties beyond communitarian or geographical boundaries; indifference to the plight of distant others is thus easy to muster. Even more disconcerting for cosmopolitanism is the historical record of the twentieth century, which is littered with instances of appropriation of the idea of solidarity-as-sameness in order to mobilize naturalized collective identities in pathological directions; the resulting effects of virulent forms of ethnic nationalism (civil and world wars, genocide, ethnic cleansing, etc.) are all too familiar to us today.

Secondly, cosmopolitans point out that a variety of global trends are challenging the nation-state's capacity to perform its regulative and distributive functions. While too much has been made of the decline of national sovereignty due to economic globalization – a claim that, at least for OECD countries, is as much a self-fulfilling prophecy as a demonstrable reality[6] – there is little doubt that the Westphalian interstate system was never designed to tackle phenomena such as dizzyingly rapid capital flows across borders, powerful transnational corporations or the globalization of risks of various kinds, such as climate change, nuclear arms, terrorism and diseases (Beck 1999; 2000; 2002). The limits of the nation-state's leverage over such forces matters to the extent that it introduces a democratic deficit. Since no global representative institutions akin to national parliaments or assemblies currently exist, popular sovereignty over transnational actors and processes is conspicuously missing. Likewise, it can no longer be assumed that the will of the people and the voices of citizens will inherently be translated into effective domestic public policy, and this precisely because governments do not hold all the levers to 'deliver' on matters of socio-economic regulation and redistribution.

Furthermore, the socio-cultural inadequacies of territorially bounded conceptions of solidarity are becoming obvious. With the existence of diasporic communities, mass migration flows, as well as the virtually instantaneous circulation of images and ideas across borders, both long-existing and newly formed supra-national sources of social integration are coming to the fore: global production and consumption circuits, to say

[6] Indeed, Euro-American nation-states are not 'victims' of the deregulation of capital flows and the (selectively applied) doctrine of free trade, but active and enthusiastic participants in these processes. It is therefore more accurate to speak of a transformation of the way national sovereignty is exercised than its disappearance or necessary erosion.

nothing of planetary dangers, are complicating functional interdependence and structural ascription; worldwide media, hybrid popular cultures and deterritorialized ideologies are increasingly contributing to processes of socialization, that is to say, the institutional transmission and acquisition of shared ways of thinking and acting. And both micro-interaction and self-identification are similarly becoming transnationalized in light of the spatial extension of interpersonal relations, lifeworlds and socio-political identities.[7] We should be wary of overstating this point, for locally and nationally based solidaristic dynamics are as strong as ever, at the same as they are being supplemented by global integrative mechanisms (Johnston and Laxer 2003).

In their focus on the first two considerations identified above, the main bodies of literature on cosmopolitanism have left the third one relatively unexplored. Accordingly, normative cosmopolitans portray solidarity as a universal ideal countering the moral dubiousness of restricted understanding of a community of reciprocal rights and responsibilities, while those who can be termed institutional cosmopolitans view solidarity as a by-product of a redesign of the structures of global governance. Yet neither framework adequately accounts for the transnationalization of the sources of and possibilities for cosmopolitanism from below, thereby neglecting the facet of enactment of solidarity that points to its representing a mode of practice through which global civil society actors can cultivate relatively thick social relations.[8]

For many normative cosmopolitans, citizens' common attachment to basic liberal democratic principles inscribed in national or supra-national constitutions – what Habermas (1996: 500; 1998: 225) terms 'constitutional patriotism' – as well as adherence to a body of international humanitarian law like the Universal Declaration of Human Rights, appear to achieve a sufficient level of social integration under globalizing conditions (Bayertz 1999; Bohman and Lutz-Bachmann 1997; Derrida 2001; Kant 1991b [1795]; Nussbaum 2002a [1996]; Singer 2002; Turner 2002). Other normative theorists have sought to extend cosmopolitanism in a Rawlsian direction, using a social-contractarian logic to make a case for

[7] See note 2 for an explanation of the terminology used here.

[8] An exception here is transnational cultural studies and anthropology, which have produced a number of analyses of globalizing processes and networks (e.g., diasporic groups, hybrid identities, travelling cultures) and offer a thicker socio-cultural treatment of cosmopolitanism. See, *inter alia*, Appadurai (1996), Clifford (1997), Friedman (1994), Gilroy (1993; 2000; 2005) and Ong (1999), as well as the special issues of the journals *Public Culture* 12(3) (2000) and *Theory, Culture & Society* 19(1–2) (2002). However, with the exception of Gilroy (2005: 58–83), these analyses have not dealt with how groups are mobilizing a sense of universal human solidarity in the name of struggles for an alternative globalization.

global distributive justice (Beitz 1999; Pogge 1992; 2001b; 2002a).[9] Therefore, in their minds, cosmopolitan solidarity implies a redistributive moral obligation in a world environment where the condition of universal equality of persons is consistently violated. Citizens of rich countries have a corresponding duty toward their less fortunate counterparts, given that socio-economic status results from the arbitrariness of a person's birth position in the existing global order, as well as from the disproportionate benefits people living in the North Atlantic region derive from the functioning of unjust multinational processes and structures.

Normative cosmopolitanism's universalism is laudable in its critique of moral parochialism, but by the same token, it tends to advocate the transcendence or shedding away of supposedly superfluous local and national ties. To be at home everywhere also means to belong nowhere in particular. This can breed a kind of jet-setting elitism, 'the class consciousness of frequent travellers' (Calhoun 2003), that fawns at its own deterritorialized sophistication while cringing at the 'provincialism' of anything it perceives to be the more rooted experiences and lifeworlds within which human beings with lower levels of economic and cultural capital actually live. Similarly, most normative cosmopolitans have misgivings about situated and particularistic social relations, which in addition to being supposedly incompatible with universalist commitments, they believe to be easily captured for tribalistic purposes.[10] And although it mounts a compelling case against the socio-economic inequalities embedded in the current world order, the paradigm of global distributive justice fails to explain how its cosmopolitan appeal can effectively be put into practice. Hence, the result is a rather anaemic version of solidarity connecting individuals on the basis of their standing as abstract bearers of universal rights and freedoms, in a manner that is at most tenuously connected to civil society struggles for an alternative globalization.

Institutional cosmopolitans, for their part, conceive of solidarity as an offshoot of new models of global governance (Archibugi *et al.* 1998; Falk 1995; 2000; Falk and Strauss 2003; Held 1995). The stress on legal institutionalization is notable in the work of Habermas and Rawls, two thinkers who have recently sought to expand their models beyond the domestic arena. Despite the fact that Rawls's notion of peoples living in discrete political-cum-cultural social formations is internationalist rather than cosmopolitan, both he and Habermas share a legalistically focused

[9] Rawls himself rejects this cosmopolitan extension of his famous argument about distributive justice at the domestic level. For his criticisms of global redistribution and his vision of a territorially and culturally circumscribed *international* order, see Rawls (1999).

[10] For notable exceptions, see Appiah (2006) and Turner (2002).

understanding of global solidarity. From their political constructivist viewpoint, putting in place and following legitimate democratic procedures is the main way – under pluralistic and post-metaphysical conditions – of justifying specific decisions and the elaboration of a particular social order. Consequently, international law becomes the institutional embodiment and rational lynchpin of a minimalist, universal political consensus organized around the dual pillars of liberal democracy and human rights. The procedural question of finding legitimate grounds for rational agreement about such a cosmopolitical programme overshadows the issue of building and performing transnational solidaristic relations between persons and groups.

How does this procedural move affect the institutional understanding of solidarity? In Rawls's contractarian scheme, it is the overlapping consensus between reasonable comprehensive doctrines that achieves a legitimate political conception of justice suited to each domestic setting (Rawls 1996: 133–72) – a consensus that, in turn, performs a socially integrative role. In the act of rationally and freely entering into agreement with one another to adhere to the principle of fairness of distributive justice, citizens living in liberal democratic societies cultivate ties of mutual commitment. 'The law of peoples' (Rawls 1999) applies a similar procedural mechanism to arrive at universal norms valid in the international arena: an overlapping consensus between independently and legitimately formulated domestic bodies of law, which draw upon particular socio-cultural traditions and worldviews, can itself produce a minimalist yet generalized political understanding of right and justice.[11] However, to make such an understanding appear plausible while avoiding the charge that it represents but another ethnocentric model falsely universalizing Western liberalism, and to remain consistent with his principle of toleration of normative pluralism, Rawls must strip his international consensus down to a thin, overarching layer. His brand of universalism must cast aside thicker conceptions of the good, social relations, and even the very principle of distributive justice upon which his domestic theory is built, lest such substantive cross-civilizational engagement threaten the viability of an international consensus of any sort or result in a law of peoples derived exclusively from Euro-American sources.[12]

[11] In his ideal theory, Rawls limits the possibility of this international overlapping consensus to two types of society, those composed of 'reasonably just liberal peoples' and those composed of 'decent hierarchical peoples'. What he terms 'outlaw states' and 'burdened societies' may, or indeed may not, eventually join the non-ideal world society of peoples (Rawls 1999).

[12] Rawls's thinking here closely follows his advocacy of a purely political conception of justice at the domestic level, where the procedure of overlapping consensus respects and leaves intact a plurality of different reasonable comprehensive doctrines. However, I would claim that when transferred to the international realm, this results in a

In Habermas's case, his recognition of the underdeveloped state of a lived cosmopolitan political culture explains the proceduralist and institutionally legalist flavour of his attempt to resolve the problem of solidarity. On the one hand, he is uncomfortable with, even mistrustful of, the density of so-called 'pre-political' identities that generate a sense of collective belonging on the basis of naturalized characteristics; given twentieth-century German history, ethnic nationalism's appeal to *jus sanguinis* understandably casts a dark shadow over his thinking.[13] On the other hand, Habermas defends cultural pluralism within and between societies and the need to respect possible differences among the substantive contents of groups' and communities' deeply held normative worldviews. The absence of agents of cosmopolitanism at the transnational level prompts him to opt for a procedural consensus, whereby the following of democratically legitimate procedures is the key mechanism through which to secure agreement among free, equal and diverse citizens about decisions regarding the laws under which they will be governed. In other words, Habermas uses procedural legitimacy as a substitute for social integration in a democratic and pluralist political culture.[14] Legal institutionalization simultaneously reflects and shapes the procedural enactment of public deliberation between citizens, whereby the discourse-ethical conditions of unrestrained and undistorted communication, as well as egalitarian reciprocity and mutual recognition, foster opinion- and will-formation in and through the public sphere.[15] Accordingly, constitutional patriotism with a cosmopolitan intent consists of a rational attachment to the democratic procedures entrenched in a domestic constitution (or, in the European case, in a prospective supra-national one) and

territorially discrete normative stance that is vulnerable to the charge of absolute relativism; if we can only argue from within our own socio-cultural horizons and traditions – which should themselves be viewed as endogenously contested and plural – then on what grounds can one group criticize another for what it believes, say, to be a fundamental violation of its conception of the good or of human dignity?

[13] See, *inter alia*, Habermas (1989b). To my mind, the distinction between 'pre-political' and 'political' identities is itself questionable, since even apparently biological traits (blood, race, sex, etc.) are discursively mediated social constructs whose use to create a sense of group identity may in reality be tangled up with procedural justifications and attachment to a democratic political culture.

[14] As Habermas puts it: 'The neutrality of the law vis-à-vis internal ethical differentiations stems from the fact that in complex societies the citizenry as a whole can no longer be held together by a substantive consensus on values but only by a consensus on the procedures for the legitimate enactment of laws and the legitimate exercise of power' (Habermas 1998 [1996]: 225). See also Habermas (1996 [1992]: 448–9).

[15] Discourse ethics specifies that a consensus is normatively and procedurally legitimate if citizens participate in its public elaboration on equal and mutually reciprocal terms. A dialogical process of publicly stating one's position, rationally and voluntarily yielding to the force of the better argument, and collective filtering out of weaker claims thus produces a justifiable and just political agreement.

international law, which serves to integrate citizens into a political community (Habermas 1996 [1992]: 499–500, 513–15; 1998 [1996]: 117–20, 225–6; 2001 [1998]: 108–9).

Habermas's procedural conception of solidarity is supplemented by his focus on a cosmopolitan legal order, the implementation of which is hampered by the underdevelopment of global deliberative institutions and mechanisms; although a supra-national public sphere and shared political culture may be gradually coming into being through the process of European integration, extending such dynamics to the rest of the planet remains both complicated and remote at this stage (Habermas 1998 [1996]: 165–201; 2003; Habermas and Derrida 2003). If a process of cross-civilizational and reciprocally egalitarian public discourse leading to the formation of a universal consensus is desirable, its realization would depend upon something more than legislation decreed from above. Being cognizant of this issue, Habermas concentrates on the institutionalization of international law, yet he ends up with an excessively formalist analysis that is deprived of the socio-cultural substance afforded by the nascent dynamics of global opinion- and will-formation about, for instance, the meaning of democracy and the content of human rights discourses (Habermas 1998 [1996]: 191–3; 2001 [1998]: 107–8). His recent writings denote the importance of a common (but so far only Europe-wide) worldview, as well as of civic associations (social movements, non-governmental organizations, and the like) and certain political parties, for the creation of supra-national solidarity (Habermas 2001 [1998]: 55–7, 102–3, 112; Habermas and Derrida 2003), yet not enough attention is devoted to the opposite problem, namely, how the aim of constructing global agreement through mutual recognition and free communication among civil society actors is a 'bottom-up' precondition for the procedural legitimacy of any body of cosmopolitan law.

All in all, then, institutional cosmopolitans aim to attend to the political limitations of the interstate system in a globalizing world, but in the process implicitly render solidarity into a 'trickle-down' outcome of proper organizational design and mechanisms, or of procedurally legitimate political consensus. While both of these aspects are important in their own right, they leave us with a version of cosmopolitan solidarity that is socially thin and thereby reminiscent of its normative counterpart. There is more to creating bonds of mutual commitment and responsibility between citizens of the world than elaborating an ideal-typical model of global governance or specifying the democratic procedures to produce a justifiable body of international law. As I am suggesting here, the creation of solidarity without bounds should be grasped as a mode of transnational practice enacted through the labour of public discourse and socio-political struggle.

We can unpack three distinctive features of cosmopolitan solidarity through which it participates in the work of global justice, along with the four other modes of practice discussed in this book. In the first place, it is necessarily dialogical because it is formed from an intersubjective process of communicative exchange and mutual recognition between civic associations in various parts of the world, which come to form a series of overlapping discursive communities where participants share their experiences and opinions, acknowledge those of others and collectively build the vision of an alternative world order; solidaristic relations can grow out of debate among groups and persons as well as from the acts of granting recognition and being granted it. Secondly, the labour of cosmopolitan solidarity forms a public practice, for civil society groups can achieve a sense of togetherness and common purpose through the voicing of their opinions and engagement in open discussion and deliberation in differently nested public spaces where all arguments and positions are intelligible to, and can be challenged by, anyone. Finally, as a mode of social action, cosmopolitan solidarity is transnational in scope. If local and national attachments remain as vigorous as ever, many global civil society actors are aiming to universalize the circle of those about whom we are concerned and toward whom we feel responsible; to the celebrated environmental slogan of 'think globally, act locally' can be added that of 'think locally, act globally', a manifestation of 'rooted cosmopolitanism' (Appiah 2002: 22; Tarrow 2005). What should also be noted is that this sort of solidaristic universalism does not merely pose an abstract ethical appeal of the 'love the stranger as much as thy neighbour' ilk. Instead, it draws upon the more laudable aspects of globalization's unleashing of socially integrative tendencies across vast distances: interdependence due to transnational risks and the functioning of global capitalism (Beck 2000); exposure to the lives of remote others via media flows and interpersonal relations (made possible by globalized public spaces); rapid exchange of ideas and information; and transborder organizing of progressive political campaigns.

To elaborate the discussion of the dialogical, public and transnational features of the labour of cosmopolitan solidarity, I want to draw upon the example of the AGM, whose interest lies in its attempts to forge attachments beyond borders by reconciling – with varying degrees of success – a commitment to global socio-economic redistribution with that of opposing cultural homogenization. By no means a panacea, the AGM nevertheless provides us with an indication of how the constitution of progressive transnational social relations is premised upon and reinforced by the incorporation of the lessons of identity politics of the past two decades with the resurgent critique of capitalism in its latest, neoliberal garb.[16] Hence, the next section of the chapter will consider the initial task of the labour of cosmopolitan solidarity, the creation of ties of mutuality that allow for a multiplicity of ways of being and thinking. In turn, the third section of the chapter will contend that the recognition of cultural pluralism need not lead to the fracturing of a shared socio-political project (such as that of an alternative globalization), which can be built upon criss-crossing networks of affinities. In the last section, I want to demonstrate that cosmopolitan solidarity does not have to be restricted to its normative or institutional dimensions. Bolstering a universal concern for the well-being of all human beings and the development of structures of global governance is the final solidaristic task beyond borders, the cultivation of the creativity of transnational public discourse and socio-political struggle that can supply cosmopolitanism with a socio-cultural robustness.

Assimilationism and the recognition of pluralism

When conceiving of solidarity as a mode of practice of global justice, the first and most common peril that we encounter emanates from what can be termed assimilationist egalitarianism, according to which cultural similarity is a precondition for the production of a sense of togetherness and responsibility for the socio-economic welfare of all. Often stated in republican terms, this logic asserts that equal treatment of citizens demands cultural sameness or neutrality, for socio-political institutions can grant individual subjects the same rights and freedoms only if they are viewed identically – whether as members of a national or a global polity. Put slightly differently, assimilationist egalitarians believe that universal

[16] The political sensibilities animating the AGM are born out of a context that differs in important ways from that of their progressive predecessors – especially the North American New Left of the 1960s and 1970s. In the first instance, an important segment of the younger generation of activists has been post-socialist from the very beginning, if only in the sense that few of them ever viewed the Soviet or the Chinese experiments of 'really existing' socialism as viable and desirable models. As such, the collapse of the Eastern bloc and the end of the Cold War in 1989–90 did not have nearly the same symbolic and ideological impact across generations of Leftists. For example, the suspicion toward utopian thinking and emancipatory discourses that fuelled much of so-called 'postmodern turn' in the last decades of the twentieth century has been replaced, at least among many of the groups that make up the AGM, by the search for contingent, fallibilistic yet reconstructive political projects and forms of action. *Das Kapital* and *One-Dimensional Man* have given way to *No Logo* and *Empire*.

socio-economic redistribution must trump the recognition of cultural identities for solidarity to be possible (Gitlin 1994; Rorty 1998b). In fact, equality and difference may stand in a relationship of incommensurability, as acknowledgement of cultural diversity is sometimes translated into a source of justification for unequal treatment of and structural discrimination against those identified as other. Moreover, the argument goes, the mobilization of persons and groups against institutionalized sources of domination and subordination is premised upon their possessing a single core identity that overcomes their specificities. Historically, three main strategies have been employed for this purpose: essentialism has turned to biologically ascribed characteristics, such as sex or race ('all women are sisters bound together by their female corporeality'); communitarianism has called upon shared socio-cultural traits, such as language, traditions and beliefs ('all Swedes are united by their history and national pride'); and structuralism has appealed to identical positions *vis-à-vis* a system of oppression, such as patriarchy, capitalism, racism and homophobia ('all workers are situated in the same way within capitalist relations of production'). Conversely, recognizing cultural pluralism supposedly erodes the socially integrative and politically effective impact of such a core identity by giving free rein to divisive expressions of particularity, and thus potentially introducing disharmony among group members.

I want to take to task the assimilationist egalitarians' key assertion, namely, that cultural uniformity carves out a path toward solidarity. If the debates surrounding identity politics during the 1980s and 1990s have taught us anything, it is that far from being a force of social integration and political mobilization, the desire to assimilate difference in the name of equality undermines the possibility of creating bonds of mutuality. Indeed, the production of a single, uniform and overarching identity to which all must adhere can simultaneously represent a process of denial or erasure of so-called secondary components of individual or collective self-identity; one is a woman, regardless of ethnicity, class or sexuality, or a worker, regardless of gender or nationality. These 'particularistic' concerns will be attended to after the revolution (against patriarchy, capitalism, etc.), or once appropriate structural reforms have been accomplished. This kind of thinking is precisely what has led to the fractious split and *dialogue de sourds* between the economic and cultural Left in North America, among other places. The first has accused the second of veering off into a brand of radically deconstructive politics of difference that is overtly hostile, or utterly indifferent, to the egalitarian grammar of socio-economic redistribution, while the reply from the cultural side consists of asserting that egalitarianism frequently resorts to symbolic violence by falsely universalizing and privileging the subject-positions and experiences of some groups over others.[17]

When translated in cosmopolitan terms, assimilationist egalitarianism implicitly expects human beings to follow a path of scaling up of their identities until they become abstract bearers of universal rights and duties, who embrace all of humankind yet are 'unencumbered' by sub-cosmopolitan attachments. To be cosmopolitan in this way is to become geographically and culturally disembedded, to adopt a view from nowhere that leaves socio-cultural specificities aside in order to unite under a generic globetrotting banner that falsely universalizes the experiences of economic and cultural elites (Calhoun 2003; Appiah 2006). Aside from the fact that it overlooks other, less rarefied cosmopolitan lifeworlds – those of Indians working in call centres answering queries from American or British clients in real time, or of Maghreban immigrants in France producing *rai* music, for instance – this cosmopolitanism from above elides the extent to which individuals and groups are hierarchically situated in intersecting structures of domination as well as unevenly able and willing to claim a cosmopolitan status. To paraphrase Orwell, all world citizens are equal, but some world citizens are more equal than others.

In order to contribute to the work of global justice, a viable practice of cosmopolitan solidarity can eschew the polarities that have racked Left politics over the past few decades by working to reconcile and demonstrate the interdependence between the emancipatory projects of recognition and redistribution (Fraser 1997; Fraser and Honneth 2003). Such a practice can be critical of the falsely universalistic and socio-culturally disembedded ideal of cosmopolitanism from above, yet it should not thereby conclude that any call to togetherness among the world's peoples inherently masks a homogenizing and self-interested will to power. The AGM hints in this direction, though not always successfully so, because it attempts to make its various constituencies coalesce around a shared vision of global distributive justice and opposition to neoliberalism that

[17] For instance, third-wave feminists have not only exposed the phallocentrism of the universal philosophical subject, but the ethnocentrism and heteronormativity of the idea of global sisterhood and the signifier 'woman' found in the discourses of their first- and second-wave Western predecessors (Collins 1991; Fraser and Nicholson 1990; hooks 1984; Mohanty 1988; 1995; Young 1995). However, we should also keep in mind that the historical legacy of 'older' social movements and forms of egalitarian politics regarding issues of cultural difference is more nuanced than admitted by most proponents of identity politics. An example of this would be the alliance between certain Anglo-American feminists and abolitionists in the nineteenth century, whereby the emancipation of women was tied to that of African-American slaves. On this point more generally, see Calhoun (1994: 22–3).

simultaneously recognizes their specific socio-cultural identities; conversely, the AGM's self-awareness of its members' cultural heterogeneity is meaningful if it endeavours to challenge transnational structural inequalities between them.

In the construction of an egalitarian and pluralist set of imagined global communities founded upon relatively thick bonds of reciprocity, two main forces already mentioned in previous chapters of this book must be at play: the moral imagination (the sense of empathy toward others that comes from the labour of trying to put oneself in their place), and reason (the cognitive capacity to learn about and come to understand others' predicaments as well as their underlying causes). Both of them can be facilitated – or indeed, hampered – by the expansion and intensification of global communication, whether in the form of media flows, new technologies or transnational meeting-places for civil society actors (such as the World Social Forum). As a result, distant strangers may no longer seem to be as morally and spatially distant – or indeed as strange – as before; to be more substantive, universalism would need to include a multiplicity of voices and experiences beyond the confines of the North Atlantic 'frequent flyer' worldview. Thus, a cosmopolitanism from below would not signify to be from nowhere or everywhere at once, but rather to engage with different lifeworlds, to partially distance oneself from one's 'native' vantage-point in order to try to see things from those of others and to reflexively locate one's position within more general frames of reference. There is thus no necessary antinomy between situated and cosmopolitan selves, for identity can be multilayered and multiscaled, as the concept of rooted cosmopolitanism suggests.[18] Groups and persons will stand side by side not because they are identical, but because they recognize in others enough similarities and spaces for difference to believe that their voices will be heard and valued.

Despite its limitations and flaws, the AGM has been explicit about tackling these questions by virtue of foregrounding the link between socio-economic power and matters of voice and representation, most comprehensively explored in the international women's movement (Who speaks and is heard? On whose behalf does one speak?, etc.). Concretely, this has meant that some Northern participants in the AGM have taken their lead from and learned about circumstances in the global South from civic associations in Asia, Africa and South

[18] Of course, this is not to imply that all parts of one's identity are always at play to the same extent. According to the situation, a particular component will be more or less prominent according to self-affirmation, external interpellation and institutional structuring.

America, to the extent that groups whose predicaments were formerly unknown or quite marginal for Euro-American audiences (e.g., Javanese female factory workers and landless male Brazilian peasants) are bearing witness to their plights and directly participating in transnational political strategizing. For instance, supporters of the Zapatistas who made the trek to the Lacandón jungle in southern Mexico to attend the International Encuentros for Humanity and Against Neoliberalism rapidly discovered that they were not expected to teach the indigenous peoples of Chiapas how to become world citizens, but to observe local ways of life and discuss the conditions in their own communities. Under the best possible scenarios, appreciating and contributing to the preservation of a variety of languages, beliefs and forms of activity thereby becomes a vital part of a different sort of globalization, 'a world where many worlds fit' as the Zapatistas themselves are fond of declaring (Marcos 2002: 250). Here, solidarity beyond borders can exist by learning to value other ways of organizing social life while being committed to universal distributive justice, not by shedding all socio-cultural particularities in order to fit into a single, generic mould. Rather than constituting traces of provincialism to be eventually transcended, these sorts of particularities and firsthand knowledges are the soil out of which can spring the normative and political resources of the work of global justice.

So far, the AGM has resisted the temptation of offering a culturally difference-blind meta-narrative. Certainly, neoliberalism has become a global phenomenon whose effects are visible and broadly comparable across the planet, while civic associations in one region have replicated political strategies of opposition to it (e.g., through alternative economic models, local representative democracy) pioneered in another region. Yet even at the cost of internal cohesion, the AGM also stresses its internal diversity, a tactic meant to distinguish itself from the generic culture spawned by neoliberal forces – a culture that would flatten out variations among human beings in the name of cultivating nondescript consumers in the planet's shopping malls and docile producers in its factories (Bové 2001; Fisher and Ponniah 2003: 346; Klein 2002; Marcos 2002). But the AGM's defence of pluralism is also visible on the ground, for as many observers have noted, the protest marches and counter-summits that have greeted various meetings of international financial and political organizations over the last few years (in Seattle, Québec City, Prague, etc.) – to say nothing of the World Social Forums themselves – have brought together a bewildering range of subaltern groups whose identities and livelihoods are threatened by the current world order: women, indigenous peoples, workers, immigrants, people of colour, gays and lesbians, environmentalists, farmers, and so on.[19] Given this heterogeneity, the AGM is not adopting the perspective of a single group as representative of the whole; its transnational coalitions are best described as patchworks grounded in the local and the national (Tarrow 2005).

Further, the AGM's pluralism merely represents a pragmatic admission on the part of its participants of their asymmetrical socio-economic statuses; the material deprivation and organized violence faced by many people from the global South remain considerably worse in degree and kind than those experienced in the North, and any effort to deny this reality would be tactically damaging. Hence, although several farmers are joining forces against genetically modified crops, the realities of subsistence farming, let alone landlessness, in South America, Asia and Africa dramatically differ from those of organic agriculture in Europe and North America; the same could be said about transnational environmentalism, with ecological preservation being a *sine qua non* for day-to-day survival for many of the earth's indigenous communities.[20] For the AGM, then, a large portion of the labour of cosmopolitan solidarity consists of striving to weave together and negotiate the intersections between a multiplicity of specific positions and subjectivities.

Splinters or webs?

In the previous section, we saw that the foundational task of a practice of cosmopolitan solidarity oriented to the work of global justice consists of articulating egalitarian universalism with cultural pluralism. Some will interpret this critique of assimilationism as invariably creating favourable conditions for the second peril of solidaristic labour, political fragmentation, because the recognition of heterogeneity supposedly strikes the death-knell of a global sense of reciprocity and the development of a shared vision of an alternative world order. There is little doubt that strong versions of identity politics are questionable on these grounds,

[19] It is in this spirit that Subcomandante Marcos, the spokesperson for the Zapatistas, has made an oft-cited remark:

> Marcos is gay in San Francisco, black in South Africa, an Asian in Europe, a Chicano in San Ysidro, an anarchist in Spain, a Palestinian in Israel, a Mayan Indian in the streets of San Cristóbal, a Jew in Germany, a Gypsy in Poland, a Mohawk in Quebec, a pacifist in Bosnia, a single woman on the Metro at 10:00 P.M., a peasant without land, a gang member in the slums, an unemployed worker, an unhappy student and, of course, a Zapatista in the mountains. (Klein 2002: 116)

[20] In addition, citizens who attend protests against neoliberal globalization face vastly different levels of personal danger and state repression – the killing or 'disappearance' of activists being quite routine in poor countries (Mertes 2002: 108).

since they promote a radical particularism that undercuts the prospects of any kind of solidaristic politics.[21] Advocating the fact that the centre does not and should not hold anymore, radical particularists fetishize otherness by championing difference for difference's sake. Hence, to the view that identities are discrete and self-contained rather than intersubjectively constituted and always already hybrid is added a presumption of incommensurability: differences are inherent and absolute, creating an unbridgeable chasm. The only way for groups to preserve cultural authenticity and uniqueness is to 'go it alone', to opt for political separatism to avoid diluting or compromising their socio-cultural essences.

However, without being buttressed by an ethos of dialogue and coalition-building, the proliferation of identity-based micro-narratives can rapidly turn into a cacophony of monological discourses that are all equally convinced of their incomparable distinctiveness and operate in isolation from each other.[22] Being preoccupied with defending their own turf against homogenizing and stigmatizing tendencies, radical particularists overcompensate in monistic directions and consequently produce politically disaggregating effects – what Ignatieff has termed, in a different context and echoing Freud, 'the narcissism of minor differences' (Ignatieff 1998). When each group tends to its own garden, what is left of the earth itself? A purely deconstructive stance does not tackle the complicated matter of how identity-based groups can forge ties with those outside of their immediate communities of interest. Likewise, it is rarely concerned with providing a general critique of the established global social order, for it views such efforts as smacking of 'totalization' while itself being more often than not at a loss to make sense of the structures that reproduce relations of domination in the world today.

Despite the fact that egalitarian assimilationism leans toward cultural homogeneity while radical particularism conceives of it pejoratively, both stances assume that it is the foundation of solidarity. What they do not wholly appreciate, however, is that collective action does not have to be framed in terms of the polarities of perfect symmetry with others or complete separation from them. And if we may be tempted to tear the heart out of overly centralizing and homogenizing notions of social

[21] For a more detailed critique of strong versions of 'postmodernism' (and by extension, of strong identity politics), see Benhabib (1992: 203–41).

[22] As Seidman has commented with reference to the predicament of the American gay and lesbian movement in the early 1990s: 'Solidarity built around the assumption of a common identity and agenda has given way to social division; multiple voices, often speaking past one another, have replaced a defiant monotone which drowned out dissonant voices in favour of an illusory but exalted unity' (Seidman 1995: 117). See also Gilroy (2005: 63–4).

cohesion,[23] we cannot simply leave in their wake a model of the social composed of isolated splinters. Better to think of cosmopolitan solidarity as a networked practice composed of a vast web of actors who labour to create nodes of commonality and points of intersection out of shifting, cross-cutting lines of affinity that remain grounded in local and national settings. This web takes the form of a patchwork pragmatically assembled and reassembled from disparate and overlapping pieces, rather than a pre-established, neatly laid out and carefully followed plan. A dialectic between convergence and decentralization is what produces common ground, as solidaristic bonds must be discursively negotiated between parties.[24]

This is where the AGM's self-description as a 'movement of movements' is worthy of attention, for – akin to the notion of 'transnational advocacy networks' (Keck and Sikkink 1998) – it suggests a mosaic of horizontal and transversal struggles simultaneously waged at different scales and in numerous settings around the world (ranging from neighbourhood councils and communal land ownership initiatives to globalized movements for women's rights and environmental protection). What commentators have described as the AGM's swarm-like quality,[25] then, stems from attempts to produce decentralized and pragmatic assemblages of diverse and unstable coalitions among actors who remain differently situated yet can occasionally unite or dissolve. None of this is entirely novel, since the AGM fits into a historical lineage of progressive coalition-building beyond territorial borders, whereby forces have tried to band together and operate across local, national, regional and global arenas.[26] Furthermore, the metaphor of the swarm captures the AGM's labour of perpetual self-reconfiguration, the growing density and expansion or contraction of the web as its member-groups discover certain commonalities or irreconcilable differences. In a network such as this, comprehensiveness of understanding comes not from vertical

[23] This would be a social-theoretical move akin to Foucault's critique of the monarchic-juridical model of power that prevails in political theory: 'At bottom, despite the differences in epochs and objectives, the representation of power has remained under the spell of monarchy. In political thought and analysis, we still have not cut off the head of the king.' (Foucault 1978 [1976]: 88–9)

[24] Feminist theory provides the most sophisticated discussion of affinity-based solidarity. See, *inter alia*, Allen (1999), Dean (1996), Fraser (1997), Fraser and Nicholson (1990), Young (1990: 172–3, 188–9, 237–41; 1995).

[25] Hardt and Negri's rich yet somewhat analytically murky concept of the 'multitude' can serve as a theoretical equivalent to the idea of a web or swarm (Hardt 2002: 117; Hardt and Negri 2000; 2004).

[26] Abolitionism, feminism, international socialism, the Popular Front during the Spanish Civil War, anti-colonial struggles in the global South and the anti-apartheid movement are but a few examples of what is a long list of multiscaled coalitions and social movements.

integration, analytical abstraction or socio-cultural disembedding, but from the aggregation of partial and situated knowledges; a 'big picture' of what is occurring in the world today may become visible by assembling the manifold smaller pictures that civic associations supply.

Within the AGM, civic associations can develop ties of mutuality by engaging in the labour of narrating their experiences and explaining their positions to others, and thus fostering a shared, albeit frequently fragile, terrain of thinking and practice. Indeed, certain progressive civil society groups originating from different locations and devoted to specific causes are realizing that they form 'transnational risk communities' (Beck 2000) integrated into global capitalism's circuits and affected by remarkably similar sets of neoliberal policies (whose prescriptions include privatization, the dismantling of the welfare state, unregulated movement of capital and the entrenchment of corporate rights).[27] Correspondingly, the AGM's opposition to these policies congeals most readily through the identification and sharing of information about what are considered to be common organizational sources of power in the global economy, such as transnational corporations and international financial institutions.[28]

Thus, in addition to the cross-border organizing of unions to stop the international race to the lowest possible wages, the AGM has witnessed the formation of a number of alliances that cut across civic associations' conventional constituencies: the Save Narmada Movement opposed to the building of dams on the Narmada River in India has drawn on support from national and international constituencies; during the 1999 WTO protests in Seattle, US ecological activists and union members marched side by side and went on to form the Alliance for Sustainable Jobs and the Environment;[29] the World Social Forum in Porto Alegre was the site

[27] Though somewhat parallel, my argument differs from Beck's in two respects. Firstly, I stress the fact that risk communities are formed less because of the existence of risks *per se* than through public dialogue and deliberation, through which individuals and groups learn to recognize such risks and may decide to organize themselves collectively in response to them. Secondly, I emphasize the affirmative dimension of the project of an alternative globalization, which cannot be completely accounted for by the more reactive tenor of risk politics.

[28] This is not to say that the neoliberal policy cocktail has identical effects everywhere, its impact on weak states and already poor societies – and within them, on the most vulnerable groups (women, ethno-cultural minorities, etc.) – being much more severe than in their richer, stronger counterparts. As argued in Chapter 4, the World Bank's and International Monetary Fund's much maligned structural adjustment programmes have further jeopardized the life prospects of millions in South America, Africa and Asia.

[29] The banner 'Teamsters and Turtles Together at Last!' was among the most memorable ones in Seattle (Cockburn and St. Clair 2000: 17). Albeit uneasy, this alliance is particularly notable in the context of the bitter 'jobs vs ecology' debates that have often pitted the green and labour movements against one another in the United States over the past few decades.

where migrant rights organizations (such as the Sans-papiers and the No One Is Illegal campaign) joined forces with Via Campesina, the global peasants' union, with regards to corporate agriculture's exploitation of an undocumented workforce; and Euro-American culture jammers, who specialize in resistance to advertising and the commercialization of public space, have linked up on occasion with unions and women's groups representing labourers in the global South who make many of the consumer goods sold in the North.

The latter coalition, which has itself given rise to the global anti-sweatshop movement, nicely illustrates the labour involved in constructing transnational solidarity from below. By learning from eyewitness accounts about the work conditions in Asian and South American factories churning out the garments and athletic shoes advertised and distributed around the globe, North American and European activists have forged links with civic associations in both hemispheres. Public information and protest campaigns (leafleting, picketing storefronts, counter-advertising, etc.) have retraced the underbelly of the global commodity chain that stretches from apparel and clothing stores to transnational corporations' affiliates and subcontractors, thereby connecting glittering products to the lives of workers employed in sweatshops, free trade zones and *maquiladoras*. Accordingly, the anti-sweatshop movement makes the case that, because they purchase these products and thus participate in the circuits of global capitalism, Euro-American consumers are bound to producers in the South whose socio-economic and civil rights must be protected (Klein 2000: 345–63; Young 2003).

None of the aforementioned coalitions is inherently stable or devoid of problems, since the labour of cosmopolitan solidarity demands continuous pursuit of the task of sustaining decentralizing tendencies and, simultaneously, an adequate level of convergence between different actors. The web form of the AGM thus represents an experiment with a mode of instituting political power that diffuses rather than concentrates the latter, with participatory democracy and the cultivation of public discourse among horizontally related civic associations acting as the principal forces of social integration – an experiment that has failed in some instances and achieved laudable outcomes in others. As such, the AGM's structural decentralization is a matter of both choice and necessity. At one level, participants in the AGM have deliberately set out to organize it against a strong, top-down executive, in order to try to avoid the bureaucratic-authoritarian dynamics that have plagued the history of many progressive political movements and parties (with their rigid divisions between leadership and rank-and-file members).[30] Within the ranks of the AGM, there is thus a marked preference for local self-management and grassroots initiatives stressing direct citizen involvement (e.g., participatory budgeting, cooperatives, neighbourhood councils), with coordinating bodies such as the World Social Forum and its regional equivalents serving to encourage the creation of transnational links – the nodes in the network – among groups from various parts of the world. In addition, the AGM's loose structure may enable civil society actors who do not hold identical positions to coalesce rapidly around particular events and issues (say, the Narmada Valley dam projects in India or the war in Iraq), and to adapt to changing circumstances and requirements (direct confrontation or the possibility of negotiations with authorities, for instance). However, as critics have pointed out, this 'hands off' approach is achieved at the price of a more solid organizational focus and of political effectiveness, since the AGM's demands have yet to impact meaningfully the formal decision-making arenas of global governance.

At another level, decentralization is a question of strategic necessity for the AGM. Given the sheer array of civic associations that participate in it and the sometimes disparate causes they represent (labour, feminism, environmentalism, indigenous rights, peace, anti-poverty, etc.),[31] the network form attempts to accommodate meaningful differences and minimize potentially divisive conflict.[32] Excessive concentration of power, prescription of an ideological outlook focusing on a 'primary' source of oppression at the expense of others – for instance, an anti-capitalism or environmentalism that ignores gendered forms of domination – or specification of a rigid programme through which to transform the existing world order would very likely threaten the viability of coalitions within the AGM. Hence, beyond a consensus about the ills of

[30] See Graeber (2002: 70–2), Notes from Nowhere (2003: 63–73) and Schönleitner (2003: 145–8). I am applying an argument proposed by Clastres, who claims that indigenous societies are self-consciously organized against a state rather than deprived of one because of supposed historical 'backwardness' (Clastres 1977 [1974]).

[31] A journalist's description of the composition of the 2004 Mumbai World Social Forum is evocative: 'At the forum, held for the first time in Asia (January 16–21), were professors from Tunisia, a Pakistani hard rock band, Irish nuns, and a woman wearing a sign reading "Australians for Peace".' (Ramesh 2004: 3)

[32] The Ninth Principle of the World Social Forum's Charter declares that it 'will always be a forum open to pluralism and to the diversity of activities and ways of engaging of the organizations and movements that decide to participate in it, as well as the diversity of genders, ethnicities, cultures, generations and physical capabilities, providing they abide by this Charter of Principles'. See www.wsfindia.org/charter.php (accessed 1 February 2004). The text of the Charter is also reprinted in Fisher and Ponniah (2003: 354–7). Of course, a gap exists between such principles and their actual implementation, yet the rhetorical commitment to the former is itself noteworthy.

neoliberal globalization, the degrees of political integration and direct collaboration between its constituent parts vary widely; they are generally highest among 'transnational advocacy networks' (Keck and Sikkink 1998), yet can extend well beyond these to incorporate broad-based alliances. Global campaigns against genetically modified foodstuffs, for example, have brought together the French Confédération Paysanne and the Indian Karnataka State Farmers' Association (Bové 2001: 93), while also drawing support from consumer protection groups and ecologists. The nodes in the AGM's network assemble and reassemble around precise issues and events, sometimes giving birth to novel communities of interest.

How does a web-like structure coordinate its numerous components? The AGM has adopted a set of horizontal organizational mechanisms designed to retain civic associations' grassroots independence while connecting them to one another in at least a minimal fashion. During meetings and fora, participants are organized in affinity groups, self-governing units composed of a small number of individuals (twenty or less) who support each other and are free to decide how and to what extent they will participate in specific forms of activity, as well as what coalitions they will join in the process. Each affinity group selects a 'spoke' who represents its members and is linked to others in spokescouncils, large public deliberative and decision-making assemblies. Whenever contentious decisional matters are raised within these assemblies, the spoke consults her or his affinity group, which takes a position that is then conveyed to the spokescouncil. Finally, a process of open debate and negotiation is initiated in order to encourage the assembly to reach a consensus.[33]

By no means are these procedures flawless, given that the objective of consensual decisional outcomes puts pressure on outliers and strong disagreements remain within the AGM. Among other things, this is why it has not yet been able to translate its critique of global neoliberalism into a coherent set of policy proposals for a different world order.[34] At the same time, the AGM's structural configuration attempts to balance the

[33] For a more detailed description of affinity groups and spokescouncils, see Graeber (2002: 71) and Notes from Nowhere (2003: 88, 215).

[34] For instance, a number of substantial differences have come to the fore in the World Social Forum. Should the latter's long-term objective be the formation of a world government or local self-management? What is the best means of achieving such an objective, reform of the world order or revolution (including armed struggle)? In the shorter term, should it encourage economic de-globalization (through the assertion of national sovereignty or de-linking), or greater insertion into the world economy? What is the role of political parties (which are formally banned from the World Social Forum) and NGOs *vis-à-vis* social movements? Should it primarily aim to formulate concrete policy proposals, or be a space for dialogue? On these questions and the relatively underdeveloped state of the AGM's policy proposals, see Bello (2002b), Brecher *et al.*

need to foster convergence of the different strands of the web with the right to dissent, the fact that participants ought not be coerced to adopt a position or commit an act with which they do not explicitly and freely agree (Graeber 2002: 70–1). In fact, I want to argue that this kind of open and decentralized process is more likely to yield sustainable and solid global alliances than top-down models of political authority and enforced unity; because it encourages collaboration, compromise and independence, it can minimize the risk of splintering off despite the fact that groups may not see eye to eye on everything.[35] Moreover, it can nurture a cosmopolitanism born out of a commitment to a dialogical widening of horizons, for individuals and groups must justify their positions to others, listen to and consider rival arguments, and thereby become exposed to a wide range of opinions and experiences out of which they can take better informed decisions and even discover previously unknown affinities and interests with other civic associations (Gilroy 2005: 67). Such outcomes are never guaranteed, of course, but they remain possible when cosmopolitan solidarity is understood as a perpetual process of construction and reconstruction of socio-political ties across borders.

The lived culture of an alternative globalization

Thus far in this chapter, we have seen how the labour of cosmopolitan solidarity can perform the task of reconciling egalitarian universalism and the recognition of cultural difference, and that of adopting decentralization without compromising the building of coalitions. Here, in the final section, I want to push these two insights further by examining how cultural pluralism and networked affinities can produce politically robust solidaristic bonds across space; the idea of a progressive political culture emerging out of global civil society is something that normative and institutional branches of cosmopolitanism, with their minimalist conception of transnational social relations, have barely touched upon. As discussed above, most normative cosmopolitans put forward principles of world citizenship and care for humankind that are weakly grounded in

(2000), Hardt (2002), Mertes (2002), Ramesh (2004), Sader (2002) and Schönleitner (2003). So far, these disagreements have been for the most part the subject of debate and negotiation rather than bitter splits and denunciations.

[35] One of the points of contention within the AGM concerns the tactics to pursue during a protest, namely, whether 'harder' direct action against security barricades or 'softer' marching around them is preferable. In response, organizers have sometimes set up coloured zones which participants are free to join according to the kind of strategy they deem most appropriate and useful. While not always effective, this solution has generally minimized bitter and divisive in-fighting between far and centrist Left forces. I would like to thank Augustine Park for drawing my attention to this phenomenon.

concrete, localized ties, given that such ties are to be transcended in the name of universalist commitments. For their part, institutional cosmopolitans either devise schemes of global governance focused on organizational design, or propose procedural norms to ensure the legitimacy of a democratic political culture. Under global conditions of normative and cultural plurality, minimalism is both a virtue (it ensures the respect of substantive differences) and a necessity (since no thicker agreement would be possible because of these differences).[36]

What accounts for the minimalist tone of such conceptions of cosmopolitan solidarity? The answer lies in their underappreciation of the sociocultural dimensions of collective existence, and more specifically, of the creativity of socio-political action through which groups and individuals weave transnational relations of reciprocity and togetherness. Normative and institutional brands of cosmopolitanism promote too narrow an understanding of global political culture, which in their eyes essentially consists of universal principles, international structures of governance and procedurally legitimate outcomes. Without denying that each of these elements is important, the idea of the work of global justice supplies a different perspective from which to underscore the significance of a cosmopolitan culture from below generating a web of solidaristic ties, themselves composed of intersecting ways of thinking and acting, values, beliefs, interests, narratives and symbols. This focus on global sociocultural practices should not be mistaken for a search for a uniform and totalizing cosmopolitan identity that would replace other layers of social experience or eliminate diverging conceptions of the good. Conversely, however, it does not treat a society or group's worldviews as internally homogeneous, discrete and static – and therefore secluded from the socio-political dynamic of the labour of cosmopolitan solidarity. Consequently, we should consider how contestations, expansions and transformations of different normative and political positions, by virtue of discursively mediated encounters between progressive global civil society participants, can give birth to a lived cosmopolitan culture made up of dense yet diverse sets of bonds of transnational mutuality.

To elaborate on this aspect of enactment of cosmopolitan solidarity, we can return to the idea of the AGM as a network of civil associations that is not pre-existing but constituted through their contestation of the established world order, and whose various constituencies (anti-poverty, feminist, labour, environmental, etc.) gradually come to form a series of

[36] Although Walzer is neither a proceduralist nor a cosmopolitan universalist, he has put forth an influential defence of moral thinness in international affairs and domestic thickness, or as he puts it, 'a thin universalism and a thick particularism' (Walzer 1994: 50).

criss-crossing and overlapping discursive spaces where the outlines of a more just globalization may emerge. Two dimensions of public dialogism come into play, since in addition to constructing this endogenous space by connecting progressive actors to one another, the AGM addresses itself and performs for an exogenous audience. This is done to widen the ranks of the AGM and draw support from ordinary citizens who may not be actively involved in it, as well as to participate in global public opinion formation. It is thus neither accidental nor trivial that many declarations emanating from the World Social Forum and other transnational civil society sites are rather grandiosely addressed to humankind and appeal to the peoples of the world, or that the AGM has developed public information campaigns to 'get its message out' among world leaders and their populations.

Because it stresses both democratic openness and agonism, an Arendtian perspective on political action is useful for our purposes. Indeed, for Arendt (1998 [1958]: 50), public realms foster ties among citizens by promoting unrestricted exchange of information and opinions, which anyone can assess and contest. Solidaristic relations within discursive communities grow out of debate and deliberation between various divergent positions, not – as is often assumed in certain communitarian arguments – from an original state of civic unanimity.[37] The cut and thrust of argumentation produces robust social relations between dialogical partners, who in the process of making their respective cases, explaining their stances and giving consideration to a range of other opinions being voiced, can develop an appreciation for them and be exposed to different realities. In other words, mutual recognition and a sense of togetherness can be nurtured in and through the communicative labour required for each party to justify its position and convince others of its merits, and in turn to try to understand their positions and be prepared to acknowledge better arguments on their part (Dean 1996: 28–32). But there is more to cosmopolitan solidarity than the formal exercise of deliberative democracy and the pursuit of rational-critical debate. Public discourse, in an Arendtian sense, is neither a purely cognitive activity nor one that is the preserve of institutional settings, since it can be undertaken in informal locations and during temporary events taking place within the fabric of civil societies (Arendt 1963; Calhoun 1997: 237).

[37] See Arendt (1963: 93–4; 1998 [1958]: 57) and Calhoun (1997; 2002: 292). Arendt contends that for the American Founding Fathers, the public realm's purpose would disappear if all citizens were of the same opinion because it would not be necessary for discursive exchange to take place (Arendt 1963: 93). Similarly, she views absolute unanimity as unhealthy to the democratic life of any people, for it breeds a political conformism that disengages citizens from public activity and speech.

By no means does the AGM embody this Arendtian-cum-Habermasian ideal of publicness, yet it occasionally approximates some of the features described here by developing a political culture according to which global civil society actors are becoming involved in overlapping and somewhat fractious communities of public debate and political action. Public arenas like the World Social Forum and the 2001 Peoples' Summit of the Americas in Québec City are more often than not the outcomes of struggles to create dialogical realms and temporary zones where subordinate social groups can voice their demands and opinions without being subjected to the same levels of state or corporate control as they otherwise would. This situation vividly contrasts with the kind of information available from mass media outlets owned by private conglomerates, as well as with the lack of decisional transparency from states, transnational corporations and international financial institutions.[38] Similarly, through the AGM, several civil society actors are voicing their demands, narrating their experiences and stating their opinions in ways that can cultivate a loosely knit collective identity and sense of belonging.[39] Such a dynamic is sustained by a growing communication infrastructure, made up of community and independent media outlets that pepper the globe.[40] And although the Internet is a contested political terrain, it remains an essential tool for organizing and exchanging

[38] In fact, the growing perception of the limited democratic character of the current world order is precisely what mobilizes the AGM's constituencies. For instance, the 1999 protests in Seattle were largely fuelled by the secrecy and 'closed-door' procedures that surrounded the World Trade Organization's negotiations at the time.

[39] On publics as sources of solidarity, see Arendt (1998 [1958]: 50) and Calhoun (2002: 287–95); on the World Social Forum's role as a public space, see Bello (2002b: 81–2). For instances of specific policy proposals resulting from the World Social Forum's participatory decision-making processes (on issues such as war, food security, the environment, AIDS, Third World debt and global migration), see Fisher and Ponniah (2003). Participatory budgeting, a policy pioneered by the Workers' Party municipal government of Porto Alegre, Brazil, and subsequently adopted by other Left-leaning city administrations around the world, represents a local example of this idea. According to its model, the process of drawing up a jurisdiction's budget is turned over to the citizens themselves via popular assemblies that encourage public debate about spending priorities and particular consideration for the well-being of subordinate social groups (Sader 2002: 91). While participatory budgeting can be contentious, it combines the virtues of decisional transparency and solidarity-building when framed in progressive terms.

[40] Two of the best examples of this alternative communication infrastructure are the Indymedia network, which is made up of local outfits in major cities and regions around the world, and *Le Monde diplomatique*, a monthly French newspaper that has played an important role in the creation of the World Social Forum and currently has sixty-eight foreign editions (and is published in the following languages: French, German, English, Arabic, Catalan, Chinese, Spanish, Esperanto, Portuguese, Greek, Italian, Japanese, Norwegian, Farsi, Russian, Serbian, Czech, Afrikaans, Bulgarian, Korean, Finnish, Hungarian, Polish, Romanian, Slovenian and Croatian). For the former, see www.indymedia.org; for the latter, see www.monde-diplomatique.fr/int.

information within the AGM. Without it, global days of action such as the 15 February 2003 marches against the war in Iraq – which were predominantly coordinated and publicized on all continents through electronic resources (websites, email listservs, etc.) – would scarcely have been conceivable.[41]

Apart from its roots in public discourse, a robust cosmopolitanism is coming into its own today because participation in the AGM is underpinned by intersecting frameworks of interpretation, symbolic systems and sets of political and normative beliefs. A vital aspect of the lived culture of alternative globalization, then, is the invention and performance of distinctive modes of political action and narrative that become familiar to participants in the AGM and identifiable by external audiences. By virtue of being repeated over time and transmitted to others, acts of protest and forms of speech (the marching and storming of barricades, the chanting of slogans, the speeches and advancement of certain arguments, etc.) become ritualized, supplying civic associations with a repertoire of strategies deployed in a variety of settings, from major events on the world stage (such as a G8 summit of world leaders) to localized struggles for basic needs (e.g., opposition to the privatization of electricity and water services in South African townships).[42] The AGM has aimed to erect this repertoire of practices as symbolic markers of resistance to global neoliberalism that affirm their constituencies' vision of a different world order, while signalling to ordinary citizens and world leaders that the current global state of affairs is neither necessary nor acceptable. Conversely, the risk of routinization that is at the root of the recent flagging of enthusiasm for the World Social Forum among some of its participants means that the AGM is trying constantly to reinvent itself and its ritualized processes.

In addition, the AGM's cosmopolitanism from below taps into the temporal dimensions of social life. Playing a socially and culturally integrative role across geographical borders, participation in gatherings at regular intervals enables actors to share common experiences, debate and collaborate whenever it is feasible in the staging of events and campaigns. And in spite of the AGM's recent formation, it has striven to develop a collective memory laden with dense iconography: the image of a masked Subcomandante Marcos and a band of indigenous insurgents (the EZLN) emerging out of the jungles of Chiapas on 1 January 1994 – the

[41] Of course, the Internet cuts both ways, as it is a prime recruitment and linking device for racist political parties and social movements, as well as for religious fundamentalists of all stripes.

[42] This is a phenomenon identified as 'diffusion' (Tarrow 2005).

date of the North American Free Trade Agreement's implementation – to declare 'Ya Basta!' to an unsuspecting world; the 'five days that shook the world' (Cockburn and St. Clair 2000) in late November and early December 1999, during the 'Battle in Seattle' that awoke many North Americans to the mass movement for an alternative globalization; the tearing down of the fence that separated protesters and citizens from official delegates and politicians during the Sixth Summit of the Americas in Québec City in April 2001; the annual World Social Forum, originally timed to coincide with (and thus act as the popular counterpart to) the World Economic Forum in Davos; the death of Carlo Giuliani, an Italian protestor killed by police during protests against the Genoa G8 Summit in July 2001;[43] and the massive 15 February 2003 marches on all continents against the US-led invasion of Iraq. Instances such as these have rapidly become part of the lore of the AGM, quasi-mythological elements that participants keep alive and revive during each new struggle. They form a mnemonic inventory that is 'fired up' during moments of socio-political intensity, and also sustain a sense of participation in a collective enterprise even when activists return to the course of their daily lives.

None the less, if the labour of cosmopolitan solidarity produced by the AGM is to move beyond the latter's confines, it will need to entrench itself among broader publics and ordinary citizens who may not be politically active or committed. This is where aesthetic cosmopolitanism is worthy of attention, in that it can nurture the formation of global imagined communities sharing an appreciation for forms of artistic expression and cultural practices from the four corners of the planet.[44] Aesthetic cosmopolitanism incorporates such broadly defined categories as world music, literature and cinema (including hybrid genres), in addition to the Euro-American phenomena of alternative overseas travel and backpacker counter-cultures (the Lonely Planet and Rough Guide audiences, so to speak). These trends should be viewed with a certain scepticism: they are invariably selective in determining what and who is worthy (or unworthy) of attention; they may encourage homogenization of distinctive styles and lineages into a cosmopolitan mish-mash, as well as superficial and fleeting encounters with exoticized cultural realities (the multicultural 'song and dance' routines, the meals at so-called

[43] At the World Social Forum in Porto Alegre, a Carlo Giuliani Plaza was created to commemorate his death – an interesting instance of the AGM's work of spatial memorialization.

[44] I am indebted to Philip Smith for many of the ideas in this paragraph, including his insistence on the importance of aesthetic cosmopolitanism.

'ethnic' restaurants, etc.); they require commodification of artistic products and are filtered through consumptive activities; and they tend mostly to represent elite preferences, those of North Atlantic groups with comparatively high levels of economic and/or cultural capital (the radical chic of Western *bhangra* or *rai aficianados*, for instance). Despite this, aesthetic cosmopolitanism should not be dismissed out of hand, for it holds a certain potential to engender an ethos of openness and substantive engagement with a multitude of ways of being in the world. We should not underestimate the significance of expanding worldviews by acknowledging the accomplishments of various civilizations, or of acquiring a sense of shared aesthetic appreciation with distant others. Moreover, under specific circumstances, aesthetic appreciation can be converted into political commitment by drawing some citizens into supporting the vision of a world where cultural diversity and distributive justice are jointly realized.[45]

The labour of cosmopolitan solidarity, then, is composed through the weaving of transnational webs of sociality and normativity sustained by structures of feeling, aesthetic preferences, substantive conceptions of the good life, as well as frameworks of interpretation and symbolic systems. Through certain forms of travel and cross-cultural contact, appreciation of different artistic traditions, or direct involvement in human rights causes and struggles such as those of the AGM, what is emerging among some segments of global civil society is a distinctive constellation of socio-cultural practices, beliefs and norms that flesh out the project of a just world order while fostering a sense of responsibility to humankind as a whole. This planetary consciousness contains an ethical kernel, for progressive global civil society participants can expand their understandings of human capabilities and of the necessary conditions for a fully realized life, as well as of the many forms of injustice and structures of domination in the world today; for instance, North Americans may learn about the aspirations, demands and forms of discrimination faced by the Dalit caste in India or the French *sans-papiers* (undocumented immigrants, primarily from the Maghreb and sub-Saharan Africa), while these two groups may gain knowledge of each other's plights and of that of North American indigenous populations.

Thus, far from being fully acquired or formed prior to public dialogue, socio-political action or cross-cultural exchange, personal subjectivities

[45] As Cohen (2001: 291) puts it: 'The astonishing successes of Bob Geldof's Live Aid and the Human Rights Now world tour show that universal altruistic messages can motivate wide audiences. Geldof's vision should not be denigrated: music is a symbolic vehicle to bypass conventional structures and reach potential supporters with disposable income, and a reservoir of undirected passion not usually targeted by charitable organizations.'

and collective identities are dynamic and constantly evolving realities constituted through such processes (Allen 1999; Calhoun 2002; Dean 1996). Some of the actors involved in the AGM are cognitively reframing their own experiences of eroding standards of living, environmental degradation or discrimination into a general narrative about the ravages of neoliberal globalization. Apparently isolated events are incorporated into this narrative and consequently invested with great symbolic meaning, to the extent that occurrences as different as the Zapatista uprising and a London street festival organized by Reclaim the Streets can be recognized as expressions of resistance. And the encounter with other ways of life and value-orientations can widen citizens' cultural and political horizons by resituating them within a global context.[46] This does not imply that the aforementioned Javanese female factory workers or landless male Brazilian peasants can or ought to shed their particularities, but that they can grasp how their specific plight is structurally parallel and connected to that of other groups around the world.

What should not be overlooked is the ludic aspect of the practice of constructing solidarity beyond borders, the fact that aesthetic and political cosmopolitanisms can be brought together under favourable circumstances. Large-scale events such as the Live 8 concerts and the Make Poverty History campaign come readily to mind, yet more effective and sustained local festivals and fundraising initiatives to support social justice and humanitarian projects are multiplying in Euro-American civil societies. For its part, the AGM has tried to foster a carnivalesque spirit, celebrating collective rebellion against neoliberalism by valuing aestheticized forms of protest and various sorts of playfully subversive, agitprop- and situationist-like performances that can join participants together to communally design and experiment with ways of thinking and acting that go beyond conventional modes of political expression.[47] In addition, street festivals and similar activities represent performances that civic associations stage for external audiences in order to reach out to members

[46] The history of the Council of Canadians is instructive in this respect. Originally a grassroots nationalist organization formed to oppose the Canada–US Free Trade Agreement, it now has a distinctively transnational hue (Klein 2001: 81).

[47] For instance, under the cry of 'Capitalism is boring!', the 20 April 2001 protest in Québec City during the Summit of the Americas was dubbed a 'Carnival Against Capitalism'; it featured groups such as the Society for Creative Anachronism and the Medieval Bloc, which wielded a 'weapon' consisting of a giant catapult lobbing stuffed toy animals over the fence. Other AGM protests have included the Radical Cheerleaders, the Revolutionary Anarchist Clown Bloc, and the Pink Bloc, consisting of individuals dressed as fairies and ballerinas. An important player here is the Reclaim the Streets movement, which organizes street parties in many cities around the world (Graeber 2002: 66–7; Klein 2000: 311–23; Notes from Nowhere 2003: 50–61).

of the general public who do not participate in protests, but may be interested and willing to join aesthetically pleasurable and culturally innovative activities with a political dimension. Through such politico-aesthetic carnivals that interrupt everyday life's regimentation and disciplining of bodies and minds, ordinary citizens can temporarily experience for themselves some of the characteristics of the kind of egalitarian and pluralist social order that the AGM has in mind. Hence, the acts of sharing these sorts of ludic public spaces and moments with others, of discussing matters of common concern with them, or yet again of being in a crowd that marches through the streets of a city, can all cultivate relations of collaboration and mutuality (Hardt 2002: 114; Mertes 2002; Schönleitner 2003: 140).

Put slightly differently, the practice of cosmopolitan solidarity is sustained by socio-political creativity. While the AGM cannot be simplistically identified as a new vanguard, the motto of the World Social Forum ('Another world is possible') is interesting to the extent that it underscores the act of radically putting into question the structural and ideological bases of the neoliberal world order. Accordingly, in claiming that the current rash of policies pursued and promoted by international economic organizations, captains of industry and certain governments (privatization, structural adjustment programmes, the deregulation of trade and financial flows, etc.) are neither self-evident nor beneficial to most of the world's peoples, progressive civic associations propose ways that the world order could be organized differently, to work toward large-scale socio-economic redistribution and the recognition of cultural pluralism – albeit without being able to arrive at a coherent and succinct programme for the precise shape of an alternative globalization.

Conclusion

As I suggested at the beginning of this chapter, the question of solidarity beyond borders has become a pressing one because of a concatenation of factors: an unbridled neoliberalism aiming to level all substantial differences interfering with the unregulated circulation of capital and the achievement of a single world market while concurrently reinscribing pervasive and structurally derived domestic and transnational socio-economic inequalities; a post-Cold War revival of essentialized ethno-religious conflicts and the growing popularity of 'clash of civilizations' scenarios; and the multiplication and intensification of cross-territorial flows and movements across the planet, often summed up by the notion of globalization. Thus the appeal of cosmopolitan discourses, which offer potentially productive modes of engagement with these tendencies and, by extension, novel ways of thinking about solidarity. Some thinkers, termed normative cosmopolitans, support the idea of an enlargement of our moral communities to embrace the whole of humankind, while other cosmopolitans of a more institutional bent are devising models for the reorganization of global governance structures or appropriate deliberative mechanisms for a democratically legitimate international political consensus.

These are important contributions, with which I am substantially in accord, yet their normative or formalist interpretations of the question of solidarity need to be supplemented by a consideration of cosmopolitanism from below, that is to say, the labour of constituting and enacting global ties of mutuality via the performance of specific socio-political tasks and the confrontation with corresponding perils. Using the AGM as a catalyst, then, this chapter has argued that cosmopolitan solidarity represents a mode of practice of global justice characterized – like its four other counterparts – by patterns of dialogical, public and transnational social action.

For progressive actors in global civil society, the first task of cosmopolitan solidarity consists of articulating and reconciling demands for socio-economic redistribution with the recognition of cultural pluralism. As an alternative to egalitarian assimilationism, a cosmopolitanism from below can thereby foreground a kind of global redistributive justice that seeks to incorporate a multiplicity of voices and experiences into a transformative socio-political project. Following from this recognition of differences, and in order to counter radical particularists' defence of cultural and political monism, entities like the AGM can pursue the second task of cosmopolitan solidarity: the construction of networked social ties that do not require activating claims about a pre-established unity with, or identical characteristics to, others. Instead, solidaristic labour aims to form transnational webs in which persons and groups pragmatically foster and constantly reconfigure nodes of affinity and converging interests. Under the best circumstances and despite its fragility, a web may be conducive to the creation of cosmopolitan bonds because of its decentralized, multi-scaled and relatively horizontal character; indeed, the negotiation of common ground among participants and of a sense of care for distant others can only result from processes of public discussion and debate through which differing positions can become mutually intelligible.

The third task constitutive of the labour of cosmopolitan solidarity is the cultivation of robust and rich bonds across borders, so as to overcome the belief that cosmopolitanism can only consist of a minimalist and formal universal consensus, leaving ways of life, aesthetic preferences and value-orientations outside its purview. By examining how certain progressive civic associations and ordinary citizens are engaging in publicly dialogical and creative political and aesthetic practices, we can obtain clues as to how thicker cosmopolitan identities may emerge out of a lived culture of alternative globalization. The exchange of opinions and deliberation among members of the AGM, the participation in ritual performances that activate shared temporal and spatial experiences and the ethos of openness to and appreciation of a wide range of forms of cultural expression can all produce a more substantive and grounded cosmopolitanism.

Of course, none of this is to proclaim that the development of these kinds of transnational relations of mutuality out of the progressive strands of a still brittle global civil society is readily accomplished, nor even that the AGM is an ideal manifestation of the practice of cosmopolitan solidarity. As argued throughout this book, the perils noted for each mode of practice of global justice are constitutive of it; consequently, cultural assimilation, political fragmentation and social thinness will persist and require perpetual engagement in solidaristic labour. The determination to recognize cultural and socio-economic differences among groups and individuals will always come face-to-face with vocal calls to unify them under a single, generic banner ('we have to leave our particularities behind in order to become good cosmopolitans'). As for the enactment of a decentred and networked solidarity, it depends upon the ongoing ability and willingness of progressive global civil society actors to negotiate points of intersection between their different political causes and stances, without this pluralism producing an incoherent muddle or deep cleavages that splinter groups off from one another (Tarrow 2005). Finally, the lived culture of alternative globalization has yet to produce a significantly thick and mainstream cosmopolitan identity, one that could be 'upwardly' institutionalized to impact the current configuration of the world order.

More concretely, a host of questions and problems remain. If the World Social Forum, say, was to eventually become the blueprint for a global peoples' parliament, would it be able to retain its character as a relatively free and egalitarian space of informal dialogue and negotiation? What precise set of policies would the AGM want to implement domestically and internationally, and which ones would be more effective in beginning to repair the devastation left behind by neoliberalism? How will the AGM insert itself into existing global structures and attract greater numbers of ordinary citizens, when many (especially in North America and Europe) perceive it less as a broad movement of peoples than a small, violent and incoherent rabble? How readily will aesthetic cosmopolitanism translate into lasting political support for struggles against global injustices? In the process of thickening, the ties that bind progressive members of global civil society will have to be porous and fluid enough to incorporate an ever-widening chorus of voices. Only greater popular participation and support will enable such a global civil society legitimately to embody the aspirations of the marginalized and pose a credible alternative to neoliberal globalization.

Clearly, these are all challenges whose seriousness and persistence we would be foolhardy to dismiss. Like other modes of practice of global justice, cosmopolitan solidarity perpetually works through a series of perils without fully accomplishing the tasks that constitute it, which remain incomplete and partially realized. Yet I would hasten to add that this need not be perceived as signifying the intrinsic impossibility of solidarity without bounds, but rather as precisely that which defines the latter as arduous and contingent labour created through processes of socio-political struggle, public discourse and cultural exploration. If cosmopolitanism is to represent something beyond a set of abstract norms or institutional arrangements, it will be articulated and expanded from below by progressive actors grounded in a variety of locales and committed to a vision of a just world order. As such, it offers a vital resource to resist rival imaginaries that threaten to engulf the globe in our era, those of human beings as isolated individuals solely concerned with economic self-maximization or as belonging to essentialized and inherently hostile religious or ethno-racial communities. In its attempt to transnationally concretize redistribution and recognition, then, the practice of cosmopolitan solidarity stands as both the underpinning of the work of global justice and its culmination.

Conclusion: Enacting a critical cosmopolitanism

Toward a substantive conception of global justice

In the preceding chapters, I have put forth a conception of the work of global justice as a substantive alternative to, and line of critique of, the formalist bent of much of the institutional, legal and philosophical literature on human rights. While useful in many regards, formalism supports a logic of attribution of human rights from above, whereby the latter are understood as entitlements prescribed and granted to citizens by official institutions (namely, states and international organizations). What results is a juridification of socio-political action, which formalists equate with or view as principally directed toward legal entrenchment (in national and supra-national constitutions, multilateral treaties, etc.) and institutional recognition of human rights; in other words, from this perspective, struggles for global justice aim first and foremost to bolster legal-political structures and principles that can advance or protect socio-economic and civil-political rights around the world. As I have claimed throughout this book, such a stance reifies human rights by reducing them to things legally and institutionally allocated to subjects according to processes that seemingly operate above their heads. Consequently, these rights are abstracted and divorced from the practices of agents in national and global civil societies, who are engaged in struggles to bear witness, forgive, prevent, assist and cultivate relations of mutuality with others, and in so doing, are enacting global justice through ethico-political labour.

Formalism effectively constrains or narrows down emancipatory projects' field of possibilities (Brown 2004), since it frames or translates political struggles in juridified terms and assesses their legitimacy by virtue of their capacity to be inserted into and contribute to the officially sanctioned legal and institutional infrastructure of human rights. Thus overlooked or marginalized is a vast array of kinds of socio-political action performed by groups and persons who may not seek official sanctioning or juridical inscription, yet are still participating in the work of global justice and its affiliated modes of practice. To take but one example, despite the fact that tasks of which the labour of bearing witness is composed (voice, interpretation, empathy, remembrance, and prevention) mostly fall outside of legal or institutional frameworks *per se*, they play essential roles in undermining structural and situational injustices in many parts of the globe. Moreover, formalists tend to favour an additive approach to global justice (which becomes a matter of trying to grant more rights to more individuals and, conversely, to reduce the numbers of persons suffering from rights violations and of rights being violated), while taking for granted or leaving unexamined structural factors that underpin socio-economic and civil-political injustices: national and global structures that create relations of domination as well as massive inequalities in the distribution of symbolic and material resources and in agents' capacities to realize whatever human rights are formally recognized. In the end, then, formalism poorly grasps processes of radically democratic participation in the making of global justice, which is more often than not produced and sustained by non-legalistic or extra-institutional claims, discourses and forms of action that may well redefine human rights beyond their established bounds.

In developing a substantive critical theory of global justice, I have sought deliberately to decentre legalistic and institutionalist frameworks in order to shift the focus from rights *per se* to socio-political and ethical action. Indeed, patterns of normatively oriented social relations – or more precisely, the specific tasks and perils defining them – constitute the core of global justice, with the juridification of human rights standing as but one route among others through which to alter systematically existing configurations of power in emancipatory directions. The notion of the work of global justice is designed to underscore the difficult labour of confronting manifestations of structural and situational violence and injustice at both socio-economic and civil-political levels, and to urge us to dereify human rights by perceiving them as components of the modes of practice that animate them in civil society arenas and thereby give them political and ethical traction. Critical substantivism simultaneously examines how concrete and particular socio-political struggles at different scales enact modes of practice of global justice, and how the latter structure and articulate the former. Hence, it opens up human rights thinking to projects and expressions of resistance that lie outside of its formalist conventions, and in fact frequently lead to demands for the structural transformation of the very legal apparatus and officially recognized institutions that produce human rights if and when these are found to sustain mechanisms of subordination.

Strongly stated, human rights only matter to the extent that agents put them into practice via forms of socio-political and ethical action that challenge relations of domination and contribute to systemic change, thereby protecting persons and groups from mass, severe and structural injustices or, more affirmatively, contributing to meeting human needs and making human capacities flourish. Further, considering the ever-widening gap between the rhetorical presence of human rights on the one hand, and the reality of severe and pervasive violations of such rights in the world on the other, formalist arguments appear to have reached the threshold of their effectivity. If institutional, procedural and legal build-up continues to be necessary, the realization and enforceability of human rights depend at least as much on the capacities of civil society participants to perform tasks advancing the work of global justice. Hitherto neglected by human rights scholars, it is the composition of these modes of practice that I have wanted to highlight and analyse. In doing so, what is brought out is the constant instituting of global justice, its creativity and remaking through the identification of previously unsuspected modalities of power and the emergence of new socio-political projects, claims and forms of struggle that are located beyond the instituted limits of juridified human rights, and thereby thicken the latter in the direction of structural change of the world order.

Centred on the study of the normative and socio-political labour that undergirds global justice, this sort of substantive thickening is most fruitfully achieved by employing critical social theory. As I argued in the introduction to this book, this distinctive paradigm can address the formalist shortcomings of normativism as well as of institutionalism and legalism, without curtailing its scope of inquiry to empiricist descriptions of already existing human rights campaigns and actors present in national and global civil societies or falling into the trap of an analytical monism that fails to connect these seemingly disparate campaigns and actors into broader configurations of social relations. Consequently, critical theorizing gains insights about global justice from its articulation of analytical and normative dimensions of the question, that is to say, from its attempts to understand the current processes pursued by emancipatory socio-political forces and what they should accomplish to bring about a just world order. The focus on modes of practice is intended to concretize this dual orientation by examining how patterns of socio-political action are contributing to the work of global justice (the existing configurations of social relations) as well as what the normative horizons and boundaries of these practices ought to be (the tasks to be performed and perils to be confronted if a just world order is to be realized). As such, the constellation of five modes of practice, with their corresponding tasks and perils forming the social labour out of which global justice exists, represents the key analytical object of a substantive and critical framework. This

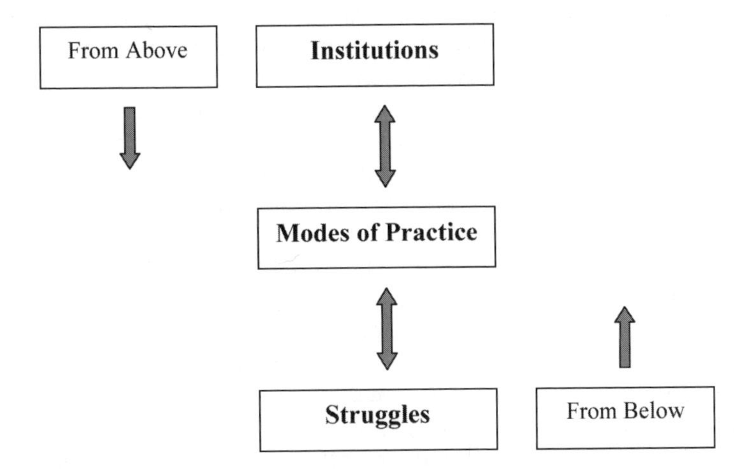

Figure 5. The levels of the work of global justice.

framework is no less sceptical of a voluntarist belief in the fact that any and all struggles and subjects have the intrinsic capacity to produce structural changes than it is of a structuralist determinism viewing such struggles and subjects as wholly derived from or generated by large-scale institutional factors; the work of global justice is neither the outcome of an actor's pure will and consciousness, nor of the operations of national and transnational structures.

As Figure 5 illustrates, modes of practice are the lynchpins of the work of global justice, the points of contact, transmission and mutual influence between national and global institutions (transnational corporations, states, international organizations, etc.), at one level, and civil society struggles (protests, public claims and campaigns, demands for prosecution, etc.), at the other. To begin, modes of practice have a direct 'upward' impact on the established social order in that the latter's degrees and kinds of reproduction and change are heavily influenced by the socio-political and normative labour accomplished through patterns of action. Furthermore, these same modes of practice serve to filter global justice struggles toward national and transnational institutions, since civil society actors tend to try to organize such struggles into publicly recognized configurations of social relations, with resource leverage and organizational networks, in order to be structurally effective by putting pressure on institutions. Hence, the first effect of this 'upward' pressure is institutionalization, whereby the enactment of various modes of practice of global justice results in the selective incorporation of national and global civil society demands within the existing official political and economic infrastructure; this would include reforms to key institutional policies and outlooks (such as the World Bank's purported move from economic growth to poverty reduction as the guiding principle of development), the legal enforcement of existing human rights by governments and multilateral organizations, as well as the recognition and inclusion of previously ignored rights into covenants and treaties (e.g., recent efforts to negotiate an Optional Protocol to the International Covenant on Economic, Social and Cultural Rights). The second possible 'upward' outcome consists of the structural transformation of existing institutions or their replacement by a new system of global economic and political governance. Here, the performance of modes of practice of global justice would help to foster an alternative world order based on principles of participatory democracy and oversight, as well as a major North–South and domestic redistribution of symbolic and material resources (through, for instance, international parliamentary bodies with civil society representation, and collective ownership and management of production).

Still referring to Figure 5, it should be clear that modes of practice do not function in a vacuum, but rather are buffered from above and below in the work of global justice. Current institutions exercise 'downward' pressure by shaping the field of possibilities for patterns of socio-political and normative labour (that is, the extent and persistence of perils faced and the kinds of tasks that are necessary), and the scale at which this labour takes place.[1] Additionally, modes of practice can become conduits through which these institutions affect several key factors in human rights struggles: the capacities of participants to have access to and mobilize resources to support their causes, the tactics they adopt and the avenues open to them in pursuit of their objectives (e.g., whether legal prosecution or public shaming is an option, and which is more likely to succeed in a particular situation), and the kinds and degrees of institutionalization or structural transformation that they achieve. From below, socio-political struggles interact with modes of practice in complex ways, for actors tend to channel and aggregate their claims and discourses toward patterns of social action characterized by modularity and spatio-temporal transferability – so that, for example, a campaign urging humanitarian responses to a case of mass famine be viewed by the general public and decision-makers

[1] For example, as was mentioned in some of the chapters, a 'boomerang pattern' may occur: civil society groups can decide to reroute their campaigns from a local or national stage to a global one if their domestic governments ignore or oppose their demands, or more, become actively involved in suppressing such groups themselves (Keck and Sikkink 1998).

as a familiar element of the labour of transnational aid because it performs tasks and confronts perils that have existed in similar situations in the past. Conversely, when cumulated and channelled in specific directions, struggles from below represent the political capillaries that feed each mode of practice, as progressive civil society elements and the forms of human rights action that they pursue supply the work of global justice with whatever sort of institutional traction it can muster. And if a sufficient number of civil society forces 'on the ground' give birth to clusters of human rights activism outside of the already existing constellation of modes of practice of global justice, this constellation may be expanded with the invention of new practices; a case in point would be the status that foresight has acquired over the last decade in the face of a perception of heightened risk, which stands in contrast to its near-invisibility in earlier renditions of human rights and whose current standing is redefining what constitutes global justice.

As briefly indicated above, one of the keys to a substantive theory of global justice is to view its practices as normatively and politically instituting. Whereas formalism reduces such practices to their juridical and institutional dimensions, that is to say, to how they statically fit into already established human rights regimes and contribute to national and transnational human rights infrastructures, I want to claim that the work of global justice is productive of the field of human rights itself and that practices are thereby simultaneously constitutive of and constituted by human rights institutions (from above) and struggles (from below). In other words, modes of practices are processes of permanent invention of social relations, searching to generate new structural arrangements and ethical principles as well as different kinds of political action connected to global justice – including the perpetual interrogation of existing human rights laws, organizations, actors and strategies to assess their constraining or stagnating effects on emancipatory labour. Accordingly, even the performance of a given mode of practice of global justice in a particular setting does not passively reproduce previously instituted socio-political relations and norms, since its enactment modifies the structures and struggles to which it is bound and may expand the project of global justice.

In the previous chapters, I have stressed a number of analytical features of the five modes of practice under consideration. Among them is the fact that they form a constellation, a coherent ensemble that captures the varied dimensions of an alternative globalization, yet whose components should be grasped together if a comprehensive picture of the work of global justice is to emerge. Similarly, these overlapping modes of practice are co-constitutive, for engaging in the labour that underpins each of them establishes the necessary conditions for others to be possible; for instance, bearing witness to civil-political and socio-economic injustices lays the groundwork for eventually forgiving those who perpetuated them, preventing their reoccurrence, assisting persons suffering from them and forging bonds of solidarity with such persons. Hence, a mutual build-up of the effectiveness of, and complementarity between, the different modes of practice exists (e.g., bearing witness to the suffering of people living with HIV/AIDS can contribute to cultivating a sense of solidarity with them, and vice versa).

Finally, this book has sought to combine synchronic and diachronic perspectives on global justice. Synchronically, I have underscored the 'modularity' of each mode of practice, which is composed of a repertoire of identifiable tasks performed and perils encountered at specific moments and places, yet diffused to other settings where human rights actors engage in similar patterns of socio-political and normative labour (Tarrow 2005). At the same time, the notion of the work of global justice is intended to underscore its diachronic character, the fact that the diffusion of a mode of practice across the globe signifies not so much mimetic reproduction of it but rather its appropriation and creative adaptation to suit specific local and national circumstances. Likewise, what we are observing is the multiplication of 'worksites' (Balibar 2004 [2001]) of global justice and the pluralization of forms of action framed in terms of human rights, to the extent that the labour supporting an alternative globalization is Sisyphean in nature: always already incomplete and in process of being made and remade anew. Global justice, then, is not a teleological end-point – the predetermined culmination of the necessary progress of human rights over time through the transcendence of the perils of each mode of practice – but a laborious and imperfect working-through without finality.

Against human rights blackmail

To my mind, a substantive critical theory of global justice refuses to play a game of intellectual blackmail according to which participants must either give unqualified support to claims made in the name of human rights lest they be deemed anti-democratic or indifferent to human suffering, or yet again wholly condemn the entire edifice of human rights to avoid charges of a naïvely idealistic, or even malevolent, liberalism. This Manichean logic sustains a politically ontologizing vision of human rights, whereby the latter are believed to contain a determinate political essence as either intrinsically and completely liberating or oppressive. By contrast, I want to contend that the relevant question is not whether one is for or against human rights *per se* – the short answer being 'it depends' on what effects and in whose interests this moral grammar is deployed – but rather how we can perform a deontologizing and politicizing turn that understands and evaluates them as socio-historical constructs produced through, and productive of, local, national and global modalities of power. Being situated on the contested and antagonistic terrains of political struggle and public discourse, human rights projects are contingent and perilous; they carry no given truths or preordained outcomes that would somehow transcend the normative and socio-political contexts of their deployment. Their substance is unstable, being constantly under dispute and remade by virtue of how they insert themselves into existing structures and how they are enacted by groups and persons in particular circumstances. Concretely, then, what matters are the effects of civil society debates and campaigns concerning human rights (from below) and of the institutionalization and juridification of human rights (from above) on the work of global justice; in what measure do such developments assist progressive agents in accomplishing the tasks underpinning modes of practice of global justice, or in sustaining their corresponding perils?

This kind of social constructivist and politicizing vision undercuts one side of the politically ontologizing blackmail of human rights discourse, which portrays them as inherently laudable because they transcend power to enter into the rarefied air of pure morality. Human rights would thereby represent an 'anti-political' and 'post-ideological' stance beyond the conventional Left–Right cleavages, one that supposedly stands for humankind as such by being solely concerned with preventing suffering and protecting the innocent or vulnerable against injustices; declaring that it refuses to 'play politics' with human lives, this stance wants to convert itself into a moralizing position above politics. However, as critics have convincingly demonstrated (Brown 2004: 453; Zizek 2005: 126), it actually marks an 'anti-political politics' that employs a rhetorical strategy trading on the moral standing of humanitarianism in order to pre-empt or disqualify any questioning of the motives of those invoking human rights and the policies or broader socio-political visions that they advocate. Who, after all, would want to be characterized as an opponent of, or apathetic toward, human rights? A substantive critical theory of global justice allows us to problematize this sort of moral ontologization by being vigilant with regards to the possible appropriation or instrumentalization of human rights to justify, or even obscure the pursuit of, a variety of projects on the world stage (principally, Western neo-imperialism, neoliberal capitalism or manufactured civilizational clashes). We need only refer to the recent appearance of hawkish, neoconservative versions of the doctrine of humanitarian intervention, which by selectively favouring the use of military force against certain states in the name of human rights, convert the latter into means of legitimation of Euro-American hegemony and 'swords of empire' (Bartholomew and Breakspear 2004; Kurasawa 2006).

If a starry-eyed perception of human rights is highly dubious, so too is its opposite in the politically ontologizing game of human rights blackmail – namely, the assertion that, far from being simply a possibility among others, the instrumental appropriation described above reveals the very essence of and underlying truth about humanitarianism. Following this line of thinking, human rights function as ideological devices through which capitalist globalization and Western military interventionism can be made to appear valid (or at least palatable to liberals), veils that distort or conceal the actual imperatives of a world system structured by the *realpolitik* of national self-interest and economic exploitation. Accordingly, to believe that human rights stand for anything beyond maintaining the West's domination (by intervening or threatening to intervene in countries of the global South whenever it may prove strategically useful) and spreading the neoliberal mantra of free trade (that is, facilitating the unregulated circulation of capital across borders and the unlimited access to an international pool of cheap labour-power) is to fall prey to the worst excesses of idealism. Often following in the footsteps of Marx's *On the Jewish Question*, critics assert that human rights under a capitalist mode of production are but abstract entitlements whose proper function is to protect and entrench private property and guarantee formal political freedom and equality, while leaving the material bases of subordination and exploitation untouched. Further, the implication is that liberal individualism represents the inalienable core of human rights, which cannot but support a thin conception of negative freedom whereby self-maximizing and monadic subjects are 'empowered' to make unimpeded choices (about who to vote for on occasion, but mostly what to purchase often) in the marketplace of civil and political life (Brown 2004: 455; Teeple 2004).

This absolutist line of thinking raises several incontrovertible problems about human rights today. Foremost among these is the ever-widening disjuncture between the consolidation of a human rights industry (consisting of mainstream NGOs and multilateral international organizations), on the one hand, and the unjust civil-political and eroding socio-economic conditions under which most persons in the global South dwell, on the other. We need not enumerate the numerous contemporary instances of structural and political violence around the world to conclude that the record of concrete human rights achievements in the last half-century is at best a mixed one; modest improvements have been realized in some spheres for certain persons, yet a vast segment of humankind has experienced either stagnating or deteriorating circumstances (due to poverty, disease, civil war, gender subordination, etc.). Some of the other major flaws, mentioned above, concern the instrumentalization of human rights for the purposes of legitimating neoliberal or neoconservative ends, and their immiseration to the point that citizens are envisaged as individualistic human rights consumers responsible for achieving, or failing to achieve, whatever freedoms they are formally granted.

A substantive critical theory of global justice must always be cognizant of the fact that these scenarios are very real possibilities on the terrain of political and discursive contestation upon which human rights are situated, without following absolutist thinking in its political essentialization of them as ontological necessities. Hence, we need not throw out the baby of the potentially emancipatory uses of human rights with the bathwater of their failed realization or dubious appropriations. For one, it is unwarranted to infer the existence of a causal relationship, instead of a simple correlation, between the ubiquity of human rights discourses and the lack of alleviation of suffering and material deprivation in the global South. Global injustices are not being reproduced because of human rights *per se* (an essentializing argument), but rather partly – although by no means exclusively – because of the excessively formalist conception and practice of emancipatory politics that many human rights advocates have hitherto pursued. Indeed, the crux of the problem lies with such advocates' excessive focus on normative and institutional matters, which has misled them into conflating the build-up of an official human rights infrastructure with structural transformations of the world order that would produce actual progress in the socio-economic and civil-political circumstances of populations on the ground. Yet as I claimed in this book, formalism is but one paradigm through which to interpret the field of human rights; the latter cannot be reduced to the former.

Nevertheless, why should emancipatory projects be connected to the notion of human rights at all? Once we distance ourselves from the political essentialism of the human rights blackmail outlined above, the answer can be found in the prospects opened up by a shift of analytical focus from formalist arrangements to practices of global justice through which groups and persons may use human rights discourses and established human rights institutions strategically. In other words, while it should not solely orient itself toward or be framed by human rights, the work of global justice can draw on their normative and organizational resources to accomplish the tasks and confront the perils that compose each of its modes of practice. This amounts to deploying what Zizek, following

Lefort, has identified as the 'symbolic efficacy of rights'; the formal dimension of human rights does not remain merely as is, for it leaves traces, and thus has important spillover effects, upon the substantive content of socio-economic and civil-political conditions (Lefort 1986: 260–1; Zizek 2005: 130). Because of their vast public recognition, high standing and institutional development, human rights offer a potent moral grammar and set of ethical horizons through which to produce an immanent critique of the existing world order, whose functioning blatantly contradicts governments' and international organizations' official commitments to the realization of such rights. Correspondingly, civil society actors are reflexively positioning their struggles 'under the sign of the defence of human rights' (Lefort 1986: 242), so that situations of genocide, extreme poverty, gender subordination and health pandemics, among others, can be conceived of and denounced as violations of the fundamental rights to which all human beings are entitled (Lefort 1986: 261–2). Rather than adopting a weakly moralizing strategy satisfied with lamenting how deplorable such situations are, progressive groups can gain a certain degree of ethical and institutional traction by presenting them as unjust conditions that deprive persons of their universally recognized rights to safety, food, shelter, gender equality, health, and so on.

In addition, the idea of the work of global justice points beyond the symbolic efficacy of human rights, toward a substantive thickening and politically progressive resignification of them to sustain a transcendent mode of critique that puts into question the current parameters of the world order. Since the meaning of human rights as a discursively mediated social imaginary is open to contestation, progressive civil society groups can subversively appropriate them against their liberal individualist roots (present since their emergence in international declarations and treaties half-a-century ago). Indeed, once formally entrenched and validated, a bundle of rights can be thickened to the point of becoming a means through which to tackle the systemic roots of situational and structural injustices. When inserted into an emancipatory politics that views them as components of practices of global justice, then, human rights can create the normative and institutional leverage to organize and legitimate demands for structural changes that support an alternative globalization. The latter becomes a *sine qua non* condition to end mass abuses of civil-political and socio-economic rights, and more affirmatively, to enact the symbolic and material underpinnings of the oft-declared principle of universal moral equality. This is precisely why certain global justice activists have pushed for the signing of enforceable international treaties on socio-economic rights and for the creation of the International Criminal Court – and conversely, why many states and fractions of capital have been opposed to both initiatives (lest a government be sued for violating the basic rights to food, shelter and health of its citizens, or that military personnel and political leaders be prosecuted for war crimes).

Therefore, rather than appealing to the aforementioned additive tendencies of formalist and liberal versions of human rights (that consist in strictly trying to increase the number of individuals with rights and the number of rights granted to each individual), a substantive critical theory of global justice strategically deploys and redefines the notion of human rights to contribute to the dense labour of radically restructuring socio-political relations at local, national and global scales via participatory political and economic democracy, the North–South and domestic redistribution of resources and of capacities for existence, the establishment of new institutions of global governance, as well as intercultural dialogue. To flesh out this vision of an alternative globalization, we need to turn to a critical cosmopolitanism.

The labour of critical cosmopolitanism

Given how ubiquitous the idea of cosmopolitanism has become in recent years and the fact that it is far from an unproblematic term, I want to begin this section by establishing what a critical rendition of it is not. Among the questionable versions of cosmopolitanism are two kinds 'from above': a formalism asserting that the legal, political and moral institutionalization of the cosmopolitan spirit will have trickle-down effects on the everyday lives of populations; and a cultural elitism whereby economically dominant and spatially mobile persons identify themselves as rootless citizens of the world in order to demarcate themselves hierarchically *vis-à-vis* locally or nationally oriented groups,[2] or according to which European civilization is elevated into the natural locus and last remaining dwelling-place of cosmopolitan thought (and, by implication, the rest of the world appears as unsophisticatedly provincial). Equally dubious is a neoliberal brand of cosmopolitanism often voiced by Western political and corporate leaders, who declare that free trade and unregulated markets are the pre-eminent vehicles by which formerly 'isolated' states can become members of the international concert of liberal, enlightened nations (Calhoun 2003; Gowan 2003). The exposure of such nations' domestic economies to foreign investments, goods and services through privatization and deepening integration into circuits of global capitalism

[2] For critiques of this position, see Appiah (2006) and Calhoun (2003).

will supposedly nurture democratization and openness to the outside world. Not to be forgotten is a neo-imperialist usurpation of cosmopolitanism, which cynically appeals to the latter to legitimate the securing of *Pax Americana*. Cosmopolitan values are thereby converted into ideological weapons aiming to justify a new civilizing mission, that of 'democratizing' a highly selective list of strategically significant 'rogue regimes' in the global South by waging war against them. To paraphrase Rousseau, it may well be necessary to force these states to become 'cosmopolitan' – that is to say, supportive of, or at least compliant with, US geopolitical and economic interests. Clearly, then, the invocation of cosmopolitanism is by no means to be taken for granted politically.

Hence, it is paramount to build upon the insights of those who have put forth the outlines of a critical cosmopolitan project articulated around principles of radical, participatory democracy and egalitarian reciprocity (Archibugi 2003; Bartholomew and Breakspear 2004; Beck 2005; 2006; Habermas and Derrida 2003). Yet I am also suggesting that we can cultivate cosmopolitanism's emancipatory potential by anchoring it in the work of global justice; the modes of practice analysed in the previous chapters represent routes to the enactment and thickening of critical cosmopolitanism, supplying it with an ethico-political substance by underscoring the social labour involved in reshaping the current world order's economic, political and cultural facets. To grasp this labour better, we can return to an action-theoretical framework in order to conceptualize how agents confront perils and perform tasks to create an alternative globalization (see Figure 6).

The economic component of critical cosmopolitanism can take aim at neoliberal capitalism's role in the reproduction of numerous instances of structural violence and distributional inequity within and between societies (chronic poverty, malnutrition and disease on a massive scale, exploitation, etc.). It can do so by supporting the establishment of a different model of governance of global economic activity, to replace the institutions of the Washington Consensus (the IMF and the World Bank) and the World Trade Organization by an infrastructure prioritizing North–South redistribution and democratic regulation of transnational financial and trade flows, as well as favouring participatory and collectivist systems of ownership and control of the means of production geared toward meeting basic needs and making human capacities flourish (such as experiments with workers' self-management). The practice of foresight lays the groundwork here, since cosmopolitan participants in national and global civil societies are seeking to cultivate farsighted anticipation and public judgement in order to prevent or reverse the continued application of neoliberal orthodoxy in poor societies; for instance, several

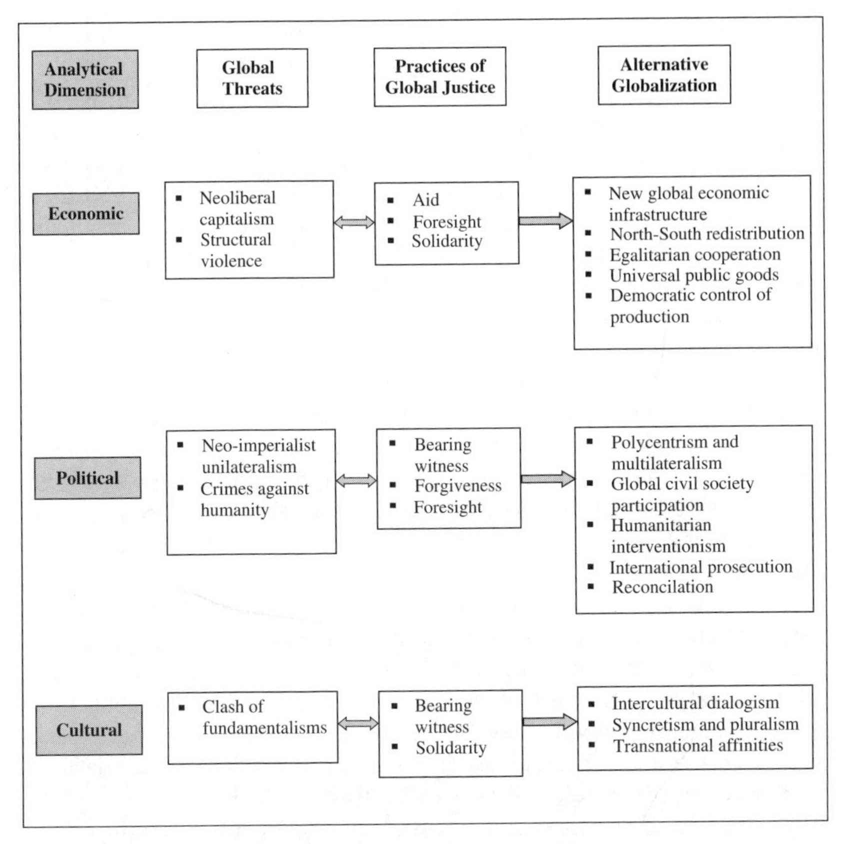

Figure 6. The labour of critical cosmopolitanism.

NGOs and social movements have mobilized popular opposition to structural adjustment programmes by building predictive models about the kind of economic havoc and social dislocation wreaked upon heavily indebted countries in the past. Likewise, the practice of transnational solidarity is vital to a critical cosmopolitanism in that its forging of a sense of responsibility for the socio-economic plight of all human beings normatively bolsters redistributive projects, while putting into question the neoliberal promotion of privatized and unregulated markets characterized by profit maximization and wealth concentration. In turn, farsighted and solidaristic action sustains the practice of aid, whose labour of reciprocity and egalitarian cooperation can foster structural transformations of the global economy by defending a notion of universal and 'non-commodifiable' public goods, as well as collective ownership and control of productive resources to meet socio-economic rights (to food, health, shelter, etc.) that are presently being grossly violated.

Politically, the principal threats to global justice today consist of a belligerent, neo-imperialist US unilateralism (exercised in the name of the 'war on terror') and the prevalence of crimes against humanity in several settings, which the labour of critical cosmopolitanism can try to offset in a variety of ways: developing a polycentric decision-making structure at the international level, in which progressive national and global civil society actors can formally participate; deterring political and military leaders from perpetrating acts of mass violence through their sanctioning and prosecution; and the enforcement and affirmation of civil-political rights in all parts of the world. The practice of bearing witness advances some of the political components of an alternative globalization, given that its tasks of giving voice to survivors of past and present atrocities, commemorating their suffering and generating empathy for them can simultaneously alert publics about the occurrence of such atrocities and urge international organizations to put an end to armed conflict and domestic campaigns of organized violence (such as civil war, ethnic cleansing or genocide). Just as importantly, the labour of foresight enables farsighted anticipation and action to prevent abuses of civil-political rights, through multilateral military intervention if necessary, while at the same time enriching civil society mechanisms to debate and assess the legitimacy of foreseeable humanitarian disasters and the means to address them – so that the cases of Rwanda and Darfur, on the one hand, and Iraq, on the other, can be clearly distinguished (Kurasawa 2006). None the less, if prevention fails, critical cosmopolitanism can turn to the labour of forgiveness because it asks that those perpetrating crimes against humanity be held responsible for their acts restoratively or retributively, including the option of their prosecution in institutions such as the International Criminal Court. Moreover, it nurtures forms of collective mourning and reconciliation that seek political paths opposed to retaliatory and ever-escalating cycles of warfare and violence (Butler 2004).

Critical cosmopolitanism's cultural labour, for its part, must face up to the resurgence and clash of ethno-racial and religious fundamentalisms in contemporary domestic and world politics, worldviews that essentialize similarities within communities and divergences between them in order to present them as incommensurable and discrete rivals doomed to entertain conflictual relations with one another. To resist these tendencies, progressive members of national and global civil society can support an intercultural dialogism that deeply engages with different ways of life and thinking (Dallmayr 1999; Kögler 2005; Kurasawa 2004a) to construct a vision of a just world order in which the recognition of the right to individual and collective difference is bound to the assertion of universal equality. As such, listening to, debating with and learning from non-Western traditions of thought and the manner in which NGOs and social movements in the global South conceptualize human rights can assist in reformulating cosmopolitanism and global justice in more inclusive directions – so that, for instance, demands emanating from poor regions of the world to consider international debt repayment as a grave injustice and the rights to food and health as paramount can become cosmopolitan values. The practice of bearing witness sustains this kind of intercultural dialogism by attempting to open up public spaces for the testimonials of distant strangers to be heard and to foster understanding of their plight through audiences' partial transposition into their shoes; the resulting humanization of such strangers can weaken stigmatizing and reductionist perceptions of them as mere representatives of threatening ideologies or group identities. But the tasks of embracing pluralism and creating webs of affinity, which inform the practice of solidarity, are equally important to the cultural dimension of critical cosmopolitanism. Indeed, global civil society actors can destabilize Manichean and purist models of collective identity by weaving solidaristic bonds that cut across apparent civilizational, religious or ethno-racial divides, and thereby demonstrate the fluidity of socio-cultural boundaries as well as the syncretism of societies. To be cosmopolitan in this sense signifies moving past an ethically thin tolerance for otherness or kindness toward strangers, toward participation in forms of political action that assert human beings' equal status while constructing a planetary consciousness according to which a shared yet diverse human condition marked by pluralism and *métissage* can thrive above and beyond absolutist categories of familiarity, sameness and proximity (Appiah 2006; Gilroy 2005: 67, 75; Sen 2006).

The idea of the work of global justice, then, is intended to materially substantiate and thicken cosmopolitanism. If the latter is to become more than an expression of socio-economic privilege or neoliberal capitalism, and if it is to resist being converted into a tool of political or cultural imperialism, it will do so by grounding itself in the forms of normative and socio-political action that inform the five modes of practice covered in the previous chapters (namely, the dialogical, public and transnational labour of bearing witness, forgiveness, foresight, aid and solidarity). Likewise, if human rights are to move down from their formalist perches to become emancipatory devices that progressive actors continue to mobilize to combat global injustices and systems of domination, we will need to begin to view them as components of modes of enactment of an alternative globalization.

Reiterating what has been affirmed throughout this book, the work of global justice is always in the making, incomplete and partial, for it dwells in inescapable aporias as well as formidable institutional obstacles and social pathologies; actors must continuously engage in the demanding tasks of which the five modes of practice are composed, to confront sources of situational and structural violence around the planet. Nevertheless, I have insisted upon the fact that the project of a just world order is neither a naïve chimera nor a doomed utopia. Despite – or better yet, precisely because of – what remains to be accomplished, this project resiliently survives as a possibility sustained by those who refuse to accept the litany of symbolic indignities and severe material deprivations to which a vast proportion of humankind is subjected, and who stubbornly cling to the conviction that another world remains possible, and indeed necessary. There is no doubt that such a possibility is fragile and contingent, as it is without ends, bounds or even guarantees. All that we have is the labour of human beings committed to each other, and to generating emancipatory paths of social action. Yet recognition of this very fact, of the socially self-instituting character of global justice, represents the fount of its robustness and vibrancy in our age.

Apart from critiques of being overly optimistic, idealistic, it is important to try (otherwise we use the idea that it can never be achieved as an excuse to do nothing)

References

Abel, O. 1991. 'Tables du pardon', in O. Abel (ed.) *Le Pardon: briser la dette et l'oubli*. Paris: Autrement, pp. 226–55.

Achmat, Z. 2003. 'Preface', in A. Irwin, J. Millen and D. Fallows, *Global AIDS: Myths and Facts*. Cambridge, MA: South End Press, pp. xiii–xvi.

ActionAid. 2005a. *Real Aid: An Agenda for Making Aid Work*. Johannesburg: ActionAid.

2005b. *Time to Act: HIV/AIDS in Asia*. Johannesburg: ActionAid.

Adorno, T. W. 1973 [1966]. *Negative Dialectics*. New York: Seabury Press.

1981 [1967]. 'Cultural Criticism and Society', in *Prisms*. Cambridge, MA: MIT Press, pp. 17–34.

1982 [1962]. 'Commitment', in A. Arato and E. Gebhardt (eds.) *The Essential Frankfurt School Reader*. New York: Continuum, pp. 300–18.

Adorno, T., *et al.* 1976 [1969]. *The Positivist Dispute in German Sociology*. New York: Harper & Row.

Agamben, G. 1999. *Remnants of Auschwitz: The Witness and the Archive*. New York: Zone Books.

Alexander, J. C. 2002. 'On the Social Construction of Moral Universals: The "Holocaust" from War Crime to Trauma Drama', *European Journal of Social Theory* 5(1): 5–85.

2003. *The Meanings of Social Life: A Cultural Sociology*. New York: Oxford University Press.

Ali, T. 2002. *The Clash of Fundamentalisms: Crusades, Jihads and Modernity*. London and New York: Verso.

Allen, A. 1999. 'Solidarity after Identity Politics: Hannah Arendt and the Power of Feminist Theory', *Philosophy and Social Criticism* 25(1): 97–118.

Allen, R. L. 1998. 'Past Due: The African American Quest for Reparations', *The Black Scholar* 28(2): 2–17.

Améry, Jean 1995 [1966]. *Par-delà le crime et le châtiment: essai pour surmonter l'insurmontable*. Paris: Actes Sud.

Anderson, B. 1991. *Imagined Communities: Reflections on the Origin and Spread of Nationalism*. London and New York: Verso.

Anheier, H., M. Glasius and M. Kaldor 2001 (eds.). *Global Civil Society 2001*. Oxford: Oxford University Press.

2002 (eds.). *Global Civil Society 2002*. Oxford: Oxford University Press.

2003 (eds.). *Global Civil Society 2003*. Oxford: Oxford University Press.

2004 (eds.). *Global Civil Society 2004/5*. London: Sage.
Apel, K.-O. 1984 [1979]. *Understanding and Explanation: A Transcendental-Pragmatic Perspective*. Cambridge, MA: MIT Press.
2000. 'Globalization and the Need for Universal Ethics', *European Journal of Social Theory* 3(2): 137–55.
Appadurai, A. 1996. *Modernity at Large: Cultural Dimensions of Globalization*. Minneapolis: University of Minnesota Press.
Appiah, K. A. 2002. 'For Love of Country', in J. Cohen (ed.) *For Love of Country*. Boston: Beacon Press, pp. 21–9.
2003. 'Citizens of the World', in M. J. Gibney (ed.) *Globalizing Rights: The Oxford Amnesty Lectures 1999*. Oxford: Oxford University Press, pp. 189–232.
2006. *Cosmopolitanism: Ethics in a World of Strangers*. New York: Norton.
Archibugi, D. 2003 (ed.). *Debating Cosmopolitics*. London and New York: Verso.
Archibugi, D., D. Held and M. Köhler 1998 (eds.). *Re-imagining Political Community: Studies in Cosmopolitan Democracy*. Stanford: Stanford University Press.
Arendt, H. 1963. *On Revolution*. Harmondsworth: Penguin.
1968. 'The Crisis in Culture', in *Between Past and Future: Eight Exercises in Political Thought*. Harmondsworth: Penguin, pp. 197–226.
1978. *The Life of the Mind*. New York: Harcourt Brace.
1992. *Lectures on Kant's Political Philosophy*. Chicago: University of Chicago Press.
1994 [1965]. *Eichmann in Jerusalem: A Report on the Banality of Evil*. Harmondsworth: Penguin.
1998 [1958]. *The Human Condition*, 2nd edn. Chicago: University of Chicago Press.
2003 [1968]. 'Collective Responsibility', in J. Kohn (ed.) *Responsibility and Judgment*. New York: Schocken, pp. 147–58.
ATTAC 2004. *Le Développement a-t-il un avenir? Pour une société économe et solidaire*. Paris: Mille et une nuits.
Atwood, M. 1985. *The Handmaid's Tale*. Toronto: McClelland & Stewart.
2003. *Oryx and Crake*. Toronto: McClelland & Stewart.
Badinter, R. 1998. 'L'Horizon moral de notre temps', in M. Bettati, O. Duhamel and L. Greilsamer (eds.) *La Déclaration universelle des droits de l'homme*. Paris: Gallimard, pp. 156–60.
Baker, G. 2002. 'Problems in the Theorisation of Global Civil Society', *Political Studies* 50(5): 928–43.
Baker, T. and J. Simon 2002 (eds.). *Embracing Risk: The Changing Culture of Insurance and Responsibility*. Chicago: University of Chicago Press.
Balibar, E. 2004 [2001]. *We, the People of Europe? Reflections on Transnational Citizenship*. Princeton: Princeton University Press.
Barber, B. R. 2003. *Fear's Empire: War, Terrorism, and Democracy*. New York: Norton.
Barkan, E. 2000. *The Guilt of Nations: Restitution and Negotiating Historical Injustices*. New York: Norton.
Barnett, M. 2002. *Eyewitness to a Genocide: The United Nations and Rwanda*. Ithaca: Cornell University Press.

Barnett, T. and A. Whiteside 2002. *AIDS in the Twenty-First Century: Disease and Globalization*. London and New York: Palgrave Macmillan.

Bartholomew, A. and J. Breakspear 2004. 'Human Rights as Swords of Empire', in L. Panitch and C. Leys (eds.) *Socialist Register 2004: The New Imperial Challenge*. New York: Monthly Review Press, pp. 125–45.

Bass, G. J. 2000. *Stay the Hand of Vengeance: The Politics of War Crimes Tribunals*. Princeton: Princeton University Press.

Bauman, Z. 1989. *Modernity and the Holocaust*. Ithaca: Cornell University Press.

1993. *Postmodern Ethics*. Oxford: Blackwell.

1995. *Life in Fragments: Essays in Postmodern Morality*. Oxford: Blackwell.

Bayertz, K. 1999. 'Four Uses of "Solidarity"', in K. Bayertz (ed.) *Solidarity*. Dordrecht: Kluwer, pp. 3–28.

Beck, U. 1992. *Risk Society: Towards a New Modernity*. London: Sage.

1999. *World Risk Society*. London: Sage.

2000. 'The Cosmopolitan Perspective: Sociology of the Second Age of Modernity', *British Journal of Sociology* 51(1): 79–105.

2002. 'The Terrorist Threat: World Risk Society Revisited', *Theory, Culture and Society* 19(4): 39–55.

2005. *Power in the Global Age: A New Global Political Economy*. Cambridge: Polity Press.

2006. *The Cosmopolitan Vision*. Cambridge: Polity Press.

Bedell, G. 2005. *Make Poverty History: How You Can Help Defeat World Poverty in Seven Easy Steps*. London: Penguin.

Beitz, C. R. 1999. *Political Theory and International Relations*. Princeton: Princeton University Press.

Bello, W. 2002a. *Deglobalization: Ideas for a New World Economy*. London and New York: Zed Books.

2002b. 'Pacific Panopticon', *New Left Review* 16: 68–85.

Benatar, S. R., A. S. Daar and P. A. Singer 2003. 'Global Health Ethics: The Rationale for Mutual Caring', *International Affairs* 79(1): 107–38.

Benhabib, S. 1986. *Critique, Norm, and Utopia: A Study of the Foundations of Critical Theory*. New York: Columbia University Press.

1992. *Situating the Self: Gender, Community and Postmodernism in Contemporary Ethics*. London and New York: Routledge.

2002. *The Claims of Culture: Equality and Diversity in the Global Era*. Princeton: Princeton University Press.

Bhargava, R. 2000. 'Restoring Decency to Barbaric Societies', in R. I. Rotberg and D. Thompson (eds.) *Truth v. Justice: The Morality of Truth Commissions*. Princeton: Princeton University Press, pp. 45–67.

Bindé, J. 2001. 'Toward an Ethics of the Future', in A. Appadurai (ed.) *Globalization*. Durham, NC: Duke University Press, pp. 90–113.

Blackburn, R. 1991 (ed.). *After the Fall: The Failure of Communism and the Future of Socialism*. London and New York: Verso.

Bohman, J. and M. Lutz-Bachmann 1997 (eds.). *Perpetual Peace: Essays on Kant's Cosmopolitan Ideal*. Cambridge, MA: MIT Press.

Boltanski, L. 1990. *L'Amour et la justice comme compétences*. Paris: Métailié.

1993. *La Souffrance à distance: morale humanitaire, médias et politique*. Paris: Métailié.

Boraine, A. 2000. 'Truth and Reconciliation in South Africa: The Third Way', in R. I. Rotberg and D. Thompson (eds.) *Truth v. Justice: The Morality of Truth Commissions*. Princeton: Princeton University Press, pp. 141–57.

Boraine, A., J. Levy and R. Scheffer 1997 (eds.). *Dealing with the Past: Truth and Reconciliation in South Africa*. Cape Town: Institute for Democracy in South Africa.

Borneman, J. 2002. 'Reconciliation after Ethnic Cleansing: Listening, Retribution, Affiliation', *Public Culture* 14(2): 281–304.

Bourassa, S. C. and A. L. Strong 2000. 'Restitution of Land to New Zealand Maori: The Role of Social Structure', *Pacific Affairs* 75(2): 227–60.

Bourdieu, P. 1977. *Outline of a Theory of Practice*. Cambridge: Cambridge University Press.

1990 [1980]. *The Logic of Practice*. Stanford: Stanford University Press.

1998. 'Pour un nouvel internationalisme', in *Contre-feux: propos pour servir à la résistance contre l'invasion néo-libérale*. Paris: Raisons d'agir, pp. 66–75.

2001. 'Pour un mouvement social européen', in *Contre-feux 2: pour un mouvement social européen*. Paris: Raisons d'agir, pp. 13–23.

Bové, J. 2001. 'A Farmers' International?' *New Left Review* 12: 89–101.

Boyer, P. 1985. *By the Bomb's Early Light: American Thought and Culture at the Dawn of the Atomic Age*. New York: Pantheon.

Bradol, J.-H. 2004. 'Introduction: The Sacrificial International Order and Humanitarian Action', in F. Weissman (ed.) *In the Shadows of 'Just Wars': Violence, Politics and Humanitarian Action*. Ithaca: Cornell University Press, pp. 1–22.

Brecher, J., T. Costello and B. Smith 2000. *Globalization from Below: The Power of Solidarity*. Cambridge, MA: South End Press.

Brooks, R. L. 1999 (ed.). *When Sorry Isn't Enough: The Controversy over Apologies and Reparations for Human Injustice*. New York: New York University Press.

Brown, W. 2001. *Politics Out of History*. Princeton: Princeton University Press.

2004. ' "The Most We Can Hope For . . .": Human Rights and the Politics of Fatalism', *South Atlantic Quarterly* 103(2/3): 451–63.

Burbach, R. 2003. *The Pinochet Affair: State Terrorism and Global Justice*. London: Zed Books.

Burkhalter, H. J. 2002. 'Round Table on Genocide Prevention: Genocide Prevention, Morality, and the National Interest', *Journal of Human Rights* 1(4): 444–8.

Butler, J. 2004. *Precarious Life: The Powers of Mourning and Violence*. London and New York: Verso.

Calhoun, C. 1994. 'Social Theory and the Politics of Identity', in C. Calhoun (ed.) *Social Theory and the Politics of Identity*. Malden, MA: Blackwell, pp. 9–36.

1995. *Critical Social Theory: Culture, History, and the Challenge of Difference*. Oxford and Cambridge, MA: Blackwell.

1997. 'Plurality, Promises, and Public Spaces', in C. Calhoun and J. McGowan (eds.) *Hannah Arendt and the Meaning of Politics*. Minneapolis: University of Minnesota Press, pp. 232–59.

2002. 'Constitutional Patriotism and the Public Sphere: Interests, Identity and Solidarity in the Integration of Europe', in P. De Greiff and C. Cronin (eds.) *Global Justice and Transnational Politics*. Cambridge, MA: MIT Press, pp. 275–312.

2003. 'The Class Consciousness of Frequent Travellers: Towards a Critique of Actually Existing Cosmopolitanism', in D. Archibugi (ed.) *Debating Cosmopolitics*. London and New York: Verso, pp. 86–116.

2004. 'A World of Emergencies: Fear, Intervention, and the Limits of the Cosmopolitan Order', *Canadian Review of Sociology and Anthropology* 41(4): 373–95.

Callon, M., P. Lascoumes and Y. Barthe 2001. *Agir dans un monde incertain: essai sur la démocratie technique*. Paris: Seuil.

Carroll, R. 2003. 'UN Envoy Attacks West for Ignoring Africa's Aids Pandemic', *Guardian Weekly*, 25 September–1 October, p. 2.

Celan, P. 2001. 'Speech on the Occasion of Receiving the Literature Prize of the Free Hanseatic City of Bremen', in *Selected Poems and Prose of Paul Celan*. New York: Norton, pp. 395–6.

Chandler, D. 2003. 'International Justice', in D. Archibugi (ed.) *Debating Cosmopolitics*. London and New York: Verso, pp. 27–39.

Chomsky, N. 1999. *The New Military Humanism: Lessons from Kosovo*. London: Pluto.

2003. '"Recovering Rights": A Crooked Path', in M. J. Gibney (ed.) *Globalizing Rights: The Oxford Amnesty Lectures 1999*. Oxford: Oxford University Press, pp. 45–80.

Clark, J. D. 2003 (ed.). *Globalizing Civic Engagement: Civil Society and Transnational Action*. Sterling, VA: Earthscan.

Clastres, P. 1977 [1974]. *Society Against the State*. Oxford: Blackwell.

Clifford, J. 1997. *Routes: Travel and Translation in the Late Twentieth Century*. Cambridge, MA: Harvard University Press.

Cockburn, A. and J. St. Clair 2000. *Five Days That Shook the World: Seattle and Beyond*. London and New York: Verso.

Cohen, J. L. 2004. 'Whose Sovereignty? Empire Versus International Law', *Ethics and International Affairs* 18(3): 1–24.

Cohen, S. 2001. *States of Denial: Knowing about Atrocities and Suffering*. Cambridge: Polity Press.

Collins, P. H. 1991. *Black Feminist Thought*. London and New York: Routledge.

Coq, C. and J. P. Bacot 1999 (eds.). *Travail de mémoire 1914–1998: une nécessité dans un siècle de violence* (Collection Mémoires, no. 54). Paris: Autrement.

Corbridge, S. 1993. 'Marxisms, Modernities, and Moralities: Development Praxis and the Claims of Distant Strangers', *Environment and Planning D: Society and Space* 11(4): 449–72.

Crocker, D. A. 1991. 'Toward Development Ethics', *World Development* 19(5): 457–83.

1992. 'Functioning and Capability: The Foundations of Sen's and Nussbaum's Development Ethic', *Political Theory* 20(4): 584–612.

1999. 'Reckoning with Past Wrongs: A Normative Framework', *Ethics and International Affairs* 13: 43–64.

2000. 'Truth Commissions, Transitional Justice, and Civil Society', in R. I. Rotberg and D. Thompson (eds.) *Truth v. Justice: The Morality of Truth Commissions*. Princeton: Princeton University Press, pp. 99–121.

Crow, G. 2002. *Social Solidarities: Theories, Identities and Social Change*. Buckingham: Open University Press.

Cullet, P. 2003. 'Patents and Medicines: The Relationship Between TRIPS and the Human Right to Health', *International Affairs* 79(1): 139–60.

Dallmayr, F. R. 1999. 'Globalization from Below', *International Politics* 36(3): 321–34.

2002. 'Globalization and Inequality: A Plea for Global Justice', *International Studies Review* 4(2): 137–56.

2003. 'Cosmopolitanism: Moral and Political.' *Political Theory* 31(3): 421–42.

Davis, P. and M. Fort 2004. 'The Battle Against Global Aids', in M. Fort, M. A. Mercer and O. Gish (eds.) *Sickness and Wealth: The Corporate Assault on Global Health*. Cambridge, MA: South End Press, pp. 145–57.

De Greiff, P. and C. Cronin 2002 (eds.). *Global Justice and Transnational Politics*. Cambridge, MA: MIT Press.

de Waal, A. 1997. *Famine Crimes: Politics and the Disaster Relief Industry in Africa*. Bloomington: Indiana University Press.

Dean, J. 1996. *Solidarity of Strangers: Feminism after Identity Politics*. Berkeley: University of California Press.

Derrida, J. 1994. *Specters of Marx: The State of the Debt, the Work of Mourning, and the New International*. London and New York: Routledge.

1996. *Archive Fever: A Freudian Impression*. Chicago: University of Chicago Press.

2000. 'Le Siècle et le pardon', in *Foi et savoir*. Paris: Seuil, pp. 101–33.

2001. *On Cosmopolitanism and Forgiveness*. London and New York: Routledge.

Digeser, P. E. 2001. *Political Forgiveness*. Ithaca: Cornell University Press.

Doyle, M. W. 2001. 'The New Interventionism', in T. Pogge (ed.) *Global Justice*. Oxford: Blackwell, pp. 219–41.

Dunne, T. and N. J. Wheeler 1999 (eds.). *Human Rights in Global Politics*. Cambridge: Cambridge University Press.

Duras, M. 1960. *Hiroshima mon amour*. Paris: Gallimard.

Dwyer, S. 1999. 'Reconciliation for Realists', *Ethics and International Affairs* 13: 81–98.

Epstein, H. 2005. 'God and the Fight Against AIDS', *New York Review of Books*, 28 April.

Epstein, S. 1996. *Impure Science: AIDS, Activism, and the Politics of Knowledge*. Berkeley: University of California Press.

Escobar, A. 1995a. *Encountering Development: The Making and Unmaking of the Third World*. Princeton: Princeton University Press.

1995b. 'Imagining a Post-Development Era', in J. Crush (ed.) *Power of Development*. London: Routledge, pp. 211–27.

Evans, G. and Mohamed Sahnoun 2001 (chairs). *The Responsibility to Protect: Report of the International Commission on Intervention and State Sovereignty*. Ottawa: International Development Research Centre.

Ewald, F. 2002. 'The Return of Descartes's Malicious Demon: An Outline of a Philosophy of Precaution', in T. Baker and J. Simon (eds.) *Embracing Risk:*

The Changing Culture of Insurance and Responsibility. Chicago: University of Chicago Press, pp. 273–301.
Falk, R. 1995. *On Humane Governance: Toward a New Global Politics*. College Park: Pennsylvania State University Press.
2000. *Human Rights Horizons: The Pursuit of Justice in a Globalizing World*. London and New York: Routledge.
Falk, R. and A. Strauss 2003. 'The Deeper Challenges of Global Terrorism: A Democratizing Response', in D. Archibugi (ed.) *Debating Cosmopolitics*. London and New York: Verso, pp. 203–31.
Farmer, P. 2003. *Pathologies of Power: Health, Human Rights, and the New War on the Poor*. Berkeley: University of California Press.
Feenberg, A. 1995. *Alternative Modernity: The Technical Turn in Philosophy and Social Theory*. Berkeley: University of California Press.
1999. *Questioning Technology*. London and New York: Routledge.
Feil, S. R. 2002. 'Round Table on Genocide Prevention: Genocide Prevention, Morality, and the National Interest', *Journal of Human Rights* 1(4): 448–52.
Felman, S. and D. Laub 1992. *Testimony: Crises of Witnessing in Literature, Psychoanalysis, and History*. London and New York: Routledge.
Fisher, W. F. and T. Ponniah 2003 (eds.). *Another World Is Possible: Popular Alternatives to Globalization at the World Social Forum*. London: Zed Books.
Foucault, M. 1978 [1976]. *The History of Sexuality*, vol. I: *An Introduction*. New York: Vintage.
1984 [1971]. 'Nietzsche, Genealogy, History', in P. Rabinow (ed.) *The Foucault Reader*. New York: Pantheon, pp. 76–100.
Frank, A. 1996. *The Diary of a Young Girl: The Definitive Edition*. New York: Anchor.
Fraser, N. 1997. *Justice Interruptus: Critical Reflections on the 'Postsocialist' Condition*. London and New York: Routledge.
2003. 'Social Justice in the Age of Identity Politics: Redistribution, Recognition, and Participation', in N. Fraser and A. Honneth, *Redistribution or Recognition? A Political-Philosophical Exchange*. London and New York: Verso, pp. 7–109.
Fraser, N. and A. Honneth 2003. *Redistribution or Recognition? A Political-Philosophical Exchange*. London and New York: Verso.
Fraser, N. and L. J. Nicholson 1990. 'Social Criticism Without Philosophy: An Encounter Between Feminism and Postmodernism', in L. J. Nicholson (ed.) *Feminism/Postmodernism*. London and New York: Routledge, pp. 19–38.
Friedlander, S. 1992 (ed.). *Probing the Limits of Representation: Nazism and the 'Final Solution'*. Cambridge, MA: Harvard University Press.
Friedman, J. 1994. *Cultural Identity and Global Process*. London: Sage.
Friese, H. 2000. 'Silence – Voice – Representation', in R. Fine and C. Turner (eds.) *Social Theory after the Holocaust*. Liverpool: Liverpool University Press, pp. 159–78.
Fukuyama, F. 1992. *The End of History and the Last Man*. New York: Free Press.
Gadamer, H. G. 1960. *Truth and Method*. New York: Continuum.
1996. *The Enigma of Health: The Art of Healing in a Scientific Age*. Stanford: Stanford University Press.

Geertz, C. 1973. *The Interpretation of Cultures*. New York: Basic Books.
Geras, N. 1998. *The Contract of Mutual Indifference: Political Philosophy after the Holocaust*. London and New York: Verso.
Gibney, M. and E. Roxstrom 2001. 'The Status of State Apologies', *Human Rights Quarterly* 23: 911–39.
Giddens, A. 1984. *The Constitution of Society*. Berkeley: University of California Press.
Gilligan, C. 1982. *In a Different Voice: Psychological Theory and Women's Development*. Cambridge, MA: Harvard University Press.
Gilroy, P. 1993. *The Black Atlantic: Modernity and Double Consciousness*. Cambridge, MA: Harvard University Press.
2000. *Between Camps: Nations, Cultures and the Allure of Race*. Harmondsworth: Penguin.
2005. *Postcolonial Melancholia*. New York: Columbia University Press.
Gitlin, T. 1994. 'From Universality to Difference: Notes on the Fragmentation of the Idea of the Left', in C. Calhoun (ed.) *Social Theory and the Politics of Identity*. Malden, MA: Blackwell, pp. 150–74.
Glasius, M., M. Kaldor and H. Anheier 2005 (eds.). *Global Civil Society 2005/6*. London: Sage.
Goffman, E. 1971. *Relations in Public: Microstudies of the Public Order*. New York: Harper & Row.
Goodman, J. 2002 (ed.). *Protest and Globalisation: Prospects for Transnational Solidarity*. Sydney: Pluto Press Australia.
Gowan, P. 2003. 'The New Liberal Cosmopolitanism', in D. Archibugi (ed.) *Debating Cosmopolitics*. London and New York: Verso, pp. 51–66.
Graeber, D. 2002. 'The New Anarchists', *New Left Review* 13: 61–73.
Gutman, A. and D. Thompson 2000. 'The Moral Foundations of Truth Commissions', in R. I. Rotberg and D. Thompson (eds.) *Truth v. Justice: The Morality of Truth Commissions*. Princeton: Princeton University Press, pp. 22–44.
Gutman, R. 2002. 'Round Table on Genocide Prevention: Genocide Prevention, Morality, and the National Interest', *Journal of Human Rights* 1(4): 452–6.
Habermas, J. 1987 [1971]. *Knowledge and Human Interests*. Boston: Beacon Press.
1989a [1962]. *The Structural Transformation of the Public Sphere: An Inquiry into a Category of Bourgeois Society*. Cambridge, MA: MIT Press.
1989b. *The New Conservatism: Cultural Criticism and the Historians' Debate*. Cambridge, MA: MIT Press.
1990 [1983]. *Moral Consciousness and Communicative Action*. Cambridge, MA: MIT Press.
1996 [1992]. *Between Facts and Norms: Contributions to a Discourse Theory of Law and Democracy*. Cambridge, MA: MIT Press.
1998 [1996]. *The Inclusion of the Other: Studies in Political Theory*. Cambridge, MA: MIT Press.
1999. 'Bestiality and Humanity: A War on the Border Between Legality and Morality', *Constellations* 6(3): 263–72.
2001 [1998]. *The Postnational Constellation: Political Essays*. Cambridge, MA: MIT Press.

2003. 'Interpreting the Fall of a Monument', *Constellations* 10(3): 364–70.
Habermas, J. and J. Derrida 2003. 'February 15, or What Binds Europeans Together: A Plea for a Common Foreign Policy, Beginning in the Core of Europe', *Constellations* 10(3): 291–7.
Hacking, I. 1990. *The Taming of Chance*. Cambridge: Cambridge University Press.
Halbwachs, M. 1994 [1925]. *Les Cadres sociaux de la mémoire*. Paris: Albin Michel.
1997 [1950]. *La Mémoire collective*. Paris: Albin Michel.
Haller, S. F. 2002. *Apocalypse Soon? Wagering on Warnings of Global Catastrophe*. Montreal and Kingston: McGill–Queen's University Press.
Hardt, M. 2002. 'Today's Bandung', *New Left Review* 14: 112–18.
Hardt, M. and A. Negri 2000. *Empire*. Cambridge, MA: Harvard University Press.
2004. *Multitude: War and Democracy in the Age of Empire*. New York: Penguin.
Hartman, G. H. 1996. *The Longest Shadow: In the Aftermath of the Holocaust*. Bloomington: Indiana University Press.
Hatley, J. 2000. *Suffering Witness: The Quandary of Responsibility after the Irreparable*. Albany: State University of New York Press.
Hayner, P. B. 2001. *Unspeakable Truths: Facing the Challenge of Truth Commissions*. London and New York: Routledge.
Held, D. 1995. *Democracy and the Global Order: From the Modern State to Cosmopolitan Governance*. Cambridge: Polity Press.
2004. *Global Covenant: The Social Democratic Alternative to the Washington Consensus*. Cambridge: Polity Press.
Heller, A. 1993. *A Philosophy of History in Fragments*. Oxford: Blackwell.
Henderson, M. 2002. 'Acknowledging History as a Prelude to Forgiveness', *Peace Review* 14(3): 265–70.
Hersey, J. 1985 [1946]. *Hiroshima*. Harmondsworth: Penguin.
Higgott, R. and M. Ougaard 2002 (eds.). *Towards a Global Polity*. London and New York: Routledge.
Hobsbawm, E. 1977 [1966]. *The Age of Revolution*. London: Abacus.
1994. *Age of Extremes: The Short Twentieth Century, 1914–1991*. London: Abacus.
Hogan, M. J. 1996 (ed.). *Hiroshima in History and Memory*. Cambridge: Cambridge University Press.
Hong, E. 2004. 'The Primary Health Care Movement Meets the Free Market', in M. Fort, M. A. Mercer and O. Gish (eds.) *Sickness and Wealth: The Corporate Assault on Global Health*. Cambridge, MA: South End Press, pp. 27–41.
Honneth, A. 1991 [1985] *The Critique of Power: Reflective Stages in a Critical Social Theory*. Cambridge, MA: MIT Press.
1995 [1992]. *The Struggle for Recognition: The Moral Grammar of Social Conflicts*. Cambridge, MA: MIT Press.
hooks, b. 1984. *Feminist Theory: From Margin to Center*. Boston: South End Press.
Hume, D. 1969 [1739–40]. *A Treatise of Human Nature*. Harmondsworth: Penguin.
Huntington, S. P. 1996. *The Clash of Civilizations and the Remaking of World Order*. New York: Simon & Schuster.

Husserl, E. 1970 [1954]. *The Crisis of European Sciences and Transcendental Phenomenology*. Evanston, IL: Northwestern University Press.

Huyssen, A. 2000. 'Present Pasts: Media, Politics, Amnesia', *Public Culture* 12(1): 21–38.

Ignatieff, M. 1984. *The Needs of Strangers*. Harmondsworth: Penguin.

1998. *The Warrior's Honour: Ethnic War and the Modern Conscience*. New York: Viking.

2001. 'Human Rights as Politics', in A. Gutman (ed.) *Human Rights as Politics and Idolatry*. Princeton: Princeton University Press, pp. 3–52.

2002. 'Intervention and State Failure', in N. Mills and K. Brunner (eds.) *The New Killing Fields: Massacre and the Politics of Intervention*. New York: Basic Books, pp. 229–44.

2003a. 'The Burden', *New York Times Magazine*, 5 January, pp. 22ff.

2003b. 'I Am Iraq', *New York Times Magazine*, 23 March, pp. 13ff.

2004. 'Democratic Providentialism', *New York Times Magazine*, 12 December, pp. 29ff.

Irwin, A., J. Millen and D. Fallows 2003. *Global AIDS: Myths and Facts*. Cambridge, MA: South End Press.

Jaar, A. 1998. *Let There Be Light: The Rwanda Project 1994–1998*. Barcelona: Centre d'Art Santa Monica.

Jameson, F. 1982. 'Progress Versus Utopia; or, Can We Imagine the Future?', *Science-Fiction Studies* 9: 147–66.

Jankélévitch, V. 1986. *L'Imprescriptible: pardonner? Dans l'honneur et la dignité*. Paris: Seuil.

1998 [1967]. 'Le Pardon', in *Philosophie morale*. Paris: Flammarion, pp. 992–1149.

Jaspers, K. 1947. *The Question of German Guilt*. New York: Dial Press.

Johnston, J. and G. Laxer 2003. 'Solidarity in the Age of Globalization: Lessons from the Anti-MAI and Zapatista Struggles', *Theory and Society* 32: 39–91.

Jonas, H. 1984. *The Imperative of Responsibility: In Search of an Ethics for the Technological Age*. Chicago: University of Chicago Press.

Joseph, S. 2003. 'Pharmaceutical Corporations and Access to Drugs: The "Fourth Wave" of Corporate Human Rights Scrutiny', *Human Rights Quarterly* 25: 425–52.

Kaldor, M. 2003. *Global Civil Society: An Answer to War*. Cambridge: Polity Press.

Kant, I. 1949 [1785]. *Fundamental Principles of the Metaphysics of Morals*. New York: Macmillan.

1991a [1784]. 'An Answer to the Question: "What is Enlightenment?" ', in H. Reiss (ed.) *Political Writings*. Cambridge: Cambridge University Press, pp. 54–60.

1991b [1795]. 'Perpetual Peace: A Philosophical Sketch', in H. Reiss (ed.) *Political Writings*. Cambridge: Cambridge University Press, pp. 93–130.

2000 [1790]. *Critique of Judgment*. Amherst, NY: Prometheus Books.

Kaplan, R. D. 2000. *The Coming Anarchy: Shattering the Dreams of the Post Cold War*. New York: Vintage.

Keane, J. 2001. 'Global Civil Society?', in H. Anheier, M. Glasius and M. Kaldor (eds.) *Global Civil Society 2001*. Oxford: Oxford University Press, pp. 23–47.

2003. *Global Civil Society?* Cambridge: Cambridge University Press.
Keck, M. E. and K. Sikkink 1998. *Activists Beyond Borders: Advocacy Networks in International Politics*. Ithaca: Cornell University Press.
Kennedy, D. 2004. *The Dark Side of Virtue: Reassessing International Humanitarianism*. Princeton: Princeton University Press.
Kidder, T. 2003. *Mountains Beyond Mountains*. New York: Random House.
Kiss, E. 2000. 'Moral Ambition Within and Beyond Political Constraints: Reflections on Restorative Justice', in R. I. Rotberg and D. Thompson (eds.) *Truth v. Justice: The Morality of Truth Commissions*. Princeton: Princeton University Press, pp. 68–98.
Klein, N. 2000. *No Logo*. New York: Picador.
2001. 'Reclaiming the Commons', *New Left Review* 9: 81–9.
2002. *Fences and Windows: Dispatches from the Front Lines of the Globalization Debate*. New York: Picador.
Kögler, H.-H. 1996. *The Power of Dialogue: Critical Hermeneutics after Gadamer and Foucault*. Cambridge, MA: MIT Press.
2005. 'Constructing a Cosmopolitan Public Sphere: Hermeneutic Capabilities and Universal Values', *European Journal of Social Theory* 8(3): 297–320.
Kouchner, B. and M. Bettati 1987. *Le Devoir d'ingérence*. Paris: Denoël.
Krog, A. 1998. *Country of My Skull: Guilt, Sorrow, and the Limits of Forgiveness in the New South Africa*. New York: Three Rivers Press.
Kumar, K. 1987. *Utopia and Anti-Utopia in Modern Times*. Oxford: Blackwell.
Kuper, L. 1985. *The Prevention of Genocide*. New Haven: Yale University Press.
Kurasawa, F. 2004a. *The Ethnological Imagination: A Cross-Cultural Critique of Modernity*. Minneapolis: University of Minnesota Press.
2004b. 'Cinema, or, An Art of Urban Memory in an Age of Forgetting.' *Public* 29: 24–49.
2006. 'The Uses and Abuses of Humanitarian Intervention in the Wake of Empire', in A. Bartholomew (ed.) *Empire's Law: The American Imperial Project and the 'War to Remake the World'*. London: Pluto Press, pp. 297–312.
LaCapra, D. 1994. *Representing the Holocaust: History, Theory, Trauma*. Ithaca: Cornell University Press.
Langer, L. L. 1991. *Holocaust Testimonies: The Ruins of Memory*. New Haven: Yale University Press.
Lanzmann, C. 1985. *Shoah*. Paris: Gallimard.
Laqueur, T. W. 2001. 'The Moral Imagination and Human Rights', in A. Gutman (ed.) *Human Rights as Politics and Idolatry*. Princeton: Princeton University Press, pp. 127–39.
Laxer, G. and S. Halperin 2003 (eds.). *Global Civil Society and Its Limits*. New York: Palgrave Macmillan.
Le Goff, J. 1992. *History and Memory*. New York: Columbia University Press.
Lefort, C. 1986. *The Political Forms of Modern Society: Bureaucracy, Democracy, Totalitarianism*. Cambridge, MA: MIT Press.
Lefranc, S. 2002. *Politiques du pardon*. Paris: Presses Universitaires de France.
Leiss, W. 2001. *In the Chamber of Risks: Understanding Risk Controversies*. Montreal and Kingston: McGill–Queen's University Press.
Levi, P. 1988 [1986]. *The Drowned and the Saved*. New York: Vintage.

1995. 'Shemá', in H. Schiff (ed.) *Holocaust Poetry*. New York: St Martin's Press, p. 205.

1996 [1958]. *Survival in Auschwitz*. New York: Touchstone.

Levy, D. and N. Sznaider 2002. 'Memory Unbound: The Holocaust and the Formation of Cosmopolitan Memory', *European Journal of Social Theory* 5(1): 87–106.

Lewis, S. 2001. 'J'accuse!' *Current Sociology* 49(6): 1–3.

2003. 'The Lack of Funding for HIV/AIDS Is Mass Murder by Complacency', *AllAfrica Global Media*, 8 January.

2005. *Race Against Time*. Toronto: Anansi.

Lifton, R. J. 1991 [1968]. *Death in Life: Survivors of Hiroshima*. Chapel Hill: University of North Carolina Press.

Lifton, R. J. and G. Mitchell 1995. *Hiroshima in America: A Half Century of Denial*. New York: Avon Books.

Linenthal, E. T. and T. Englehardt 1996 (eds.). *History Wars: The Enola Gay and Other Battles for the American Past*. New York: Metropolitan Books.

Lipschutz, R. D. 1992. 'Reconstructing World Politics: The Emergence of Global Civil Society', *Millennium* 21(3): 389–420.

Luban, D. 2002. 'Intervention and Civilization: Some Unhappy Lessons of the Kosovo War', in P. De Greiff and C. Cronin (eds.) *Global Justice and Transnational Politics*. Cambridge, MA: MIT Press, pp. 79–115.

Lurie, P., P. Hintzen and R. A. Lowe 2003. 'Socioeconomic Obstacles to HIV Prevention and Treatment in Developing Countries: The Roles of the International Monetary Fund and the World Bank', in E. Kalipeni, S. Craddock, J. R. Oppong and J. Gosh (eds.) *HIV and AIDS in Africa: Beyond Epidemiology*. Oxford and Malden, MA: Blackwell, pp. 204–12.

Lyotard, J.-F. 1988 [1983]. *The Differend: Phrases in Dispute*. Minneapolis: University of Minnesota Press.

Maclear, K. 1999. *Beclouded Visions: Hiroshima–Nagasaki and the Art of Witness*. Albany: State University of New York Press.

Mann, J. M. 1997. 'Medicine and Public Health, Ethics and Human Rights', *Hastings Center Report* 27(3): 6–13.

Marcos, S. 2002. 'Fourth Declaration from the Lacandón Jungle', in T. Hayden (ed.) *The Zapatista Reader*. New York: Thunder Mouth's Press, pp. 239–50.

Margalit, A. 2002. *The Ethics of Memory*. Cambridge, MA: Harvard University Press.

Marshall, T. H. 1950. *Citizenship and Social Class*. London: Pluto Press.

Matthews, E. 1988. 'AIDS and Sexual Morality', *Bioethics* 2(2): 118–28.

McAdam, D., S. Tarrow and C. Tilly 2001. *Dynamics of Contention*. Cambridge: Cambridge University Press.

McGary, H. 2003. 'Achieving Democratic Equality: Forgiveness, Reconciliation, and Reparations', *Journal of Ethics* 7: 93–113.

Meadows, D. L., *et al.* 1972. *The Limits to Growth: A Report for the Club of Rome's Project on the Predicament of Mankind*. New York: Universe Books.

Menchú, R. 1984. *I, Rigoberta Menchú: An Indian Woman in Guatemala*. London and New York: Verso.

Mertes, T. 2002. 'Grass-roots Globalism: Reply to Michael Hardt', *New Left Review* 17: 101–10.

Minear, R. H. 1990. 'Introduction', in R. H. Minear (ed.) *Hiroshima: Three Witnesses*. Princeton: Princeton University Press.

Minow, M. 1998. *Between Vengeance and Forgiveness: Facing History after Genocide and Mass Violence*. Boston: Beacon Press.

Moeller, S. D. 1999. *Compassion Fatigue: How the Media Sell Disease, Famine, War and Death*. London and New York: Routledge.

Mohanty, C. T. 1988. 'Under Western Eyes: Feminist Scholarship and Colonial Discourses', *Feminist Review* 30: 61–88.

1995. 'Feminist Encounters: Locating the Politics of Experience', in L. Nicholson and S. Seidman (eds.) *Social Postmodernism: Beyond Identity Politics*. Cambridge: Cambridge University Press, pp. 68–86.

Morin, E. 2000. 'Pardonner, c'est résister à la cruauté du monde', *Le Monde des Débats* 11: 24–6.

Morin, E. and B. Kern 1993. *Terre-Patrie*. Paris: Seuil.

Morris-Suzuki, T. 2000. 'For and Against NGOs: The Politics of the Lived World', *New Left Review* 2: 63–84.

Murphy, J. G. and J. Hampton 1988. *Forgiveness and Mercy*. Cambridge: Cambridge University Press.

Nachtwey, J. 1985. 'Statement from James Nachtwey', www.war-photographer.com/warum_e.htm (accessed 11 July 2003).

Nagy, R. 2002. 'Reconciliation in Post-Commission South Africa: Thick and Thin Accounts of Solidarity', *Canadian Journal of Political Science* 35(2): 323–46.

National Inquiry into the Separation of Aboriginal and Torres Strait Islander Children from Their Families 1997. *Bringing Them Home: Report of the National Inquiry into the Separation of Aboriginal and Torres Strait Islander Children from Their Families*. Sydney: Human Rights and Equal Opportunity Commission.

Niemöller, M. 1995. 'First They Came for the Jews', in H. Schiff (ed.) *Holocaust Poetry*. New York: St Martin's Press, p. 9.

Noddings, N. 1984. *Caring: A Feminine Approach to Ethics and Moral Education*. Berkeley: University of California Press.

Nora, P. 1984–92 (ed.). *Les Lieux de mémoire*, 3 vols. Paris: Gallimard.

Notes from Nowhere 2003 (eds.). *We Are Everywhere: The Irresistible Rise of Global Anticapitalism*. London and New York: Verso.

Ntsebeza, D. B. 2000. 'The Uses of Truth Commissions: Lessons for the World', in R. I. Rotberg and D. Thompson (eds.) *Truth v. Justice: The Morality of Truth Commissions*. Princeton: Princeton University Press, pp. 158–69.

Nussbaum, M. 1992. 'Human Functioning and Social Justice: In Defense of Aristotelian Essentialism', *Political Theory* 20(2): 202–46.

2002a [1996]. 'Patriotism and Cosmopolitanism', in J. Cohen (ed.) *For Love of Country?* Boston: Beacon Press, pp. 2–17.

2002b. 'Capabilities and Human Rights', in P. De Greiff and C. Cronin (eds.) *Global Justice and Transnational Politics*. Cambridge, MA: MIT Press, pp. 117–49.

Oliver, K. 2001. *Witnessing: Beyond Recognition*. Minneapolis: University of Minnesota Press.

O'Neill, O. 2002. 'Public Health or Clinical Ethics: Thinking Beyond Borders', *Ethics and International Affairs* 16(2): 35–45.

Ong, A. 1999. *Flexible Citizenship: The Cultural Logics of Transnationality*. Durham, NC: Duke University Press.

Packer, G. 2002. 'The Liberal Quandary over Iraq', *New York Times Magazine*, 8 December, pp. 104ff.

Perlesz, A. 1999. 'Complex Responses to Trauma: Challenges in Bearing Witness', *Australian and New Zealand Journal of Family Therapy* 20(1): 11–19.

Petchevsky, R. P. 2003.*Global Prescriptions: Gendering Health and Human Rights*. London and New York: Zed Books.

Peterson, M. J. 1992. 'Transnational Activity, International Society and World Politics.' *Millennium* 21(3): 371–88.

Phillips, M. M. and M. Moffett 2005. 'Brazil Refuses U.S. AIDS Funds, Rejects Conditions', *Wall Street Journal*, 2 May, p. A3.

Pianta, M. 2003. 'Democracy vs. Globalization: The Growth of Parallel Summits and Global Movements', in D. Archibugi (ed.) *Debating Cosmopolitics*. London and New York: Verso, pp. 232–56.

Pieterse, J. N. 1997. 'Sociology of Humanitarian Intervention: Bosnia, Rwanda and Somalia Compared', *International Political Science Review* 18(1): 71–93.

Pogge, T. 1992. 'Cosmopolitanism and Sovereignty', *Ethics* 103(1): 48–75.

1994. 'An Egalitarian Law of Peoples', *Philosophy and Public Affairs* 23(3): 195–224.

2001a (ed.). *Global Justice*. Oxford: Blackwell.

2001b. 'Priorities of Global Justice', in T. Pogge (ed.) *Global Justice*. Oxford: Blackwell, pp. 6–23.

2002a. 'Human Rights and Human Responsibilities', in P. De Greiff and C. Cronin (eds.) *Global Justice and Transnational Politics*. Cambridge, MA: MIT Press, pp. 151–95.

2002b. *World Poverty and Human Rights: Cosmopolitan Responsibilities and Reforms*. Cambridge: Polity Press.

2002c. 'Responsibilities for Poverty-Related Ill Health', *Ethics and International Affairs* 16(2): 71–9.

Poku, N. K. 2002a. 'The Global AIDS Fund: Context and Opportunity', *Third World Quarterly* 23(2): 283–98.

2002b. 'Poverty, Debt and Africa's HIV/AIDS Crisis', *International Affairs* 78(3): 531–46.

Power, S. 2002a. *'A Problem from Hell': America and the Age of Genocide*. New York: Basic Books.

2002b. 'Raising the Cost of Genocide', in N. Mills and K. Brunner (eds.) *The New Killing Fields: Massacre and the Politics of Intervention*. New York: Basic Books, pp. 245–64.

Rabinow, P. and W. M. Sullivan 1987 (eds.) *Interpretive Social Science: A Second Look*. Berkeley: University of California Press.

Rabinowitz, P. 1993. 'Wreckage upon Wreckage: History, Documentary and the Ruins of Memory', *History and Theory* 32(2): 119–37.

Rajagopal, B. 2003. *International Law from Below: Development, Social Movements and Third World Resistance*. Cambridge: Cambridge University Press.

Ramesh, R. 2004. 'Place in the Sun for Everyone – Except George Bush, Coca-Cola and Windows', *Guardian Weekly*, 22–28 January, p. 3.

Rawls, J. 1971. *A Theory of Justice*. Cambridge, MA: Harvard University Press.

1996. *Political Liberalism*. New York: Columbia University Press.

1999. *The Law of Peoples*. Cambridge, MA: Harvard University Press.

Ricoeur, P. 1981. *Hermeneutics and the Human Sciences*. Cambridge: Cambridge University Press.

2000. *La Mémoire, l'histoire, l'oubli*. Paris: Seuil.

Rieff, D. 2002. *A Bed for the Night: Humanitarianism in Crisis*. New York: Simon & Schuster.

Rivière, P. 2004. 'Vivre à Soweto avec le sida', *Manière de voir: Le Monde diplomatique*, February–March.

Rorty, R. 1989. *Contingency, Irony, and Solidarity*. Cambridge: Cambridge University Press.

1998a. 'Human Rights, Rationality, and Sentimentality', in *Truth and Progress: Philosophical Papers*, vol. III. Cambridge: Cambridge University Press, pp. 167–85.

1998b. *Achieving Our Country: Leftist Thought in Twentieth-Century America*. Cambridge, MA: Harvard University Press.

Rostow, W. W. 1960. *The Stages of Economic Growth*. Cambridge: Cambridge University Press.

Rotberg, R. I. 1996 (ed.). *Vigilance and Vengeance: NGOs Preventing Ethnic Conflict in Divided Societies*. Washington, DC: Brookings Institution Press.

2000. 'Truth Commissions and the Provision of Truth, Justice, and Reconciliation', in R. I. Rotberg and D. Thompson (eds.) *Truth v. Justice: The Morality of Truth Commissions*. Princeton: Princeton University Press, pp. 3–21.

Rotberg, R. I. and D. Thompson 2000 (eds.). *Truth v. Justice: The Morality of Truth Commissions*. Princeton: Princeton University Press.

Rousseau, J.-J. 1973 [1755]. 'A Discourse on the Origin of Inequality', in *The Social Contract and Discourses*. London: Dent.

Royal Commission on Aboriginal Peoples 1996. *Looking Forward, Looking Back: Report of the Royal Commission on Aboriginal Peoples*. Ottawa: Department of Indian Affairs and Northern Development.

Ruddick, S. 1989. *Maternal Thinking: Toward a Politics of Peace*. Boston: Beacon Press.

Sachs, W. 1992 (ed.). *The Development Dictionary: A Guide to Knowledge as Power*. London: Zed Books.

Sader, E. 2002. 'Beyond Civil Society: The Left after Porto Alegre', *New Left Review* 17: 87–99.

Sampson, S. 2003. 'From Reconciliation to Coexistence', *Public Culture* 15(1): 181–6.

Scarry, E. 1985. *The Body in Pain: The Making and Unmaking of the World*. New York: Oxford University Press.

Schaap, A. 2001. 'Guilty Subjects and Political Responsibility: Arendt, Jaspers and the Resonance of the "German Question" in Politics of Reconciliation', *Political Studies* 48: 749–66.

Scholte, J. A. 2002. 'Civil Society and Democracy in Global Governance', *Global Governance* 8(3): 281–304.

Schönleitner, G. 2003. 'World Social Forum: Making Another World Possible', in J. D. Clark (ed.) *Globalizing Civic Engagement: Civil Society and Transnational Action*. London: Earthscan, pp. 127–49.

Seckinelgin, H. 2002. 'Time to Stop and Think: HIV/AIDS, Global Civil Society, and People's Politics', in H. Anheier, M. Glasius and M. Kaldor (eds.) *Global Civil Society 2002*. Oxford: Oxford University Press, pp. 109–36.

2003. 'HIV/AIDS, Global Society, and People's Politics: Update to Chapter 5, 2002', in H. Anheier, M. Glasius and M. Kaldor (eds.) *Global Civil Society 2003*. Oxford: Oxford University Press, pp. 423–4.

Seidman, S. 1995. 'Deconstructing Queer Theory or the Under-theorization of the Social and the Ethical', in L. Nicholson and S. Seidman (eds.) *Social Postmodernism: Beyond Identity Politics*. Cambridge: Cambridge University Press, pp. 116–41.

Sell, S. K. and A. Prakash 2004. 'Using Ideas Strategically: The Contest Between Business and NGO Networks in Intellectual Property Rights', *International Studies Quarterly* 48: 143–75.

Sen, A. 1999. *Development as Freedom*. New York: Anchor Books.

2006. *Identity and Violence: The Illusion of Destiny*. New York: Norton.

Sen, G. and C. Grown 1987. *Development, Crises, and Alternative Visions: Third World Women's Perspectives*. New York: Monthly Review Press.

Sheth, D. L. 1987. 'Alternative Development as Political Practice', *Alternatives* 12(2): 155–71.

Short, D. 2003. 'Reconciliation, Assimilation, and the Indigenous Peoples of Australia', *International Political Science Review* 24(4): 491–513.

Shriver, D. W. J. 1995. *An Ethic for Enemies: Forgiveness in Politics*. Oxford: Oxford University Press.

Silber, M. 2003. 'Ricardo Cavallo, ancien militaire argentin, a été extradé du Mexique vers l'Espagne', *Le Monde*, 1 July.

Singer, P. 2002. *One World: The Ethics of Globalization*. New Haven: Yale University Press.

Smith, A. 2002 [1759]. *The Theory of Moral Sentiments*. Cambridge: Cambridge University Press.

Smith, A. K. 1965. *A Peril and a Hope: The Scientists' Movement in America, 1945–47*. Chicago: University of Chicago Press.

Smith, J. 1998. 'Global Civil Society? Transnational Social Movement Organisations and Social Capital', *American Behavioral Scientist* 42(1): 93–107.

Sontag, S. 1966. 'The Imagination of Disaster', in *Against Interpretation*. New York: Anchor, pp. 209–25.

1990. *Illness as Metaphor and AIDS and Its Metaphors*. New York: Farrar, Straus and Giroux.

Starr, A. 2000. *Naming the Enemy: Anti-corporate Movements Confront Globalization*. London: Zed Books.

Sturken, M. 2002. 'Memorializing Absence', in C. Calhoun, P. Price and A. Timmer (eds.) *Understanding September 11*. New York: New Press, pp. 374–84.

Tarrow, S. 2005. *The New Transnational Activism*. New York: Cambridge University Press.

Tavuchis, N. 1991. *Mea Culpa: A Sociology of Apology and Reconciliation*. Stanford: Stanford University Press.

Taylor, C. 1985 [1971]. 'Interpretation and the Sciences of Man', in *Philosophy and the Human Sciences: Philosophical Papers*, vol. II. Cambridge: Cambridge University Press, pp. 15–57.

1989. *Sources of the Self: The Making of the Modern Identity*. Cambridge, MA: Harvard University Press.

1995. 'To Follow a Rule', in *Philosophical Arguments*. Cambridge, MA: Harvard University Press, pp. 165–80.

Taylor, C., *et al.* 1994. *Multiculturalism: Examining the Politics of Recognition*, ed. A. Gutman. Princeton: Princeton University Press.

Teeple, G. 2004. *The Riddle of Human Rights*. Aurora, ON: Garamond Press.

Terry, F. 2002. *Condemned to Repeat? The Paradox of Humanitarian Action*. Ithaca: Cornell University Press.

Tester, K. 1997. *Moral Culture*. London: Sage.

Thomas, C. 2002. 'Trade Policy and the Politics of Access to Drugs', *Third World Quarterly* 23(2): 251–64.

Thompson, E. P. 1985. *The Heavy Dancers: Writings on War, Past and Future*. New York: Pantheon.

Todorov, T. 1996 [1991]. *Facing the Extreme: Moral Life in the Concentration Camps*. New York: Metropolitan Books.

2000. *Mémoire du mal, tentation du bien: enquête sur le siècle*. Paris: Robert Laffont.

Toffler, A. 1970. *Future Shock*. New York: Bantam Books.

Toge, S. 1990. 'Poems of the Atomic Bomb', in R. H. Minear (ed.) *Hiroshima: Three Witnesses*. Princeton: Princeton University Press.

Touraine, A. 1997. *Pourrons-nous vivre ensemble? Égaux et différents*. Paris: Fayard.

Tronto, J. C. 1993. *Moral Boundaries: A Political Argument for an Ethic of Care*. London and New York: Routledge.

Turner, B. S. 2002. 'Cosmopolitan Virtue, Globalization and Patriotism', *Theory, Culture and Society* 19(1–2): 45–63.

Tutu, D. 1999. *No Future Without Forgiveness*. New York: Doubleday.

UNAIDS/WHO 2004a. *2004 Report on the Global HIV/AIDS Epidemic* (UNAIDS/04.16E). Geneva: Joint United Nations Programme on HIV/AIDS and World Health Organization.

2004b. *AIDS Epidemic Update: December 2004* (UNAIDS/04.45E). Geneva: Joint United Nations Programme on HIV/AIDS and World Health Organization.

2005a. *A Scaled-Up Response to AIDS in Asia and the Pacific* (UNAIDS/05.15E). Geneva: Joint United Nations Programme on HIV/AIDS and World Health Organization.

2005b. 'Access to HIV treatment continues to accelerate in developing countries, but bottlenecks persist, says WHO/UNAIDS report'. www.who.int/mediacentre/news/releases/2005/pr30/en/index.html (accessed 6 July 2005).

2006a. *2006 Report on the Global AIDS Epidemic* (UNAIDS/06.20E). Geneva: Joint United Nations Programme on HIV/AIDS and World Health Organization.

2006b. *AIDS Epidemic Update: December 2006* (UNAIDS/06.29E). Geneva: Joint United Nations Programme on HIV/AIDS and World Health Organization.

UNDP 2003. *Human Development Report 2003*. Oxford and New York: Oxford University Press and United Nations Development Programme.

Vidal-Naquet, P. 1992 [1987]. *Assassins of Memory: Essays on the Denial of the Holocaust*. New York: Columbia University Press.

Villa-Vicencio, C. and W. Verwoerd 2000 (eds.). *Looking Back, Reaching Forward: Reflections on the Truth and Reconciliation Commission in South Africa*. London: Zed Books.

Virilio, P. 1997 [1995]. *Open Sky*. London and New York: Verso.

Walzer, M. 1983. *Spheres of Justice: A Defense of Pluralism and Equality*. New York: Basic Books.

1992. *Just and Unjust Wars*. New York: Basic Books.

1994. *Thick and Thin: Moral Argument at Home and Abroad*. Notre Dame, IN: Notre Dame University Press.

2002a. 'Arguing for Humanitarian Intervention', in N. Mills and K. Brunner (eds.) *The New Killing Fields: Massacre and the Politics of Intervention*. New York: Basic Books, pp. 19–35.

2002b. 'Can There Be a Decent Left?' *Dissent* 49(2): 19–23.

2003. 'Editor's Page', *Dissent* 50(2): 1.

2004. *Arguing about War*. New Haven: Yale University Press.

Weber, M. 1946 [1921]. 'Politics as a Vocation', in H. H. Gerth and C. W. Mills (eds.) *From Max Weber: Essays in Sociology*. New York: Oxford University Press, pp. 77–128.

Weiss, T. G. and Don Hubert 2001. *The Responsibility to Protect: Research, Bibliography, Background*. Supplementary Volume to the Report of the International Commission on Intervention and State Sovereignty. Ottawa: International Development Research Centre.

Weissman, F. 2004 (ed.). *In the Shadow of 'Just Wars': Violence, Politics and Humanitarian Intervention*. Ithaca: Cornell University Press.

Wheeler, N. J. 2000. *Saving Strangers: Humanitarian Intervention in International Society*. Oxford: Oxford University Press.

Wiesenthal, S. 1976. *The Sunflower*. New York: Schocken.

Wieviorka, A. 1998. *L'Ère du témoin*. Paris: Plon.

Wilson, Richard A. 2001. *The Politics of Truth and Reconciliation in South Africa: Legitimizing the Post-Apartheid State*. Cambridge: Cambridge University Press.

Wittner, L. S. 1993. *The Struggle Against the Bomb*, vol. I: *One World or None*. Stanford: Stanford University Press.

1997. *The Struggle Against the Bomb*, vol. II: *Resisting the Bomb*. Stanford: Stanford University Press.

Wolfe, S. A. 2003. 'Will AIDS Finally Teach Us the Meaning of Sustainable Human Development (for All)?' *IAPAC Monthly* 9(2): 37–44.

Woodiwiss, A. 2005. *Human Rights*. Oxford and New York: Routledge.

World Commission on Environment and Development 1987. *Our Common Future*. Oxford: Oxford University Press.

Yavenditti, M. J. 1974. 'John Hersey and the American Conscience: The Reception of "Hiroshima"', *Pacific Historical Review* 43(4): 24–9.

Yoneyama, L. 1999. *Hiroshima Traces: Time, Space, and the Dialectics of Memory*. Berkeley: University of California Press.

Young, I. 2003. 'From Guilt to Responsibility', *Dissent* 50(2): 39–44.

Young, I. M. 1990. *Justice and the Politics of Difference*. Princeton: Princeton University Press.

1995. 'Gender as Seriality: Thinking About Women as a Social Collective', in L. Nicholson and S. Seidman (eds.) *Social Postmodernism: Beyond Identity Politics*. Cambridge: Cambridge University Press, pp. 187–215.

1997. 'Asymmetrical Reciprocity: On Moral Respect, Wonder, and Enlarged Thought', *Constellations* 3(3): 340–63.

Young, J. E. 1993. *The Texture of Memory: Holocaust Memorials and Meaning*. New Haven: Yale University Press.

Zalaquett, J. 1993. 'Introduction to the English Edition', in *Report of the Chilean National Commission on Truth and Reconciliation*. Notre Dame, IN: Center for Civil and Human Rights, Notre Dame Law School, pp. xxiii–xxxiii.

Zanetti, V. 2001. 'Is Interventionism Desirable?' in T. Pogge (ed.) *Global Justice*. Oxford: Blackwell, pp. 204–18.

Zizek, S. 2005. 'Against Human Rights', *New Left Review* 34: 115–31.

Index

Cambridge Cultural Social Studies

Other books in the series (continued from page iii)

Luc Boltanski, translated by Graham D. Burchell, *Distant Suffering*

Mariam Fraser, *Identity Without Selfhood*

Carolyn Marvin and David W. Ingle, *Blood Sacrifice and the Nation*

Nina Eliasoph, *Avoiding Politics*

Bernhard Giesen, translated by Nicholas Levis and Amos Weisz, *Intellectuals and the Nation*

Philip Smith, *The New American Cultural Sociology*

Meyda Yegenoglu, *Colonial Fantasies*

Laura Desfor Edles, *Symbol and Ritual in the New Spain*

Ron Eyerman and Andrew Jamison, *Music and Social Movements*

Scott Bravmann, *Queer Fictions of the Past*

Steven Seidman, *Difference Troubles*

Lynn Rapaport, *Jews in Germany after the Holocaust*

Michael Mulkay, *The Embryo Research Debate*

Lynette P. Spillman, *Nation and Commemoration*

Sarah M. Corse, *Nationalism and Literature*

Darnell M. Hunt, *Screening the Los Angeles 'Riots'*

Paul Lichterman, *The Search for Political Community*

Alberto Melucci, *Challenging Codes*

Alberto Melucci, *The Playing Self*

Kenneth H. Tucker, Jr., *French Revolutionary Syndicalism and the Public Sphere*

Roger Friedland and Richard Hecht, *To Rule Jerusalem*

Suzanne R. Kirschner, *The Religious and Romantic Origins of Psychoanalysis*

Linda Nicholson and Steven Seidman, *Social Postmodernism*

Ilana Friedrich Silber, *Virtuosity, Charisma and Social Order*